Come Lovely and Soothing Death

*The Right to Die Movement
in the United States*

SOCIAL MOVEMENTS PAST AND PRESENT

Robert D. Benford, Editor

Come Lovely and Soothing Death

The Right to Die Movement in the United States

*Elaine Fox, Jeffrey J. Kamakahi,
Stella M. Čapek*

Twayne Publishers
New York

Come Lovely and Soothing Death
The Right to Die Movement in the United States
Elaine Fox, Jeffrey J. Kamakahi, Stella M. Čapek

Twayne Publishers
1633 Broadway
New York, NY 10019

Library of Congress Cataloging-in-Publication Data
Fox, Elaine.
    Come lovely and soothing death : the right to die movement in the United States / Elaine Fox, Jeffrey J. Kamakahi, Stella M. Capek.
        p.   cm. — (Social movements past and present)
    Includes bibliographical references and index.
    ISBN 0-8057-1645-9 (alk. paper)
    1. Right to die—Social aspects—United States.   2. Euthanasia—Social aspects—United States.   I. Kamakahi, Jeffrey J.
II. Capek, Stella M., 1953– .   III. Title.   IV. Title: Right to die movement in the United States.   V. Series.
    [DNLM: 1. Hemlock Society U.S.A.   2. Right to die—United States.
3. Organizations—United States.   4. Social change—United States.
W 85.5 F791c   1999]
R726.F69   1999
179.7—dc21
DNLM/DLC
for Library of Congress   99-29556
                                                                                   CIP

This paper meets the requirements of ANSI/NISO Z3948-1992 (Permanence of Paper).
10 9 8 7 6 5 4 3 2 1

Printed in the United States of America

Come lovely and soothing death,
Undulate round the world, serenely arriving, arriving,
In the day, in the night, to all, to each,
Sooner or later delicate death.

Prais'd be the fathomless universe,
For life and joy, and for objects and knowledge curious,
And for love, sweet love—but praise! praise! praise!
For the sure-enwinding arms of cool-enfolding death.

Dark mother always gliding near with soft feet,
Have none chanted for thee a chant of fullest welcome?
Then I chant for thee, I glorify thee above all,
I bring thee a song that when thou must indeed come, come
    unfalteringly.

Approach strong deliveress,
When it is so, when thou hast taken them I joyously sing the dead,
Lost in the loving floating ocean of thee,
Laved in the flood of thy bliss O death.

From me to thee glad serenades,
Dances for thee I propose saluting thee, adornments and feastings for
    thee,
And the sights of the open landscape and the high-spread sky are
    fitting,
And life and the fields, and the huge and thoughtful night.

The night in silence under many a star,
The ocean shore and the husky whispering wave whose voice I know,
And the soul turning to thee O vast and well-veil'd death,
And the body gratefully nestling close to thee.

Over the tree-tops I float thee a song,
Over the rising and sinking waves, over the myriad fields and the
    prairies wide,
Over the dense-pack'd cities all and the teeming wharves and ways,
I float this carol with joy, with joy to thee O death.

                          —Walt Whitman

Contents

Preface

In recent years, there has been growing public interest in the United States and worldwide in the Right to Die movement. Both passive euthanasia (avoiding artificially prolonging the life of a terminally ill patient), and the more controversial active euthanasia (deliberately terminating life to avoid suffering, sometimes known as "assisted suicide") are the subject of much debate. A variety of groups have sprung up in the United States to offer help and support to people who want some choice over the manner in which they, or those close to them, die.

The only national organization willing to support voluntary active euthanasia in the United States until recently has been the Hemlock Society, founded in 1980 in Los Angeles. Initially operated out of a garage on a shoestring budget, this nonprofit national organization was headquartered in Eugene, Oregon, and recently relocated to Denver, Colorado. Boasting a membership of over 25,000 people, the Hemlock Society stands out as a key player both organizationally and philosophically in the emerging Right to Die movement.[1] Despite the movement's increasing media visibility (Singer and Endreny 1993), and despite growing public support for euthanasia in the United States (Williams 1989)—including voter approval of the first "right to die" law in Oregon in November 1994 and again in 1997—it has yet to receive systematic sociological attention.

We feel that such an analysis is long overdue and offer this case study of the Hemlock Society (HS) as a means of enriching the study of social movements. Previous books on euthanasia have primarily either a philosophical or an applied orientation (for example, Clark and Kutscher 1992; Humphry 1981, 1991; Humphry and Wickett 1986). Although the sociological literature reflects a growing interest in the topic of death and dying beginning in the late 1960s (Dumont and Foss 1972; Glaser and Strauss 1975; Kubler-Ross 1969, 1975; Sudnow 1967; Denzin 1992), and medical sociology increasingly incorporates discussions on life and death decisions (Kurtz and Chalfant 1984; Williams 1989), we found no evidence of an organizational analysis of the Right to Die movement. Nor were we able to find a sociological analysis of the HS, which has played such a key role in this movement. Suber and Quinn (1993) examined demographic characteristics of HS members, but at the time of the study, the organization was small and based mostly in California. Holden (1993) compared demographic characteristics and attitudes between HS members and an antieuthanasia group (both in California) but did not focus on the organization itself. Thus, we offer our work as a step toward a systematic understanding both of the HS as an organization and the broader social movement within which it is embedded.

Our case study permits us to focus ethnographically on a key social movement organization (SMO) while sketching out the broader contours of a burgeoning but factionalized Right to Die movement; in this wider "field," a variety of organizations cooperate and compete for material resources, as well as symbolic identities, against a backdrop of changing cultural and technological forces. In mapping this terrain, our study breaks new empirical ground. Moreover, we find that the shifting fortunes and organizational dilemmas of the HS—including the 1992 departure of its charismatic founder, Derek Humphry, and subsequent debates over tactics—reflect structural tensions and practical debates faced by a variety of U.S. SMOs in the 1980s and 1990s (Benford 1993a; McCarthy, Britt, and Wolfson 1991). These issues point us beyond the case itself and toward the broader universe of social movements. At the same time, our focus on the HS highlights a moment of transition, or "goal reorientation," in a particular organization and reveals a shift in the Right to Die movement as a whole.

Social Movements Theory

We see our opportunity in this book as theoretical as well as empirical. Our case study feeds into the ongoing theoretical dialogue about social movements. As social movements theory continues to gain in diversity and richness, there is no longer one dominant explanatory model. Recent assessments of social movements theory concur on the need to move beyond a previously dominant "resource mobilization" tradition while retaining its insights (Benford 1993b; Buechler 1993). We believe this reflects a trend toward an integrative understanding of complex social movements. Such an understanding requires simultaneous insights from multiple theories—a kind of theoretical "triangulation" (Denzin 1989). We join with those who view multiple perspectives as a strength for the field of sociology (Nash and Wardell 1993) rather than a weakness (J. Turner 1989; S. Turner and J. Turner 1990).

Our approach hinges on a triangulation between three prominent theoretical models—the "resource mobilization," "framing," and "new social movements" perspectives. We are particularly interested in how the issues identified by each theory condition the issues identified by the others, revealing new interfaces between the theories themselves as well as new empirical connections. We use data from our HS study—both qualitative and quantitative—to illustrate the usefulness of such an approach. Although we are not the first to identify complementarity between social movements theories, we feel that actual examples of theoretical triangulation are rare and much needed.

Our primary purpose here is not to prove that one theory is better than another; indeed, our study attempts to bypass the theoretical and methodological dogmatisms that often constrain sociological investigations. We are concerned primarily with how well theoretical notions and qualitative and quantitative methodological analyses shed light on our understanding of the phenomenon under study. We share Howard Becker's view of sociological theory: "[T]he real test has always been how useful or interesting that way of looking at things is to an audience. If you look at things from a sociological perspective, what can you see that used to be invisible?" (1986, 2) We suggest in the present study how each theory contributes unique as well as complementary tools for an analysis useful to the sociological student of social movements, thought provoking to the general reader, and resonant for those whose link to the movement is more direct.

Data and Methods

This book grew out of a paper that was presented by Elaine Fox and Stella Čapek at the 1993 meetings of the American Sociological Association (Fox and Čapek 1993). As it underwent revisions, Jeffrey Kamakahi joined the project, and it became a three-way collaboration. Our collaboration is enhanced by the fact that one of the authors (Fox) has been a member of the national HS almost since its inception. Fox founded the only Arkansas chapter of the HS over six years ago and served for several years as its chapter leader. She has also engaged in participant observation and has conducted a number of interviews with key players in the HS. Her insider status has given her entry into local, regional, and national communication networks. Čapek has participated in and analyzed a variety of grassroots social movements using qualitative techniques. Kamakahi brings to the project a background in medical sociology as well as the quantitative skills that permitted us to design and analyze a national survey of HS members. This enabled us not only to collect new data on the Right to Die movement but also to cross-check the findings from our ethnographic study.

Qualitative Analysis

We rely on a variety of qualitative methods for our case study, including informal content analysis of documents, participant observation, and interviews. The documents we have used are generated by the HS both at the national and local levels. These include the quarterly newsletter of the Hemlock Society USA, available to all members, and newsletters sent to chapter leaders, which have more of an in-house character. We also have access to correspondence and various communications within and between chapters of the HS. As more communication takes place on the Internet, we have also made use of electronic media documents. We have been careful to balance access to important information with a respect for the privacy of particular individuals involved in the HS.

Although we have collected a broader range of data, we focus in greater detail on the period since early 1992, when, after establishing itself as a successful SMO, the HS began to undergo leadership and structural changes. Such moments of transition are particularly valuable from a sociological perspective; our "ethnographic window" on this process reveals how HS members see their organization and how they think it should fit into the overall Right to Die movement. Some of the changes and resulting crises in the HS were experienced only at the highest levels of the organization because a number of chapters chose not to disseminate many details to rank-and-file members. The paucity of media coverage of the various events at the national level reveals that relatively little information leaked out to the public at large. Thus, our ethnographic focus and analysis of the organizational changes unavoidably assumes an "official" stance. At the same time, we are committed to incorporating as broad a range of voices as possible. Thus, where appropriate and available, we provide a glimpse of both levels of HS involvement, national leadership as well as rank-and-file membership. Documents and interviews give us information about the former; our entry into the local setting through participant observation provides insight into the latter and helps fill out the picture of social patterns within and surrounding the organization.

Another qualitative dimension of our book is the inclusion, in chapter 1, of a narrative based on the true story of an act of euthanasia, with names and revealing facts changed to protect the privacy of the participants. We have named our character "Ellen," and she speaks in the first-person voice. No other method could capture the drama of this scenario. First, people are often thrown into active-euthanasia decisions unexpectedly and against their will. Moreover, the secrecy surrounding euthanasia, as well as respect for privacy, makes such moments difficult to observe. Through our participant-observer involvement in the Right to Die movement, however, we are familiar with such stories and know of their significance. To capture this aspect of the movement, we chose to present a narrative based on our intimate knowledge of a personal experience that would otherwise be unavailable to us in this book. This is a theoretical as well as a methodological choice; by expanding our methodological tools, we broaden the scope of our theory because we are only able to see that our theoretical "triangulation" works by using a variety of methods. This then opens up the possibility for further theorizing.

Quantitative Analysis

We were fortunate to have been involved in the creation, collection, and analysis of a national survey of the HS membership in 1995. One of the authors (Fox) approached the HS with the idea for such a survey. The HS responded favorably because the leadership was interested in learning more about its membership and agreed to mail the survey in one of its newsletters. Both the HS and the authors had input into the design and content of the questionnaire. Although the two agendas were different, the overlap between them permitted the final survey instrument to represent an amalgam of both scholarly and practical concerns. Thus, the survey project represents a cooperative effort by the HS and sociological researchers. Interestingly, this interaction itself constitutes an example of an SMO navigating its environment, a subject of great interest to us in this book.

One of the authors (Kamakahi) played the major role in the quantitative analysis of survey results. This verified for us some of our more intuitively based ethnographic findings while at other times challenging us with surprising and unexpected results. The data from the approximately 6,000 respondents of the survey yielded information of many kinds: for example, demographic information, members' attitudes toward and participation in various organizational and extraorganizational activities, and attitudes toward particular aspects of the Right to Die movement. We also used national survey data of the general population as a backdrop, enabling us to compare the characteristics of HS members with the U.S. population at large. Although some of our preliminary findings have been reported elsewhere (Kamakahi, Fox, and Čapek 1997; Kamakahi and Fox 1996; Wilson, Fox, and Kamakahi 1998), this book represents our first effort to compile our results and present a holistic picture of the HS and the Right to Die movement more broadly.

Our Hopes for This Book

Our goal in this book is to break new empirical ground in a case study of a key SMO in the Right to Die movement and to enrich the study of social movements more generally by offering a productive integration of three usually separate traditions. We believe that the Right to Die movement will continue to grow in significance at both local and national levels. We see it as representative of a category of movements increasingly visible on the social horizon—movements that make "contested terrain" out of life and death as bureaucracy and technology become more invasive and pervasive. Our hopes in writing this book are that the reader will become more informed about social movements in general and the Right to Die movement in particular. We have attempted to make the book accessible to the general adult reader, useful for undergraduate and graduate college students interested in social movements, and insight provoking for our colleagues in academia. In writing the book, we also address those who are directly grappling with the right to die issue at a personal level. Given the demographic realities of our society and the organization of our health care and technology, few of us remain directly untouched by this difficult issue. Although each situation is unique, many will face a scenario such as the one presented in our first chapter. The Right to Die movement and the HS in particular have created new resources and also raised new questions about the appropriate conditions surrounding death in our society. Our book identifies some of these important questions, suggests some answers, and in the process, provides a model for the holistic study of a social movement.

In chapter 1, we present a scenario based on a true story of a woman's struggle to assist with her mother's request for active euthanasia. In chapter 2, we suggest some important sociological questions that emerge from "Ellen's" story to be explored in our book. We introduce the theoretical lenses that we will use for understanding the Right to Die movement and conclude with a brief overview of the emergence of the movement. Chapter 3 discusses the changing role of medical and public health practices in the United States and considers how this provides a backdrop for the Right to Die movement. Chapter 4 delves into the organizational biography of a key SMO, the HS, showing how theoretical triangulation can provide insight into the movement. In chapter 5, we present the results of our national survey of HS members. Chapters 6 and 7 consider the recent flurry of activity in the Right to Die movement both nationally and internationally. We conclude in chapter 8 by revisiting our sociological questions and presenting conclusions about the movement.

Acknowledgments

We wish to thank our families, friends, and colleagues for their help, support, and understanding as we worked through the various phases of this book in Minnesota and Arkansas. Stella would like to extend special thanks to the Hendrix College Travel Grants Committee, to Lynne Sittig Cossman at the University of Central Arkansas, and to Britt Johnsen at the Bailey Library at Hendrix College. She would also like to thank her mother, Stephanie Čapek, who, in the closing days of her life as this book was being written, reminded her of the importance of a person's right to die with dignity and to refuse the artificial prolongation of life. Jeff thanks Katie, Lindsay, and Hattie for being constant sources of love and inspiration, as well as the College of Saint Benedict and Saint John's University community, especially the Sociology and Social Work Department, for their support. Elaine would like to acknowledge the research grant from the University of Central Arkansas, which supported the development of part of this book, her son for being such a great human being, and her coauthors for shared laughs and frustrations. We also appreciate Rob Benford for being a catalyst and advocate for this project, and Jim Lilly of the HS and its Arkansas chapter for his valuable input. Finally, we want to thank Jan Strange, without whose expertise this book would still remain on 18 diskettes and 3 word-processing programs.

Chapter One

An Act of Euthanasia

My name is Ellen. On a Tuesday in March six years ago I killed my mother. She asked me to do it, so I did. I could be kinder to myself and use less harsh words. I delivered my mother from her pain. Yes, that falls more gently on the ear. And, of course, this is the language used by those who advocate for a right to die for persons suffering from a terminal illness. But, whatever terms I use to describe the act that caused my mother's life to end, I committed the act. My intention was for her to die and she did. Depending upon the perspective of the listener, I murdered my mother or I humanely prevented her from suffering any further from the cancer that was devouring her brain.

In this chapter, we present a story of an act of euthanasia based on an actual experience, but with the names and some significant details changed to assure confidentiality. Although our goal as sociologists is to find patterns in the Right to Die movement, every social movement is experienced in a highly personal way by people struggling to make sense of their lives. We begin our study of the movement with Ellen's narrative for two reasons: first, to remind ourselves of the real people who form the movement, and second, to open the door to more systematic sociological questions. Here, then, is Ellen's story.

The Beginning

This is really my mother's story; it is a tale of courage, humor, foresight, fear, pain, and personal power. I wish she were here to tell it. But she isn't, so I will do this for her.

1

I was 43 when my mother first experienced health problems. Mom was visiting my sister Julie, who lived with her husband and son in Hong Kong. Developing a cough and some slight shortness of breath that seemed to linger longer than a typical viral upper respiratory infection, Mom, ever the adventurer, visited a traditional Chinese physician. She returned back home from that appointment with a sack full of herbal medicines and the firm conviction that she would soon be better. After all, this experience provided her with great material with which to entertain her bridge club back home. It had been an experience that none of her friends in the South could match. And, surely the cough would go away soon.

It didn't. Back home in the states several weeks later, my mother went to her family doctor. X rays indicated a potential spot on one of her lungs, and she was scheduled into the hospital for a bronchoscopy. Another of my four sisters lives in the same town as my mother, and it was Debbie who called to tell me about Mother's hospitalization. "You need to come home for this. I talked to the doctor and it doesn't look good so you have to come home! You are the nurse. You have to be here."

I hadn't really been too concerned about Mother's health. She had been a smoker for 40 years. Of course she had a cough. However, with Debbie's dark hints of deeper problems and the degree of hysteria I detected in her voice, I knew I should go. It is my role, my place. I am the family "quack."

As a registered nurse, I am the sister called upon for all family medical concerns. Usually, my role requires little more than supporting the information already provided by a physician. On occasion, it requires a bit of anxiety reduction among my siblings. Despite my dubious title of resident quack, I still end up involved in all family health matters and am consulted on all decisions. So when Debbie issued orders to come home, I knew I needed to go.

The timing was good for a sudden departure: I was due some lengthy vacation time. My only real problem was my 16-year-old son, Ryan, who insisted on accompanying me. I didn't want him to miss any school. However, claiming his rightful title as the "favorite grandchild" of my mother, he protested being left behind, insisting that, if anything was seriously wrong with Grandma, she would want to see him. I knew the truth of that statement, so we both climbed in the car and began the long drive home. Little did I realize that this journey would ultimately take two years and engage me in the mapping of my own personal hell.

Ryan and I arrived in Alabama in the midmorning, after driving all night. We went immediately to the hospital where my mother was a patient. As we exited the elevator on the third floor, my sister Debbie was waiting at the doors. She had been watching for us. Debbie looked at me and broke into tears. "It's cancer. She has lung cancer."

I felt the breath leave my body in one great rush. "You are sure? The path report is definite?" Debbie nodded, tears streaming down her face. "How did Mom take it?" I asked her. Debbie looked at me quizzically. "I didn't tell her. I've been waiting for you to tell her. I told the doctor not to tell her, that you would tell her."

My knees almost gave way as I felt my stomach do a flip-flop. "Do you mean to tell me you have known since yesterday it was cancer and no one has told her yet?" I yelled. "I knew you would want to tell her. She would want to hear it from you," explained my sister, defending her actions.

I would want to tell her? Why would anyone think I would want to be the conveyer of bad news? But I wasn't really surprised. The quack was being called upon again. With a sigh of resignation, I acknowledged this assigned responsibility. After looking at the pathology report and talking to her doctor, I trudged towards Mother's room.

Mom was sleeping, her hospital sheets tossed around in her restlessness. I touched her shoulder. She awoke with a start, her eyes staring wide into my face. "What is it? What's wrong with me?" Bypassing any pleasantries, her questions drove straight to the heart of the matter. "Mom, you have cancer in your lung," I said as gently as possible. Tears filled my mother's eyes. "Am I dying?" she asked, in the small pleading voice of a child. "No, Mom. There is treatment. There is chemotherapy. There is radiation. There is surgery. It isn't the time to have no hope." Mom gazed deeply into my eyes. "Are you telling me the truth?" she asked, her voice stronger. I reassured her I was. She cried quietly for a few minutes. I held her.

After a few moments, she looked at me, her eyes unblinking. "I don't want to live if cancer goes to my brain. You know I don't want that. If I have cancer in the brain, you must promise to help me. I don't want to go like that. If my mind is gone, I am gone."

Her hand tightened around my arm like a tourniquet. Desperately searching for calmness I did not feel, I sought to give her comfort with the words I knew she needed to hear. "Mom, I will help you. You don't have to worry about that. I promise you. But it won't ever come to that."

Later, after Mom fell asleep, a stab of anxiety gripped me. I had promised my mother I would help her die! No, I shook my head, *it won't come to that. It will never come to that.* Little did I know that it would, indeed, come to that.

With the diagnosis of cancer came my mother's journey into the pain, fear, and physical humiliation of chemotherapy and radiation treatments. I was, of course, not able to stay with her for the duration of these treatments that were designed to spare her, but which slowly stole her strength and vitality in exchange for lengthening her life. It was Debbie, as well as my youngest sister, Annie, who accompanied her on those trips into the cold, stainless-steel world of medical technology. Annie had been living in Europe when Mother was diagnosed, and on learning the news, she quickly reordered her life. She quit her job in Germany and flew home to be with Mother for the duration of the war on cancer. So I wasn't the one with Mother when she spent days throwing up, her head hanging over the toilet, her body slowly wasting away in response to the "poison" being injected into it. The radiation therapy burned her, but it was a burn that was felt internally; there was no obvious blister for the world to observe and comment on. However, her hair loss was visible, and the bald head wrapped in a turban really didn't fool anyone.

When I visited her during this time and we would venture out to a shopping mall, I watched as people, strangers in public spaces, glanced at her turbaned head, only to quickly avert their eyes in other directions. It was strange; I remember thinking how readily recognizable the results of chemotherapy are to the mass public. The covered head announces a body in rejection of itself, the ultimate shameful stigma in a society that worships slim, healthy bodies.

However, slowly, despite the enormous personal and emotional costs, the medical wizardry worked, and my mother was pronounced cured of her cancer. In time, she regained her lost weight and regrew her hair and took up her old life again, feeling victorious over her brush with death. For two years, she felt well and every cancer checkup brought good news.

As Mom approached her third cancer-free year, we were all lulled into a false sense of well-being. Surely, three years is equal to forever.

But the day of reckoning arrived, catching us all unaware and unprepared. I received the news while working a special job assignment on an Indian reservation in Arizona. My son had graduated from high school and had joined the Marine Corps. I felt unfettered and happy, permanently freed from the responsibilities of parenthood of a minor child. Life was vastly entertaining.

The phone call from Annie wrenched all that from me. I was working in the research project office when I answered the telephone and was surprised to hear Annie's voice. "What are you doing calling me in the middle of the day? What's wrong?"

How quickly we forget to maintain vigilance when we have been lulled into a sense of well-being. "Mom just came back from her checkup and she has cancer in her brain. It has metastasized from her lungs."

I was stunned into silence. Annie quickly continued, "I am going to put Mom on the phone now." Before I even had a chance to process this news in my mind, my mother was talking to me, her voice strong, proud, and insistent. "I am not going to have treatment this time. I won't go through chemotherapy again. The cancer is in a place where surgery won't do any good, so I am going to spend these last few months doing as much as I can. I can't go through chemotherapy or radiation again. Besides, it really isn't an option. It will only prolong my life and it won't cure it."

I remember mumbling some type of response to my mother, hoping it was appropriate words of comfort. But at that moment, I felt like I was the one who needed comforting. My mother was dying? How could she die? In retrospect, it is strange how I immediately viewed my mother's impending death as *my* loss. How could my mother die on me?

Promising to call that evening, I hung up the phone. I remember thinking that, when my mother dies, I will be an orphan. I was immediately ashamed that I was dwelling on what this news meant to me. I was losing a mother, but my mother was losing her life.

That evening, on the telephone, we again discussed my mother's decision not to have medical treatment for her cancer recurrence. I assured her I supported her decision not to simply prolong her existence in misery, but rather to spend what time she had left as freely as she could. I wasn't surprised by her decision. Stimulated by the personal situations I had encountered in my nursing career, Mother and I had spent many a conversation focused on the "what ifs" of life. For example, I remember relating to her the story of a young patient of mine who was dependent on life support machines. He had been in an automobile accident and was essentially brain dead. "What if that were you, Mom? What would you want to have happen?" For both of us, the denying of medical treatment that only prolongs life without any hope of cure was something we held strong convictions about, particularly when the medical treatment would only rob the person of their remaining quality of life.

While on the telephone that evening, my mother reminded me of the promise I had made to her when she was first diagnosed with cancer three years back. "Remember, when the brain goes, I am no longer in that body and I do not want my body to continue on. You will help me, won't you? You will do as I asked, won't you?"

I quickly assured Mother that I would help her when the time came. "But it won't really come to that," whispered a voice softly in my head as I loudly vocalized assurances to my mother that I would comply with her wishes. After hanging up the phone, I sat and reflected on the big "what if" I had pledged myself to.

The first time, a number of years in the past, in pre-Kevorkian days, and in more optimistic times, my mother and I addressed that particular "what if" when we were both in good health and had no idea what the future held for us. How effortlessly that promise of an easy death had rolled off my lips. I can do this, I told myself firmly, while believing that it would not come to pass. Fortune or fate would intervene, and I would not be placed in a situation where I would be forced to act. Sure, I could do it if I had to, but I wouldn't have to. *It wouldn't come to that. It would never come to that.*

Thanksgiving Eve 1990

Mother was diagnosed in early September 1990. The remaining moments of her life had been estimated to be but a few short months. She was told she probably would not see the coming Christmas, so she decided that all of her children would come to visit her on Thanksgiving. She wanted us all to be together as a family one last time. Thus, it was with mixed emotions that I made airplane reservations to fly home for the holiday. I was excited and looking forward to having all my family together under one roof at the same time. It had been years, well over a decade and a half since my father's death, that we had all been together as a family. My sisters and I were scattered all over the map; our geographies and biographies make it difficult to find a common time to steal away together. But this Thanksgiving was that time.

For us, as for many Americans, it was a death in the family that was bringing us all together again. But in a bittersweet mixture, the death had not yet arrived, although our family gathered in honor of its imminent arrival.

It was late in the evening, past nine o'clock, when I arrived at my mother's house. As I walked in the door, the living-room lamp gave off a small, warm glow. Debbie and her husband, Ben, were waiting for me. After hugs and smiles, we sat down and Debbie told me how Mother was feeling.

According to Debbie, Mom was tiring easily and going to bed very early but had not experienced any mental abnormalities from her brain tumor yet.

As Debbie was talking to me, relaying various doctors' reports and so forth, my eye caught sight of a small tag taped to the living room lamp. Curiously, my eyes scanned the room. I noticed that almost every object in the room had a tag clinging to it. I stood up and went to peer at a painting hanging on my mother's wall. The tape attached to it had my sister Marsha's name written on it. The tape on the painting next to it identified itself as my sister Julie's. The crystal ashtray on the coffee table had my name taped to it. I turned to my sister in wonderment. "What's going on? What does all this mean?"

Debbie laughed. "Mother has been busy. Everything anyone has ever given her over the years or has specifically asked her for she is labeling so there will be no mistakes or hard feelings over who gets what." My eyes shot around the room, identifying various objects I had given Mother over the years, in some cases so long ago I didn't remember the item until I saw my name tag on it. With that stimulus, the memory of the gift giving burst in my mind like a multicolored rainbow. What a wonderful present Mother was giving us by returning our gifts. We not only got the items back that we had given, but more than that, we had the memory attached to the item refurbished in our minds.

I remembered the story surrounding the ashtray. I had bought it for her one Christmas to replace an earlier version of the ashtray that my son, then not quite a year old, had broken during one of his first stumbling steps. I had forgotten how young he was when he first walked, only eight and a half months old, and how determined his small face looked as he attempted to move across the room on his shaky small legs.

In amazement, I wandered from one room to the next, glancing at the various name tags. On some items, there were two or more names, and a very few family antiques had no names identifying their owners. Questioningly, I turned to my sister. "See that chest?" she explained. "It has both our names on it. At some time, we both told Mom how much we liked that chest. She couldn't give it to both of us or one of us and not the other, so after Thanksgiving dinner, Mom is going to have a family drawing and will pull a name out of a hat, and that is how it will be decided who gets what."

I laughed. How like my mother to turn a family gathering into a celebration. I suppose I should have felt sad at the stark reminder of Mother's impending death, the distribution of personal items to survivors. I had arrived at my mother's house expecting to be immersed in sorrow, but now I realized that she had refused to define this gathering as a time of sadness. Clearly, we were not to spend our last moments together as a family in sorrow. Tomorrow, the celebration would be held.

Thanksgiving 1990

Glancing around the dinner table, I saw the light from the patio reflecting off the many layers of shiny necklaces Debbie wore around her neck. Annie had entangled a string of pearls in her hair, and Julie's wrist was loaded with multiple bracelets. I had placed several rings on a couple of my fingers, and Marsha's earrings tinkled as she moved her head.

Mother was the only woman at the table devoid of jewelry, and she smiled radiantly as she looked at her daughters in their newly acquired finery. After we had all arrived at Mom's house, she presented each of us with a pile of jewelry. Like all other items she had been given throughout her life, she was returning the various pieces of jewelry we had all given to her over the years. With five daughters giving presents of jewelry over some 40-odd years, it made a fairly impressive pile. Mother had obviously neither lost nor thrown away a single piece. As she distributed the jewelry, my sister Julie sniffed back a few tears. Mother's eyes flashed in anger. She would not tolerate crying. I glanced over at Julie's pile of items and spied a beautiful shell necklace that I had always admired in Mother's jewelry box over the years. Julie had always had great taste in accessories.

"I'll trade you something of mine for that necklace," I proposed to her, holding up a pair of earrings I had once heard Julie admire. "Sold," she cried loudly, as she snatched the earrings with one hand and tossed me the shell necklace with the other. Annie joined in the revelry. "I want that pearl ring to go with my necklace! What will you take for it?" I peeked at my mother out of the corner of my eye. She was smiling contentedly as she watched her laughing daughters toss jewelry around the room at each other.

Thanksgiving Evening

Dinner was also a boisterous affair. Daughters, sons-in-law, and grandchildren all joined in the raucous mood. Now, with full stomachs and jaws aching from laughing so much, we all sprawled in the living room. Mother prepared her drawing. She carefully wrote each daughter's name on a slip of paper and placed it in her hat. "The first drawing will be for the French antique chest," she announced as she blindfolded my niece with a carelessly tied scarf, pressing her into duty as the name drawer. "Let it be me," prayed Debbie out loud, "please let it be me. I want that chest so much!" My niece drew a slip of paper from the hat and handed it to Mother. Turning to Debbie, Mom held the slip up for all to see. "For some reason, your prayers have been answered." Debbie sprang up from her chair, jumping up and down and waving her arms in the air, she screamed, "I won! I won! I won!" The rest of us clapped for her while the drawing for the rest of the family heirlooms began again. Each of us won something.

After the drawing, Mother motioned for all of us to gather around her. "I want to say goodbye to each of you now. I don't know when I will see some of you again, and I want to say goodbye today. I had the drawing and have every item in the house labeled so everyone knows who gets what. I have seen too many families split up over arguments about who gets what after someone dies, and that will not happen to my family. In my will, everything is divided equally among all the daughters, and everything else not noted in the will has been distributed today. But in addition to that, I have a few words to say to each one of you."

Turning to my nephew, the oldest grandchild, my mother's words caressed him. "Dave, I know you have had your set of problems and seem to be finding it hard to find your own direction in life. My advice to you is to give up the drugs, learn to work harder, and stop allowing your relationship with your father to prevent you from doing what you need to do with your life. You have a large heart that you try to hide. Let it show sometimes and you will be happier."

To each of her descendents, Mother related a brief but personal message. Sometimes it was one of hope, at other times it was a message of warning, but each ended with love. I remember looking at my mother and admiring her style. "Damn," I thought, "When my time comes, I hope I can pull it off with just half her class."

Suddenly, like an unexpected clap of thunder in a clear, blue sky, my mother stunned me. Reaching into a drawer she pulled out a signed and witnessed living will and placed it on the coffee table with a flourish. "Now look. I have brain cancer, and when my mind goes, as far as I am concerned I am already dead and I do not want to remain living without a mind. Ellen has promised to help me at that time. I am not telling you to open this up for discussion. I am telling you so each of you will know what I have decided for me. If anyone has a problem with it, it is your problem and not my problem and not Ellen's problem. Do you understand?" She surveyed the group with a stern eye.

I was paralyzed. I had no idea she would do this. Yes, I had agreed to help her, but I had no notion that she planned to share this with the whole family! This was supposed to be our secret, our very own private agreement. I momentarily was unable to breathe. Rapidly, I scanned the faces of each of my family, desperately trying to read the expressions of shock. I quickly surmised that my nieces and nephews didn't understand what Mother had meant. Their eyes showed confusion. Julie was expressionless, her face a mask of stoicism. Debbie and Marsha were staring at me with terror, eyes huge and round, much like those of a deer startled by headlights. Annie, knocking over a glass as she lunged off the floor into a standing position, cried out in anguish, her face breaking into thousands of tiny lines. "I can't stay here and listen to this. I can't. You are talking about murder. No one but God can take a life. I can't hear my family plan this."

She looked pleadingly into Mom's face. Mom, with firm resolve, turned to Annie and quietly said, "I am sorry you feel that way. But it doesn't change anything, and I suppose you will need to leave the room." With tears flooding her face, Annie ran from the room. Mother, with a small sigh, turned back to the group. "Does anyone else need to leave?" No one moved—no one even took a breath. "Good," Mother nodded, "Do we need to discuss this anymore?" Everyone slowly shook his or her head; not one word or sound was uttered. "Okay, then let's get on with the funeral arrangements. I have written down what I want and what I don't want.

"Debbie," she looked quickly in my sister's direction, "If I don't look good, you will not have a viewing at the funeral home. There will only be a viewing if I still look good." Debbie nodded her head to acknowledge acceptance of her assignment. Mother continued, "Ben." Ben sat up as if poked with a cattle prod. "Ben, I will not have my age printed in the newspaper. A lady's age should never be printed in the newspaper. No one is going to have the satisfaction of knowing my age! Agreed?" Ben nodded acceptance of his orders. Mother continued on, delineating all aspects of her funeral arrangements.

I sat by Mother, still dazed. I heard her voice as she talked with others, but in a sense, it was like the small buzzing of a mosquito. I heard the discussion, but my mind was reeling from the public disclosure my mother had made. I was still astonished and dismayed. I guess I thought this would be a covert act between the two of us. I never realized that other people would know and be involved. My mother had made my task so much harder. Before, it was a small, private pledge between just two people, shrouded in secrecy. But now I had to deal with my family's knowledge. I knew each person in that room that evening would have some personal, cherished conviction regarding the rightfulness or the wrongfulness of what Mother and I were contemplating, and now I would be forced to confront the emotional baggage of all those people. I experienced a flash of anger at the unfairness of this situation. I shouldn't have to do this. I was filled with rage at my mother. It was unjust. I had been assigned the hardest task of all and now my mother had made it so much more difficult. But then, the small voice whispered in my mind's ear: *it won't come to this after all.* I clung to that tiny fragment of hope. *No, it won't come to that.*

Later that evening, with everyone in bed, I crept down the stairs to the kitchen to find something to soothe my warring nerves. I was an emotional wreck. Part of me wanted to cry out in sorrow at the pain of losing my mother in the near future, while another part still fueled the fires of outrage at my mother's public disclosure. I walked into the kitchen and was startled to find Julie sitting in the dark, the side of her face partially outlined by the moon's glow. She silently handed me the bottle of whiskey she held. Without preface, she said, "You know you can go to jail if you do this and word of it gets out." I turned to her. "Then we will have to make sure it doesn't get out, won't we?" Her face remained impassive. Slowly she nodded grimly. We sat in silence for several moments slowly sipping our drinks.

I pondered going to jail. I didn't want to go to jail. Sifting through the anger I felt toward my mother at that moment, I recognized a source of fear. I could go to jail for doing what my mother wanted me to do. I imagined myself in jail, imprisoned in a small concrete cell. I envisioned the waste of the rest of my life, the years of education thrown away unused and the wealth of my life's experiences wasting away to nothingness in prison. I did not want to go to jail!

Even though I had doubts as to my ability to comply with my mother's wishes, I also knew that, should it come to that, I did not think it would be fair for me to go to jail for helping her die at her own request. It was her life; she should have the right to make the final decision as to when she wanted it to be completed. I thought about this woman, my mother, who had made all her arrangements already, getting her will updated, making her own funeral plans, giving away her possessions, and realized that she was planning her death just as she had planned her life. For the very first time in my own life, I realized that death truly was the final act of life, and that people should have the right to preplan the completion of that life in situations such as my mother's. So why was I sitting in the moon's glow with my sister, contemplating perhaps having to go to jail? Why was I feeling so guilty and afraid about an act I had not even committed? This wasn't right. People should have the right to make these decisions for themselves, and family members such as me should not have to face jail as a result of an act of love. I shouldn't have to be angry with my mother for disclosing our agreement to the entire family and now live in fear of jail.

One very clear thought stuck me as sharply as a knife's edge. I shouldn't be feeling like a criminal. This act we were contemplating should be legal, done in the bright sunshine with all family members gathered. It should not have to be a sinister plot contrived and executed in darkness.

There ought to be a law!

February 1991

The telephone rang insistently at home. The voice of my sister Debbie on the other end of the line cut through my morning drowsiness. "It's time for you to come home. I can't do this anymore. I need help."

My mother was still alive. She had lived past the prognosis date offered by her physician. While her mental faculties were failing, she was still cognizant of her surroundings and herself. However, her over-all physical condition had weakened, and she constantly needed some-one with her. She would stumble and fall without help. Annie had given up her job in Europe to move in with mother until her death, and along with Debbie, who lived in the same town, had agreed to take care of mother for as long as they could. But we all knew that at some time the situation would deteriorate beyond their ability to assist. Mom wanted to die at home. She did not wish to be admitted to a hospital and had asked us to help fulfill her wish to remain at home. We agreed to help. And now my sister was telling me it was my time to come home. My mother's physical state was such that she needed professional nursing care to remain in her own home. Neither of my sisters could provide that for her, but I could. As my sister Annie had done earlier, I packed my bags and went home to help my mother die as she wished to die.

When I arrived at my mother's home, I quickly assessed the med-ical situation. I called her physician and requested hospice services. My mother's doctor told me there was nothing more he could do for her, so she need not come back for any more office visits. A visiting hospice nurse could provide the services my mother would need in the coming weeks. My mother had been sleeping for several weeks in a large lounger in her living room. It was too difficult for her to climb the stairs to her bedroom. My sisters had been giving her sponge baths downstairs, again due to the difficulty of scaling the stairs to the upstairs bathrooms.

My first task was to order a hospital bed to be set up in the living room, as well as the delivery of a wheelchair. My mother agreed that these would be helpful items for her mobility. She would like to go out to dinner at her favorite restaurant a few more times but was unable to walk from the car to the restaurant. The wheelchair was a guarantee of some continuing mobility and normalcy of her lifestyle. I knew that very soon the wheelchair would be her only source of movement. So I was completely unprepared for my mother's tears at the arrival of the bed and wheelchair. "I hate them," she sputtered, "I hate them."

I realized the arrival of these objects represented for her a new, declining phase in her slow journey to death. Despite the tears, she slept in the hospital bed that night and was strengthened a small bit the next morning by a good night's rest.

That day, we got her wheelchair upstairs, and she enjoyed the first real bath she had had in several weeks.

March 1991

One day slowly turned into the next, with each few days bringing a deterioration of bodily and mental functions and more medical decisions to be made. No, we won't tube feed her. She will eat what she can and what she wants and that will be it. No, we won't insert a urine catheter. That might be distressful for her, and I can change her sheets as much as needed. And so on and so on. I concentrated on nursing procedures. I turned her every two hours. I got her out of bed into her wheelchair every morning and evening. I allowed her to sip as much wine as she wanted and refused to hear Annie's protests about Mother's drinking.

My son, Ryan, fresh out of the marines with a broken knee and on crutches, soon came to stay with us. He wanted to be with his grandmother. He was an amazing source of help. Even with his one casted leg, he could still lift Mother from the bed to the chairside commode. With infinite patience, he fed her, taking as much time as she needed to eat. He slept on the floor by her bed in case she needed something in the night. I felt so much love for my young humanitarian son. I didn't know many young men who could have helped bathe, turn, lift, feed, and clean a dying grandmother with as much gentleness. Watching the man my son had become was my source of pride and comfort during those final days. I tried not to think too much about Mother's dying.

Without recognizing what I did, I began to engage in childlike magical thinking. If you don't name it, it doesn't exist. If you ignore the monster in the closet, then it isn't there. If you don't say the time is soon coming when your mother should die, then the time won't come. Every time I started to think about my promise to her, my mind clamped down hard. It isn't time yet. Don't think about it. It won't come to that. Something else will happen first—although I would have been hard pressed to name that something else I was so strongly counting on.

I remember the day so clearly that I first admitted to myself that it was time to think about my pledge to my mother. It was my birthday, and I asked my Mom what we should do to celebrate. She turned and faced me. "Let's go on a snake hunt." Her words were shaky and slurred. I laughed. I thought she was making a joke. But with a sense of terror as I stared into her empty eyes I realized her words had voiced her disjointed thoughts. I recognized at that point that I had been minimizing the deterioration of her mental condition. I had not wanted to accept her declining mental cognition, for to do so would bring me face to face with the promise I had been avoiding. Guiltily, I dissected the meaning of her words. "Is she calling me a snake because I haven't fulfilled her wishes yet? Is she asking me to act? Had it come to this, finally?"

An overwhelming sense of anxiety permeated me. I went outside and sat down on the ground. I told myself to breathe slower and more deeply. Never having experienced one before, I intuitively fought to overcome a panic attack. It was as if all I could hear was a large bell tolling the impending time over and over again in my brain. The time is coming, the time is coming. But as I calmed myself down, I knew the time was coming, but it wasn't today.

Julie and I had had an argument the previous night. Whereas I was always stretching to find meaning and cognition where none existed, Julie in her more practical applied approach to living had evaluated my mother's mental condition astutely. "She isn't there anymore. Her mind is gone and she isn't there anymore." With tears of frustration, pain, and anger, she whispered to me, "When? When are you going to do it? It kills me to see her like this. Look at her. She doesn't know what is going on. You promised her. When?"

I was outraged at Julie. How dare she question me? "It isn't time yet," I flung back at her. "I will do it when it is time, but it isn't time yet." Julie dissolved into tears. "Then when will it be time?" I grabbed my sister and held her close to me as I whispered in her ear. "Julie, if I could spare you the pain of watching Mom like this I would. But I can't do it to ease your pain. This is between Mom and me and I have to do it to ease her pain. Don't you think I am tired of the bedpans, the enemas, the hand feedings, the lack of sleep, and the damn ritual of getting her up in a wheelchair every day and the continual changing of her sheets? I want it to end, too. I am sick of it, too. But don't you see, I can't do it to end my pain and I can't do it to end your pain. I can only do it when the time is right, and all I know is the time isn't right now. If I did it now it would be to end *my* suffering and your suffering. I couldn't live with myself if I did it to save myself one more bedpan. It has to have more meaning than that."

That interchange with my sister threw me into a state of despair. When was the right time? Would there be some puff of smoke or some flash of lightning to draw my attention? I was so confused and so physically and emotionally worn out. I was afraid of ending my mother's life one second before it should end. I called a physician friend who lived in another state. Unlike most doctors I was acquainted with, I knew that my friend strongly believed in patient autonomy in decision making with regard to medical care, and I knew she also supported giving pain medication to patients even if it hastened death. I explained to her, "Mother has the cognition of maybe a five-month-old baby now. But, when I take her outside she seems to enjoy the breeze, and while she isn't coherent anymore, she still smiles in recognition when old friends come to visit. She didn't want to live if she didn't have her mind left. But she is enjoying some things still, I can see she does. But she doesn't have her mind anymore. Is it time?"

My physician friend asked, "Can five-month-old babies enjoy life with their limited cognition?" "Of course they can," I responded fitfully. What a foolish question she had asked me when I needed her to console me. There was only silence on the telephone line. I suddenly realized what she was telling me without words. "You will know when it is time," she assured me as she hung up the phone.

The next evening as I was turning my mother over to change her sheets, I heard a faint pause as she drew in a deep breath of air. I grabbed my stethoscope and listened carefully to her lungs. Yes, I could hear a tiny rattle in her left lung. It was very tiny, but I immediately recognized it. I thanked whatever gods were listening for that small sign from heaven. It was pneumonia, very early, just beginning, easily fixed with modern miracle drugs, but in the end, like historical times in the past when worn-out old people prayed for something to take them from life, still the "old man's best friend." "This is it. This is the sign. Now is the time," I sighed with relief. The waiting and the anguish were almost over. There was a light at the end of the tunnel after all. Now I could act. As a nurse, I knew the suffering pneumonia would bring. My mom would soon begin to struggle for each gasp of air as her lungs slowly filled up with fluid. I didn't know how to define a quality of life for my mother, but I knew what suffering was and I knew my mother would not suffer!

A few hours later, the hospice nurse came for her daily call. I greeted her at her car. "Mom is developing pneumonia." The hospice nurse looked at me and asked, "Are you going to treat her for it?" I shook my head no. This was my long-awaited sign. Now the time had arrived. Now there would be deliverance, both for my mother and for me.

My sister Marsha was due to arrive sometime the next morning. I wanted her to have the opportunity to see Mom alive one more time. That night, I slept my first night of good sound sleep in a number of weeks. The guilt was gone, the struggle for a decision was over. For me, I knew the time had come, and calmness had descended over me. The next morning, my sister arrived and spent a few quiet moments with Mother. She had been traveling all night on a train and soon left to go upstairs to sleep. Annie woke up and came downstairs. She noticed that Mother's breathing was becoming a bit labored and she was concerned. I told her Mother only had a short time to live. Debbie and her husband Ben arrived just as the hospice nurse did. I told them also that Mom's condition had worsened and she wasn't expected to live long.

I then asked Annie to go to the grocery store to pick up some items for Mother's care. I watched her with a deep well of sadness in my heart as she drove away, knowing that from today for the rest of our lives, I could no longer ever be completely honest with her. I was going to help my mother die, and Annie could never know that.

I love my sister very much, and because I love her, I will forever lie by remaining silent. It would cause her too much pain to know that I had "murdered" our mother, and so she will never know. And the rest of my family must also join me in this duplicity, our love for each other somehow tainted by the lie we all share. This makes me feel so very lonely.

I turned and looked at the hospice nurse. "You know she has pneumonia." The hospice nurse nodded. "I think that might be painful for her," I remarked as I walked into the kitchen to mother's medical supplies. I took up Mom's narcotic, glanced at Debbie. Ben walked across the room and put his arms around her. Debbie quietly began to cry. I walked into the living room with her medication. I looked at the hospice nurse.

I wasn't alone at the moment of my mother's death. The hospice nurse witnessed my actions. She didn't cry out in anger or outrage, nor did she attempt to stop my hand as I administered that overdose of morphine. She only nodded to me with empathy, silently giving her consent to my illegal act and pledging herself to the conspiracy of silence.

I sat by Mother's bed and listened to her chest with my stethoscope. I could hear her heartbeat begin to slow down and I heard her lungs slowly cease to fill sufficiently. I listened to her because I wanted a close physical connection with my mother. I wanted to be as close to her and as connected to her as I could be. Somehow, listening to her as she slowly ceased to live did not seem clinically cold; rather, it seemed as if she wasn't alone, that I was with her, that I was accompanying her on her journey from life. I listened until there was nothing more to hear. Somehow it seemed right. Mother was there with me when I drew my first independent breath as a newborn, and it was fitting that I should be with her when she drew her last.

From Private Troubles to Public Issues: Ellen's Story and the Right to Die Movement

Ellen's story takes us into the private world of a person facing painful decisions about active euthanasia and death with dignity in the late-twentieth-century United States. Yet, as C. Wright Mills (1967) and others have recognized, private stories are always embedded in a set of social patterns and practices. For example, had Ellen lived in another country or in another time, her circumstances would most likely be quite different. The fact that her actions are constrained by particular legal, political, economic, medical, religious, and other systems gives her common ground with others in the United States who must make decisions about euthanasia. This by itself does not create a social movement, however; for that to occur, as Mills noted, private troubles must be translated into public issues. Ellen grasped this when, in despair at her social isolation, she said, "There ought to be a law!"

Ellen eventually took the next step. It is part of her story that, two years after her mother's death, she joined the Right to Die movement. She became an active member of the Hemlock Society, at that time the only U.S. organization that supported active euthanasia. Like many others, she began to work for social change. Her personal story expanded as she joined the groundbreaking individuals and organizations pushing to define the right to die with dignity as a basic human right on the eve of the twenty-first century. As sociologists, it is our task to understand this link between personal experience and the emergence of a powerful social movement.

Chapter Two

The Emergence of a
Right to Die Movement:
A Sociological Framework

Some Sociological Questions

Our task in this book is not to make claims about the rightness or wrongness of active euthanasia. Rather, it is to make sociological sense of the growing Right to Die movement. In order to do so, we must listen carefully to the questions embedded in Ellen's story that reveal how her personal experience is connected to broader social issues. Indeed, because euthanasia is such a volatile issue, a sociological framework that locates the euthanasia debate in a larger context is particularly useful.

Ellen's narrative in chapter 1 raises some important sociological questions: What are the sociocultural circumstances that produce scenarios such as hers, where isolated individuals face criminal sanctions for engaging in active euthanasia? What difference does it make to face questions of death, dying, and euthanasia in a community (i.e., a network of supportive relationships) rather than alone? How are people's personal identities and interpersonal relationships transformed by encounters with right to die issues?

With regard to the social movement that emerged as a response to situations such as Ellen's—a movement that she herself joined—her narrative leads us to ask questions such as these: How did a Right to

Die movement emerge in the United States? Who are the key players in the movement? Why has the Hemlock Society (HS) had such an important leadership role in the movement, and how is its role evolving? More specifically, we can ask the following: Who joins the HS, and why? How are they different from other people in society? And finally, How is the movement changing? What is its future? What kinds of resources is it creating both locally and globally?

As we explore these questions throughout this book, our entire project is shaped by two underlying questions that relate to sociology itself: How can the theoretical tools developed by social movement theorists give us insight into the Right to Die movement? And more generally, how does a sociologist effectively study the Right to Die movement? In this chapter, we discuss the theoretical framework that, along with the questions identified above, will guide our subsequent discussions of the movement. We conclude this chapter with a brief overview of the emergence of the Right to Die movement up to the point of the founding of the Hemlock Society. Later chapters explore new developments in the movement.

Interpreting the Right to Die Movement: Social Movement Theories

We begin with a definition of the term *social movement*. Social movements have been variously defined; here, we use McAdam and Snow's definition: A social movement is "a collectivity acting with some degree of organization and continuity outside of institutional channels for the purpose of promoting or resisting change in the group, society, or world order of which it is a part" (1997, xviii). By this definition, organizations such as the Hemlock Society clearly fall into the realm of social movements. (Later in this chapter we acquaint the reader with some of the major players in the Right to Die movement and set the context for our discussion of the special role played by the HS.)

As we noted in the preface, our approach hinges on theoretical "triangulation," that is, the simultaneous use of three different sociological theories—the "resource mobilization," "framing," and "new social movements" perspectives. This triangulation yields important insights not only into the movement as a whole but also into the significance of the HS as a key actor in the movement. Below, we introduce the main components of each perspective, identifying the central question(s) posed by each.[1] Our triangulated framework will provide a foundation for our discussions of the HS and the movement as a whole in our later chapters.

Resource Mobilization   The resource mobilization (RM) theory of social movements, often characterized as the dominant model of the last several decades, emerged in the wake of the 1960s movements in the United States. Unlike earlier traditions that painted social movement actors as irrational or motivated by deprivation and "social strains," RM theory focuses on rational motives, successful organizational strategies, and the importance of "structural opportunities" for mobilization (McCarthy and Zald 1973, 1977; Zald and Ash 1966; Gamson 1975; Tilly 1978). RM theorists such as McCarthy and Zald have emphasized the professionalization of social movement organizations (SMOs), giving particular attention to leadership and the organizational manipulation of resources. To a large extent, social movements came to be studied through the organizations that constituted them.

RM studies have paid a great deal of attention to meso-level (interorganizational) relationships among SMOs, including the multiorganizational field in which SMOs compete and cooperate for scarce resources related to a particular movement (Curtis and Zurcher 1971; Klandermans 1992; Zurcher and Snow 1981). The organizational field includes not only promovement SMOs but also "countermovement" SMOs, those organizations that actively oppose social change (Gale 1986; Mottl 1980; Zald and Useem 1987). RM theorists have also noted the role of social actors who may not benefit directly from a movement but who are spokespersons, conduits for resources, or "conscience constituents" that support it (Harrington 1968; Lipsky 1970). More recently, theorists such as Tilly (1978) and McAdam (1982) have delineated a "political process" model that traces the two-way relationship between macrolevel "structural opportunities"—such as political, legal, and economic changes—and social movement mobilization.

On the whole, RM theory succeeded in redirecting attention toward the SMO as a significant unit of analysis and away from such issues as ideology, identity, and social-psychological considerations. A central question for RM theory is, *How do organizations (SMOs) acquire resources and negotiate the social movement field?* An additional question is, *How do their successes and failures relate to structural opportunities in a particular society?*

The Framing Perspective   The framing approach to social movements focuses on how social actors employ "interpretive schemata," or "frames," to make sense of social reality (Snow and Benford 1988, 1992; Snow et al. 1986). Drawing on a social construction of reality perspective (Schutz 1962; Berger and Luckmann 1966; Spector and Kitsuse 1973) and on an expansion of Erving Goffman's (1974) frame analysis work, it is centrally concerned with questions of meaning. Frames "focus attention on a particular situation considered problematic, make attributions regarding who or what is to blame, and articulate an alternative set of arrangements including what the movement actors need to do in order to affect the desired change" (Hunt, Benford, and Snow 1994, 190).

Frames can operate on several different levels. At one level, frames help individuals clarify and construct meaning out of the situations they encounter (such as the scenario presented in chapter 1). A successful frame will make sense of an ambiguous situation and will resonate with the "lifeworlds" of those who adopt it (Klandermans 1992). On another level, frames can be used to organize a movement's "presentation of self" to its public (Benford 1993a; Gamson 1988; R. Turner and Killian 1972; R. Turner 1969). Thus, they may be used in a persuasive manner to generate public support and, no less important, to strategically ward off countermovement attacks that attempt to discredit the movement. There is also a historical dimension to frames. Frames from earlier movements (such as the civil rights movement) can supply "master frames" for later movements (Snow and Benford 1992). For example, the disability rights movement draws on civil rights language to claim a role for the government in protecting the rights of the disabled. We will suggest in chapter 6 that the Right to Die movement also uses a civil rights model of institutional protection.

The framing approach has contributed to the systematic study of ideas and symbols as they relate to social movements. It emphasizes the ongoing process of frame construction as individuals and groups interact to negotiate meanings. Snow et al. (1986) suggest that the manipulation of interpretative frames, or "frame alignment" processes that connect individually held beliefs with the frames of an SMO, is a key element in explaining the ongoing and dynamic character of movement participation (for example, in chapter 4, we show that the HS frame defines active euthanasia as a compassionate and rational avenue to death with dignity, whereas its opponents frame it as murder). Studying how social movements frame reality both for participants and opponents is a crucial task for the student of social change. A central question for framing theorists is, *How are interpretive frames connected to the creation of private and public meanings in a social movement?*

The New Social Movements Approach   The new social movements (NSM) approach emerged largely in Europe in response to a somewhat different set of social conditions than those experienced by U.S. theorists (Klandermans 1986; Klandermans and Tarrow 1988; Kriesi 1988). Like RM theory, NSM theory represents various constellations of theoretical and empirical work (Buechler 1995; Larana, Johnston, and Gusfield 1994). Less concerned with the organizational aspects of movements, NSM theory focuses on the connection between broad societal changes and the emergence of new individual and collective identities, which in turn form the basis for a new type of social movement. Some typical examples of NSM concerns include the natural and built environment, planetary survival, physical and psychic health, the control of information, gender relations and sexual identity, peace, and more recently, ethnic and separatist movements (Klandermans 1986; Offe 1985; Larana, Johnston, and Gusfield 1994).

NSM theorists suggest that new social movements arise in response to postindustrial societies that are shaped more by information than by the economic class relations typical of industrial societies. The United States and Europe are representative of such complex and relatively affluent advanced capitalist societies (Habermas 1975; Inglehart 1977; Touraine 1985). Here, NSM theorists argue, struggles over power are no longer primarily class based or workplace based (as conceptualized by traditional Marxist theory), nor are they focused exclusively on material demands, such as money or income. Instead, symbolic identity becomes a key mobilizing issue. One reason for this, according to theorist Jurgen Habermas (1975), is that advanced capitalist societies are characterized by the "economic and administrative colonization of life space," an invasive process in which both the state and the economy invade and attempt to control private space (such as, we argue, the experience of death and dying).

In response, social movements resist by inventing spaces (both physical and metaphorical) in which "self-production" of identity, both individual and collective, can be affirmed (Cohen 1985; Hunt, Benford, and Snow 1994; Touraine 1985). In a modern complex society, actors also respond to "confusion over the wide horizon of available cultural alternatives" and the inability of social systems to provide solutions that make sense (Ronald Inglehart, quoted in Larana, Johnston, and Gusfield 1994). The struggles generated by these issues are diffused into a broad range of sites that can include neighborhoods as well as identity-based networks organized around lifestyle, culture, or social problems.

For NSM theorists, these social movements represent new constituencies, new values, and new action "repertoires" that are qualitatively different from the older, class-based movements such as labor unionism (Eder 1993; Luke 1989; Melucci 1980, 1985; Touraine 1971, 1985). NSM theory claims, for example, that the new social movements are likely to generate coalitions that cut across traditional class lines and that frequently bypass the institutionalized political sphere. According to Alberto Melucci, these movements "cannot survive without the mediation of political actors, but cannot be reduced to them" (1980, 190). Instead, they rely on periodically mobilized "submerged networks" of activism that may be more cultural or lifestyle-based than explicitly political (Melucci 1985).

The newness of these movements is disputed by some who claim that identity has always been an important part of social movements, or that class relations are as important as ever (Calhoun 1993; Plotke 1990, Tarrow 1991). Many NSM participants, for example, are relatively affluent members of their societies, suggesting that economic class is still a relevant variable. A lively debate also addresses the degree to which NSMs are merely reactive or have truly radical potential.

These debates aside, NSM theorists have succeeded in drawing attention to the problem of macrolevel social changes (such as a shift to a more information-based society) and their connection to emerging collective identities that often have a tenuous relationship to conventional social movement repertoires based on class structure and institutionalized politics. A central question for NSM theorists is, *How are broad sociocultural changes linked to movements of collective identity?*

Interpreting the Role of the Hemlock Society   Throughout this book, we use the above three theories to sociologically interpret the role of the HS and the broader sociocultural phenomenon of the Right to Die movement. This integrated approach will help clarify the highly intertwined processes of resource competition, issue framing, and identity negotiation taking place in the movement. For example, RM theory is best used to analyze organizations, not reality construction or broad shifts in collective identity; yet issues raised by one theory often condition the issues raised by another, such that they are complementary. Our goal is to interweave these theories and demonstrate how their simultaneous use enriches our understanding of the Right to Die movement. In chapter 4, we will apply our framework to the qualitative data that we collected on the HS. Chapter 5 will tap a more quantitative data set collected from surveys. First, however, we need to place the HS—as well as Ellen's story—in the historical context of the emergence of the Right to Die movement in the United States. The remainder of this chapter provides a brief sketch of this movement.

The Emergence of a Right to Die Movement in the United States

Although evidence of social acceptance of the right of individuals to control the circumstances of their deaths goes back to ancient societies, the Right to Die movement in the United States did not assume any formal structure until 1938, with the formation of the Euthanasia Society of America. The Euthanasia Society was politically active but ineffective during the next few decades, failing to gain public or political support (Marker 1993; Humphry 1981). Indeed, some sociological theorists have characterized the United States prior to the 1960s as being in a state of denial about death (Dumont and Foss 1972). The palpable silence around issues of death and dying began to be challenged in the 1950s, as breakthroughs in medical technology and organ transplant science inspired a need for a new definition of death. The harvesting of organs from the clinically brain dead in the still physiologically alive proved more successful than harvesting organs from the already dead, thus necessitating the legal ability to remove an organ from a "body" still being ventilated by machines (Kurtz and Chalfant 1984; Simmons, Marine, and Simmons 1977). In addition, such simple procedures as cardiopulmonary resuscitation (CPR) and the Heimlich maneuver were heralded as lifesavers. As we show in chapter 3, for the demographically expanding population of the elderly, there was an increasing probability of an extended life span due to technology, but in circumstances that were not always desirable.

The shifting boundaries between life and death stimulated a reexamination of existing social norms and practices. As the prolongation of life through advanced medical technology became institutionalized in medical settings, public concern emerged over the appropriate role of medical science. For example, by 1974, health care institutions were setting protocol for nonphysicians to initiate CPR without a physician order, and by 1978, articles were appearing that questioned the unrestrained use of such medical technology (Humphry and Wickett 1986). An important distinction was drawn between passive euthanasia (avoiding artificially prolonging the life of a terminally ill patient) and the more controversial active euthanasia (deliberately terminating life to avoid suffering, sometimes known as "assisted suicide"). Religious organizations naturally had a stake in the debate. In 1957, Pope Pius XII foreshadowed the Right to Die movement by differentiating between "ordinary" and "extraordinary" means of medical care (Pius XII 1957a, 1957b). In doing so, he gave tacit permission to millions of Catholics to forego medical care that only prolonged a painful existence (passive euthanasia).

The debates on prolongation of life became so energized that, in 1968, the World Medical Association adopted a statement confirming their opposition to active euthanasia. The British Medical Association followed suit in 1969. Concurrently in the United States, Louis Kutner proposed the concept of a living will in an article in the *Indiana Law Review* (Kutner 1969). California would become the first state to recognize this instrument. The groundswell of a movement began in earnest, encouraged by such works as Elizabeth Kubler-Ross's *On Death and Dying* (1969) and Barney Glaser and Anselm Strauss's *Awareness of Dying* (1975). From 1960 to 1969, more than four dozen articles and some one dozen books were published on euthanasia, the terminal patient, and the laws (or lack thereof) applying to mercy killing (Humphry and Wickett 1986). The emergence of journals such as *Omega* (in 1969), *Death Education* (in 1977), and *The Journal of Thanatology* (in 1973) indicates not only the professionalization of the study of death (Clark and Kutscher 1992) but also its growing public visibility. In 1976 the Karen Ann Quinlan case dramatically focused public attention on the passive euthanasia issue. Quinlan, admitted to an intensive care unit at age 21, was kept alive for nearly a decade in a "persistent vegetative state." Although her parents wanted her to be removed from a respirator, they were opposed by medical staff. Only after several years of legal battles did the New Jersey Supreme Court permit Quinlan to be removed from life support; she continued to live, however, for another decade.

Beginning in the 1970s, a variety of SMOs began to surface, creating a network, or field, of organizations. Some of these SMOs cooper-

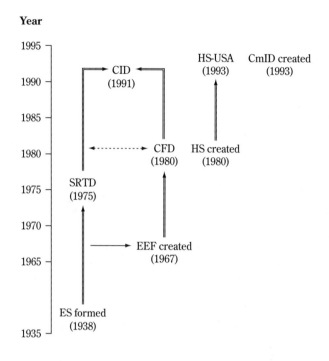

FIGURE 2.1.

Chronological Diagram of Right to Die Organizations.

ated with each other, while others competed (McCarthy and Zald 1973, 1977). In 1967 the Euthanasia Society, worn out from pressing for political results without success, established a tax-exempt organization called the Euthanasia Educational Fund (referred to as the Council). The Council concentrated on distributing information about dying and was successful in fund-raising, providing funding for the Euthanasia Society (after 1975 called the Society for the Right to Die [see Figure 2.1]). Using the concept of the living will as a common focus, these two organizations operated as separate arms of the U.S. Right to Die movement, sharing offices and concentrating on passive euthanasia until their relationship eroded in 1979.

In 1980 the Council (now called Concern for Dying) issued a statement indicating its disapproval of indiscriminate or ill-conceived "right to die" legislation by activist groups. The Society for the Right to Die sued Concern for Dying for breaching joint fund-raising agreements, wanting its share of money to continue the legislative and activist battles in opposition to Concern for Dying's direction (Humphry and Wickett 1986). In the same year, the World Federation of Right to Die Societies was founded with 27 groups from 18 countries (Humphry and Wickett 1986), signaling a global dimension to the Right to Die movement. Concern for Dying and the Society for the Right to Die both joined, although the latter (unsuccessfully) opposed the application of the former. Concern for Dying and the Society for the Right to Die eventually rejoined forces under the umbrella name of Choice in Dying (see Figure 2.1). They apparently continued their previous division of labor, with Concern for Dying focusing on education and the Society for the Right to Die concentrating on passive euthanasia legislative issues (Marker 1993).

The Emergence of the Hemlock Society

Also in 1980, the first real splinter group in the euthanasia movement emerged. Former British journalist Derek Humphry and his wife and coauthor Ann Wickett established the Hemlock Society as a tax-exempt educational organization advocating *active* as well as passive euthanasia. The founders of the HS deliberately set it up to fill an organizational niche that no other SMO was willing to claim, as no other group in the United States supported active euthanasia. With its motto "Good Life, Good Death," the organization's name was intended to call up associations of Socrates drinking hemlock to take his life, an act of "rational suicide" accepted in some societies (HS n.d.b). It offered to members a support network and pragmatic advice in the form of a quarterly newsletter, a federated chapter structure at the state level, and resources such as a free living will.

A stated goal of the HS was, among other things, to "provide a climate of public opinion which is tolerant of the rights of people who are terminally ill to end their own lives in a planned manner" (HS n.d.a). The founders hoped to accomplish this by raising public awareness through the media, through public meetings, and by working with the medical, legal, and other professions. A broader goal was to have physician aid in dying (active voluntary euthanasia) made lawful through passage of a "Death with Dignity" act. As an educational 501(c)(3) tax status organization, however, the HS could have only limited political goals (see chapter 4 on the implications of IRS tax code classifications). Although it was periodically able to secure national media attention when various individuals acting separately engaged in "mercy killings" of family members, the HS found itself in a constant battle to gain financial stability and legitimacy during the first few years of its existence.

Derek Humphry, who served as executive director of the HS from the organization's inception until 1992, was a charismatic leader with the credibility of having personal experience with active euthanasia. He had directly assisted his terminally ill first wife with her suicide, an experience documented in the book *Jean's Way* (Humphry and Wickett 1978). Humphry proved to be a highly effective spokesperson for the organization; as a former journalist, he was well acquainted with manipulation of the written and visual media and sensitive to the presentation of issues to the public. He was, moreover, an entrepreneurial leader able to articulate a problem, gather financial support, and promote action toward its solution (Herrmann 1991). He also authored a number of books on active euthanasia that, despite being repeatedly criticized by the Concern for Dying organization, eventually reached a broad audience and created revenues for the HS (Humphry 1981, 1991; Humphry and Wickett 1978, 1986).

By 1991, 11 years after its founding, membership in the HS had expanded from 2 individuals operating out of a garage to over 25,000. With its growing membership and increasing public visibility, the HS had found not only a successful niche but also a leadership position in the Right to Die movement. A statement by former HS president John Westover reflects the convergence of social forces and organizational energy that made this possible:

In the 1980s, active euthanasia was a cause "whose time had come." Several organizations were promoting passive euthanasia and, in so doing, were raising the expectations of a nation whose people were becoming aware of the dilemma created by the growth of hi-tech medicine that could keep bodies alive at a time when antiquated laws prevented a dignified death. Derek and Ann did not create the dilemma, but their new organization addressed it. Hemlock, riding a tide of events and court decisions, became successful beyond their expectations. (HS 1993, 1)

The Hemlock Society's entry onto the scene shifted the dynamics between the various organizations in the Right to Die movement, just as, more recently, the isolated activism of retired pathologist Dr. Jack Kevorkian has altered the social movement landscape by directly assisting patients with planned suicides. Existing SMOs criticized the HS for its "radical" stance on euthanasia even as they recognized its potential as a successful competitor in an increasingly crowded social movement field.

We see, then, the gradual emergence of a Right to Die movement represented by a number of organizations as well as by individuals unaffiliated with any specific organization, with a range of goals varying from working for greater acceptance of passive euthanasia to advocacy of the legalization of active euthanasia. With the founding of the HS, a new chapter opened in the Right to Die movement in the United States. Chapter 4 examines in more detail the HS as a major actor in the movement. First, however, we will look in chapter 3 at how changes in medical practices and technology provide a backdrop for the private and public issues surfacing in the Right to Die movement.

Chapter Three

Medical Technology: Friend and Foe

As noted in our discussion of the emergence of the Right to Die movement in chapter 2, a striking aspect of innovation in the twentieth century is the potentially volatile relationship between human beings and technology. One facet of this relationship involves control. Where are the boundaries that define appropriate use of technology vis-à-vis individuals? What is the appropriate role for medical technology? As illustrated in chapters 1 and 2, an individual's choices for using medical technology may be at loggerheads with existing cultural norms, legal structures, and the orthodoxy of established medical practice. This issue is crucial to understanding the Right to Die movement. In this chapter, the role of medical technology is examined further.

Striving and Constraint

"The best way to conceive of the fundamental project of human reality," philosopher Jean-Paul Sartre once stated, "is to say that man is a being whose project is to be God" (1965, 70). Although many would dispute this, Sartre's words certainly characterize the driving force behind Western biomedicine's quest for total omniscience, immortality, and power. But consider also, as Sartre did later, that human beings are born into a preexisting world and bound by the vagaries of history and society (Sartre 1976). Human existence, he realized, is the struggle between the desire for control and the limitations that envelop us.

The dialectical battles that pit striving and constraint against one another are not new. They animate the legends, myths, and epics of humankind. Often, the consequence of "pushing the envelope" is severe. In the biblical Eden, for instance, Adam and Eve are expelled for eating of the fruit of knowledge. In the Greek legend, the wax-winged Icarus plummeted from the sky for attempting to fly "too high." Yet there are also hints of ultimate success. After all, Faust skirted eternal damnation when he bargained with Mephistopheles and tasted victory. What are the risks of striving? Are the potential benefits worth the risks?

Substitute the word *technology* for striving and *nature* for constraint. We can conceive of technology as an "applied knowledge" whose goal is to increase our control over nature. We can conceive of nature as the great unknown. Our love-hate relationship with technology is highly visible. George Orwell's *1984,* Charlie Chaplin's *Modern Times,* and even Arthur C. Clarke's *2001: A Space Odyssey* display our nascent fears about the technology/nature tandem, especially with its consequences for human beings. Interest in human-versus-machine contests—for example, the recent chess matches between chess champion Garry Kasparov and computers—demonstrates the same point. Technology is seen as a partner for human development but also as laden with potential dangers.

A recurrent theme emerges. In striving, humankind discovers its limits. However, with the nagging pessimism, hope springs eternal that those limits will become less and less significant. Many topics of international concern involve the (potential) dangers of technology: for example, greenhouse gas emissions, nuclear weapons, deforestation, overpopulation, and so on. Despite the problems, humankind has embraced technology as a tool for creating a better world. It has continued to apply new knowledge to everyday living, and "technological optimism" remains strong.

Human Bodies   Substitute *medical technology* for technology and the *human body* for nature. Humankind has made monumental strides with regard to knowledge of the human body and its structure and dynamics. Although vestiges of beliefs in auras, the four humors, and faith healing persist, the "scientific" orientation toward the human body predominates in the Western industrialized world. This scientific orientation involves the following premises: (1) that disease is a function of identifiable, material causes; (2) that human bodies function in similar ways across races, sexes, and social classes; (3) that human agency (intervention) can treat (perhaps even prevent and/or cure) afflictions; and (4) that these interventions do not conflict with some otherwise beneficent divine plan (see Abercrombie, Hill, and Turner 1988).

Nested within this scientific model for the body is the striving for immortality and perfect existence. Indeed, the measurement of and striving for longevity has become a hallmark of the modern medical era. Governments and international agencies are preoccupied with the aggregate longevity of populations. Vital statistics such as life expectancies or infant mortality rates are collected. Copious records are kept regarding not only how long people live but where they were born, where they lived, what ailed them, and what they eventually died from. Records of birth and death, once used to keep track of souls, are now used to monitor human longevity and societal development (Sivard 1991).

Although working toward the goal of immortality and perfect existence, medical technology and the scientific orientation focus on the study and treatment of *medical deficit*. A medical deficit is any deviation from immortality and perfect bodily functioning. In the real world, all have deficits. Even mental problems are treated in accordance with this medical model through psychiatry (Mechanic 1989). Virtually any deficit can be medically treated (although not all treatments are effective or lead to cures). Within the medical orthodoxy (i.e., the scientific orientation, medical technology, and the medical establishment), the dialectical battle waged pits medical technology against human deficit.

A short life is a paramount deficit. It is indicative of failure: the failure to control the hazards that surround us; the failure to treat afflictions effectively; and the failure to live an immortal and perfect existence. In the real world, even the highest aggregate life expectancies (and life spans) pale in comparison to immortality. The ailments that circulate (and recirculate) throughout human populations also represent deficiencies with respect to perfect existence. In the real world, all have had ailments. However, from the perspective of the medical orthodoxy, living and dying make failures of us all.

Our general social and cultural norms predate and have evolved along with the medical orthodoxy's values for human longevity and medical treatment. These norms were formulated and maintained when youth was an especially hazardous stage of life and when pandemics devastated whole populations in large fell swoops. Although pandemics of that magnitude have all but disappeared from our lives, our cultural orientation has remained unchanged. Our present infant mortality rates are infinitesimal when compared to those of even a century ago (U.S. Bureau of the Census 1975). The top 10 causes of death in the United States have shifted to chronic ailments and away from infectious diseases. Life expectancies in the United States reach beyond the length of time for which the present pension systems and social welfare systems were originally designed (Weeks 1996).

The proportion of the aging population grows as the hazards of youth have been controlled. The young are advised that the current Social Security system will likely be minimized or defunct, that the age of retirement will be increased, and that their tax burden will be greater than that of preceding generations (B. Turner and Samson 1995). The medical costs for the elderly, on the other hand, have skyrocketed; the costs for their last six months of life will probably be greater than for their previous 70-plus years (Cockerham 1991). The aggregate increases in longevity engender their own societal dilemmas.

Such social change reverberates throughout the entire social fabric. As we seem to be nearing a limit of practical longevity, as the threshold of medical orthodoxy's efficacy in increasing aggregate longevity approaches, and as the social and economic costs of holding on to our last mortal breath increase, people have begun to question whether longevity equals the good life. Some have even suggested that voluntary suicide may be a rational alternative to depleting one's physical, mental, and financial resources for impossible dreams of immortality and perfect existence.

Within the framework of the medical orthodoxy, voluntary suicide is certainly an enigma. Who in their "right mind" would want to end their own life? (Notable are the rarely discussed exceptions for martyrs and heroes.) Medical technology, focused on increasing the average aggregate human longevity, finds the notion of rational, voluntary suicide preposterous. For it, voluntary suicide is an oxymoron. A long life is the sacred and unquestioned goal for which the medical orthodoxy strives.

A Question of Privilege   The quest for human longevity lies at the core of the Western medical orthodoxy and is ingrained in the cultural ethos of the United States. But there is an emerging social movement, the Right to Die movement, that voices a new "heresy": that longevity is not the sine qua non of the good life. It questions whether the medical orthodoxy strives for what is best for the individual patient or what is best for itself. It questions whether the medical orthodoxy has the right to impose its values and assumptions on individuals. The Right to Die movement is garnering significant support among the populace (Wood 1990).

Substitute *individual empowerment* for striving and *the medical orthodoxy* for constraint in order to place the orientation of the Right to Die movement in its proper context. The situation described in chapter 1 demonstrates that individuals presently must fight against the boundaries of cultural norms, legal entanglements, and medical practice in order to engage in voluntary suicide. How did any of this come to be?

To answer this question, we must take a few steps back. It is the turn of the twentieth century. The United States is becoming a key player in the world economy. Large dams have been constructed that are harnessing energy and changing the landscape. Waves of immigrants, mostly from Europe, have settled and are expanding the country's agricultural and industrial bases (Parrillo 1997). Something else is also occurring; resources are being mobilized to combat the scourge of epidemics and malnutrition that exist. A national priority is to increase the longevity of the population and create an active, healthy workforce. This era begins two important shifts in the nation's population dynamics: the *epidemiological* and *demographic transitions.*

The Epidemiological and Demographic Transitions

In the broad scope of human history, acute infectious diseases have been a major nemesis of human populations. There are other dangers, of course (for example, warfare or natural disasters), but the impact of diseases has been tremendous and largely underestimated.

It did not take much contact between social groups to produce epidemics and pandemics of huge proportions. Empire building (Wallerstein 1974–1989) and civilization building (Couch 1984) facilitated the process by which microbes were increasingly transferred between previously isolated and insulated populations. At the cost of great suffering and tremendously high levels of mortality and morbidity, exposures to virulent foreign microbes were eventually transformed into immunities shared across (and between) populations. In their wake, native populations and cultures were often decimated (see Stannard 1989; Bushnell 1993).

Although deadly infectious diseases still exist, their place within the pantheon of leading causes of death has dwindled worldwide. In the industrialized world and now throughout the world, the acute infec-

TABLE 3.1.

Leading Causes of Death in the United States, 1916 and 1991.

Rank	Year of 1916	Rate	%
1	Other	220.8	15.2
2	Organic heart disease	150.1	10.7
3	Tuberculosis of the lungs	123.8	8.8
4	Acute nephritis	105.2	7.5
5	Violent deaths (except suicide)	90.9	6.4
6	Pneumonia	88.3	6.3
7	Cerebral hemorrhage	82.6	5.9
8	Cancer and malignant tumors	81.8	5.8
9	Congenital debilities	77.5	5.5
10	Diarrhea and enteritis	65.6	4.7

Rank	Year of 1991	Rate	%
1	Diseases of the heart	285.9	33.2
2	Malignant neoplasms	204.1	23.7
3	Cerebrovascular diseases	56.9	6.6
4	Chronic pulmonary	35.9	4.2
5	Accidents	35.4	4.1
6	Pneumonia/influenza	30.9	3.6
7	Diabetes mellitus	19.4	2.3
8	Suicide	12.2	1.4
9	HIV	11.7	1.4
10	Homicide	10.5	1.2

Leading causes of death, 1916 versus 1991. Note the predominance of infectious, environmental, and accidental deaths in 1916 and the predominance of chronic and accidental deaths in 1991. Rates refer to deaths per 100,000 population. Percentages refer to percent of total deaths in that year attributed to a category.

Sources: Data for 1916 were taken from the U.S. Bureau of the Census (1918). Data for 1991 were taken from U.S. Department of Health and Human Services (1991, Hyattsville, MD, 1996)

tious diseases are of secondary concern (see United Nations Population Fund 1990, 1991; Garrett 1994). A brief look at the leading causes of death in the United States during this century bears this out (see Table 3.1).

The causes of death have changed dramatically in the United States during the twentieth century. At the beginning of the century, infectious diseases predominated. At the end of the century, infectious diseases have been displaced by chronic ailments. Epidemiology, the study of the relationships of various factors determining the frequency and distribution of diseases in the human community (Anderson 1989), has duly noted the changes. This societal shift from acute to chronic ailments is referred to as the epidemiological transition.

What brought the epidemiological transition about? The answer is fourfold. First, there were the natural abilities of the human body to create immunities once exposed to microbes. As interactions between groups became more frequent, immunities eventually became shared across (and between) populations. The immunities present among survivors could be intergenerationally passed along—genetically and behaviorally (e.g., by breast feeding). Of course, the process was slow and carried a high price in terms of mortality and morbidity: those without immunities were either lucky to survive or they perished.

A second factor in the epidemiological transition involved public health measures. Although some ancient taboos served a public health function, the identification and correlation of environmental conditions to diseases is a fairly recent phenomenon (Cockerham 1995). The importance of sanitation practices was paramount for the health of groups. Activities such as waste disposal, the monitoring of the water supply, food storage and distribution, pest control, and the isolation of the sick were and are all important measures for preventing, or at least controlling, the spread of acute diseases (McKeown 1965, 1979).

Social organization is a third important factor in the epidemiological transition. As society became more complex and resource sharing became more widespread, the notion that health care was an entitlement rather than a privilege began to emerge (Navarro 1986). The ethos that health care is a quasi-public entitlement rather than strictly an individual privilege has far-reaching implications. In cities, public utilities and services arose. In the streets, public sanitation involved pest control, garbage pickup, and street cleaning. The social organization of the workplace raised concerns about occupational hazards and possible employer liability for work-related injuries. Social welfare legislation began to include health services to nonemployed portions of the population (e.g., the young and elderly) and/or the poor (free meal programs, Medicaid, Social Security, etc.) that are rare for developing nations (Doyal and Pennell 1981).

The advances of medical technology and medical practitioners is the fourth factor in the epidemiological transition. The evolution of a scientifically based model of medical intervention and its institutional- ization in education (medical schools, nursing degrees, etc.) has been important (E. R. Brown 1979; Starr 1982). The monitoring of health and the intervention of medical practice have allowed for the preven- tion, diagnosis, and treatment of numerous ailments. Over the past century, the creation of vaccines and other pharmaceuticals, the devel- opment of diagnostic procedures and machinery, the improvement of surgeries and other medical procedures, and the increased under- standing of the functioning of the human body have indeed been aston- ishing (Thomas 1983).

The emergence of the epidemiological transition has had far- reaching effects on how people in the United States live out their lives. Its effects reach beyond the circumstances of our present living situa- tion and into the structure of society itself and are reflected in the changing population profile.

After many infectious diseases were controlled, youth became a much less hazardous period of life. When agencies for the social good became entrenched in the social organization of life, hazards of work- ing life also decreased. With these reductions in hazards came changes in the demographics of the United States. The equilateral tri- angle that represented the age structure of the country at the turn of the century changed into more of a population "cylinder" as the pro- portion of elderly increased relative to the proportion of young (see Table 3.2).

This demographic change was occurring as the U.S. population was becoming more urbanized and commodified (see U.S. Bureau of the Census 1994; Giddens 1981; Baudrillard 1988). The movement away from the agrarian lifestyle, the decrease in the hazards of youth, and the greater degree of social entitlements changed our orientations toward the family and altered our practices with respect to education and work. Succinctly, people's livelihood and security in later life no longer depended on their offspring (Weeks 1996). In urban, market- driven societies such as the United States, children became more of an economic liability. Social security was now to be found in pension

TABLE 3.2.

U.S. Population, Percentages by Age.

YEAR

Age	1900(%)	1950(%)	1990(%)
65 and over	4.10	8.10	12.60
55–64	5.30	8.80	8.50
45–54	8.50	11.50	10.10
35–44	12.20	14.20	15.10
25–34	16.00	15.80	17.40
15–24	19.60	14.70	15.20
5–14	22.30	16.10	14.20
Under 5	12.10	10.70	7.40
Total %	100.10	99.90	100.50
Pop (mil.)	76.10	151.70	248.70

Source: Kurian 1994.

plans, government transfers, personal investments, and personal savings.

The movement from the farm to the city decreased the importance of children as social security and hence the incentive for people to have large families. High fertility rates also declined as the survival rates of offspring increased. One significant result of fewer and safer childbirths was a decline of maternal mortality (i.e., deaths due to pregnancy and childbirth) (U.S. Bureau of the Census 1975). Female mortality rates fell because women were now decreasing the number of times they went through the life-threatening process of childbirth. Structurally, the population's profile was changing. In the parlance of those who study human populations, the United States underwent a demographic transition.

In the three stages of the demographic transition theory, as societies become industrialized, they concomitantly make a shift between two different types of population equilibriums (see Figure 3.1). Stage one involves agrarian societies with high birthrates and high death rates. Because infectious diseases predominate, death rates are high. Many of the deaths occur among the young—especially infants. To

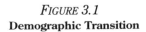

FIGURE 3.1
Demographic Transition

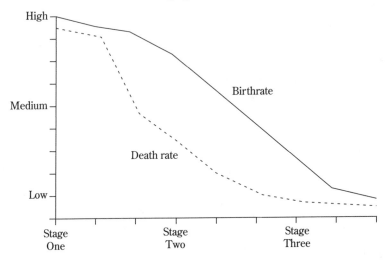

counteract the high mortality among the youth, people have many children—so that enough young people will survive to adulthood. The shape of the population's age structure resembles an isosceles triangle. At the base, there are many young; at the apex are the few who have made it to "old age." The slant of the sides reveals those who have survived the hazards of the previous age group.

In stage two of the demographic transition, effective measures for addressing infectious diseases are adopted among a population, resulting in a significant decrease in death rates. However, while the death rate declines, the birthrate continues unabated. People have yet to adjust their procreation habits to match the reduction in societal hazards. The result is a "baby boom." The shape of the population pyramid remains roughly the same except for this baby boom "bulge" as the cohort moves upward through the age gradient.

In the final stage of the demographic transition, birthrates decline, balancing the low death rates. The population has again reached equilibrium. At this point, the population shape is more columnar. Because there are relatively few hazards, the life expectancies are higher for individuals and the society as a whole. Fertility decreases, infant mortality decreases, life expectancy increases, and the social organization of the population becomes ever more important. The distribution of resources in society also becomes a function of an anonymous social and economic marketplace, a series of political agencies, and one's position in the world of human capital.

The demographic transition theory, although perhaps not universal, is certainly an adequate depiction of what happened in the United States during the nineteenth and twentieth centuries. But the theory itself only scratches the surface of the demographic transition's total social impact. The transition did more than allow people to live longer. Indeed, it has forced us to live in an entirely different world than that of preceding generations. The economic market envelops us. Wages and benefits are our tickets to goods and services. Technology continues to grow by leaps and bounds. One's immediate family is a means toward establishing one's own level of human capital. People are adrift within a sea of information. Society has changed dramatically, but we are essentially the same human animal who has existed for millennia (see Morris 1996; Gould 1981).

In the realm of medical practice, medical technology has ushered in a new era. In the words of physician and essayist Lewis Thomas, we live in an era of "halfway technology" (1983)—that is, we now have the means to keep people alive for longer periods of time, but the chronic ailments we now treat, as well as some infectious diseases, cannot be cured. Perhaps medicine and health technologies have altered medicine's function from a curative endeavor to a palliative one.

Medical Knowledge and Health

A common assumption in the contemporary United States is that medical care and health care are synonymous. For instance, discussions of health care or health services tend to focus exclusively on medical care and services. Likewise, when health industries are discussed, images of pharmaceutical companies, medical equipment manufacturers, hospitals, nursing homes, and so on come to mind. Interestingly, anything that is remotely related to health has been symbolically appropriated as part of the medical orthodoxy. In other words, we tend (wrongly) to view health care as revolving around medical care.

The equating of health with medicine has far-reaching implications. It elevates the social and material statuses of physicians, leading to large public investments into the cost of their training, high fees for their services, and high prestige associated with their activities. Furthermore, they are granted authority by the government over the use of certain types of technologies—and as such are the primary consumers of medical services (services ordered for and paid for by the patients) (B. Turner and Samson 1995). The grand implication of this identity between health practice and medical practice is that it assumes that medical practitioners are primarily interested in serving the health needs and wishes of patients. In matters of health, the public has tended to blindly accept medical opinion as scientific, unbiased, and well considered.

However, when one looks into the social history of medicine in the United States, there are more than a few unpleasant surprises. Among the litany of medical opinions are the endorsement of tobacco smoking, the recommendation of high-fat diets, the experimentation upon unknowing subjects (e.g., the Tuskegee experiments in which some syphilis patients were involuntarily given placebos instead of receiving approved treatment), the use of lobotomies for several mild mental disorders, and the involuntary sterilization of minorities. Although these may represent notable anomalies, they nonetheless demonstrate chinks in the medical armor.

Also of note has been the medical orthodoxy's initial opposition toward client-centered developments such as third-party health insurance, informed-consent procedures, national health insurance, and patients' rights initiatives. In short, the medical orthodoxy controls access to technologies, with physicians as official gatekeepers. One rarely thinks of physicians as human beings who have vested interests in promoting their occupations and livelihood while keeping other groups from encroaching on their territory (Friedson 1970). Some, however, have defined medical practitioners as primarily interested in having the needs and wishes of patients fit into the predefined medical regimes that the former have created (Illich 1976; Foucault 1973; B. Turner and Samson 1995).

Because health and medicine are often equated, the general understanding of health is that it refers exclusively to the "absence of disease." However, there are alternative definitions of health. Health can be the state of "maximum functioning." Or, health is the state of "optimum functioning" within a given context. Health is "normal functioning." Health is "adequate functioning." Health is "subjective well-being." Health is "survival." As some of the latter definitions indicate, there is no inherent reason why medical practice or disease must include the assessment of health proclaimed by the medical orthodoxy.

Health issues and medical issues, then, are not synonymous. Health issues involve a wide array of concerns, of which medical issues constitute only a subset.

The Medicalization of Living

As discussed in the previous section, medical practice is a technology, whereas health is an assessment. In contemporary society, however, medical technology has dominated the discussion of health issues (McKinlay 1984; Illich 1976). The medical orthodoxy has been able to appropriate the gateway to medical technology. It is also well positioned to determine much of the national health policy agenda. Its mind-set pervades mass education and government policy. Our lives are often portrayed as different clinical phases—each requiring its own brand of medical intervention (G. Rosen 1983; Ehrenreich and Ehrenreich 1970).

In sum, our lives have become medicalized. We keep a constant vigil over our deficits, bringing them to medical attention, maintaining a regimen of approved diets and treatments, and by doing so, hope to "live long and prosper." Medical specialties bear out this division of life course: for example, pediatrics and gerontology. Other specialties focus around lifestyle: for example, sports medicine.

But if there are alternative ways of defining health, are there also different orientations for achieving health? What are the major models for viewing and achieving health? In deference to space, we will discuss only three models: the *medical model,* the *public health model,* and the *heretical model.* The medical model is the approach of the medical orthodoxy. The public health model addresses the needs of a population at large through management of the community resource base. Heretical models depict the alternatives to the two mainstream approaches or orthodoxies and include the Right to Die movement (see Table 3.3).

The Medical Model   The medical model is the foundation of the medical orthodoxy. It assumes an authoritarian, paternalistic relationship between two individuals: the physician, who possesses skills and knowledge, controls the patient (the afflicted person who seeks to be

TABLE 3.3.
Chart of Models.

	Medical	*Public Health*	*Right to Die*
Focus	Disease or trauma	Community resources	Individual choice
Stage one	Symptoms	Complaint	Ailment
Stage two	Diagnosis	Measurements	Monitoring
Stage three	Invasive treatment	Search for cause	Quality of life assessment
Stage four	Cure	Penalty or rectification	Possible end-of-life decision

healed). Because we are referring to individuals, the model assumes face-to-face interaction with individuals being treated serially and only after they are suspected of having a deficit. Behind the medical orthodoxy and medical technology stands the edifice of the scientific method. The scientific method involves the systematic testing and analysis of the relative effectiveness of treatments under controlled conditions. By comparing treatments to nontreatments and/or treatments to each other, tentative recommendations can be made about the most effective technologies and treatments to be used on patients in the general population. Ideally, and except for the experimental tests themselves, probable treatment outcomes are based on empirical findings. More effective technologies are continually being developed to identify, diagnose, and treat ailments. Data measurements and the tracking of cases are very important.

There are four specific and unalterable stages involved in the medical model. Stage one involves the appearance of a disease (i.e., the deficit) within an individual. It is important to note that the medical model imputes a biologically disease-based or trauma-induced cause for ailments. It was formulated to deal with identifiable biological pathologies and physical trauma, disease, and injury. The medical model is not interested in illness (i.e., the subjective, personal accounts that individuals have about their own health) or sickness (i.e., the socially legitimized "excuses" relieving someone from usual duties and obligations) (B. Turner and Samson 1995). Rather, it looks for and treats organic aspects of ailments.

In stage two of the medical model, the physician or other medical technician diagnoses the ailment through an analysis of the described and/or observed symptoms. A multitude of diagnostic equipment (e.g., stethoscopes, blood pressure gauges, X-ray machines, magnetic resonance scanners) may be used. These megaliths of diagnostic technology monitor the processes of the human body. Symptomatology is an essential aspect of diagnosis. Whether subjectively described or objectively measured, information is gathered sequentially. Diagnosis begins with the simplest and most-likely conditions and tests and moves slowly toward more-complicated (and less-probable) informational searches. If no definitive diagnosis can be made, this process is reiterated until at least some tentative possibilities are identified (Friedson 1970).

Assuming a tentative diagnosis has been made, a treatment regimen is decided upon. This is stage three. The regimen is ideally a cure—that is, it is designed to eradicate the organic cause of the ailment. With the eradication of its cause, the ailment is supposed to disappear. As with the scientific method, the quest for the ailment's cause is seen as essential. The medical model is, therefore, not a holistic approach to health. The efficacy of the treatment has much to do with the congruence of the diagnosis to the ailment, the individual characteristics of the patient, and the compliance of the patient to the treatment regimen. The regimen can range from the very mundane ("take two aspirin") to the complex (organ transplant). There is always the chance, of course, of misdiagnosis, nondiagnosis, noncompliance, or treatment complications to be reckoned with. Iatrogenic diseases (e.g., those that occur as a result of treatment)—such as postoperative infections—may also occur. These, however, are often treated as separate and distinct ailments.

The fourth and final stage of the medical model is (ideally) the disappearance of the organic cause and its symptomatology, resulting in the eradication of the ailment. Because the ailment is the focus of the model, success is achieved by destroying the pathology—and only secondarily by the health of the patient. Tests attempting to confirm the destruction of the pathology may be performed at this time.

The forte of the medical model is identifying, isolating, and eliminating pathogens. In a context of acute, infectious diseases, the medical model is a "magic bullet." It is also very effective in treating physical traumas.

During the latter part of the nineteenth century and the first half of the twentieth century in the United States, the medical model was tremendously useful in helping to elevate the aggregate health of the population. As the coalition between surgeons and physicians (the former being descended from barbers and the latter from apothecaries) became consolidated, the efficacy of incision and excision improved as well. There is no doubt that many of the perils of everyday life have dissipated with the advance of medical knowledge and technology. Conditions that would have previously killed have been tamed and now represent mundane conditions that may even be treated by over-the-counter remedies or by simple outpatient procedures.

In an age when deadly pathogens are being held at bay, the medical model has been expanded to deal with chronic ailments such as cancer and heart disease. Within such a context, the medical model has not fared as well. It can treat but not necessarily cure. Conditions can be identified but not eradicated through short-term specific procedures. Also, the reductionist orientation toward "cause" has been modified to include various organic and behavioral "factors." The medical orthodoxy, with its technology and political might, still talks about cure but moves more and more toward accepting palliative treatment. It speaks about organic causes but moves more toward behavioral ones. It visualizes elimination of ailments but speaks more about prevention, prosthetics, and longevity (Thomas 1983).

In short, in an era of chronic ailments, the medical model has lost center stage. It continues to hold on, however, to its recent glorious past and its very real political foothold.

The Public Health Model   The public health model is quite similar to the medical model, and its four stages even parallel the medical model's stages (see Table 3.3). There are, however, important differences between the two. The public health model focuses on a community rather than an individual as its "patient." The public health model is concerned with the prevention of ailments rather than in post hoc cures.

The public health model is another national orthodoxy of health praxis. Its existence is often hidden because contact with public health practitioners is usually indirect. However, we are often aware of its presence in other ways: health regulations, mass media education programs, environmental quality measurements, water treatment and sanitation plants, vaccination programs, and so forth. The public health model is primarily involved in the monitoring and treatment of a community's shared resources. The scientific method plays a significant role in the public health model, as experimental results are meticulously gathered and are then matched with field data in the assessment of resource quality.

In stage one of the public health model, suspected deficiencies in the community resource pool are identified for possible monitoring, or conditions that have come to the attention of public health officials (by complaints within the community) are looked into. As with the medical model, the focus is on specific organic pathogens. What are the deficits (including the excesses of toxic substances) that may play a role? (Note that deficits can refer to excesses in harmful substances as well as low levels of beneficial ones.)

Once a problem area is targeted, the machinery and technologies of measurement are employed. This is stage two. What are the norms? What are the deficiencies? Are they serious? Are they short-term? Measurements are taken, compared to baseline values, and evaluated.

Purported causes are considered in stage three. Is it a natural fluctuation? Is it caused by industrial wastes? Was storage inadequate? Where did the pathogens originate—within the community or outside the community? As the answers to these questions are considered, the treatment is formulated—it is often a function of the political authority of public health institutions to identify violations (and violators) of health policy and regulations. Will a warning be issued? Will a fine be levied? Will a business be shut down? Will an area be quarantined? Much depends on the seriousness of the circumstances and its effect on the community. There may be trade-offs to consider—for example, continual pollution versus unemployment (or underemployment).

In the final stage, based on determinations made in stage three, a penalty is imposed or rectification takes place. The resource condition is monitored to see if it has returned to acceptable levels. Acceptability levels may change over time because of increased knowledge, better technology, and/or political expediency.

The public health model participates in the orthodoxy of deficit, diagnosis, treatment intervention, and cure. As populations share resources, the role of the public health orthodoxy has expanded. Public health serves as the primary means by which many potential organic pathogens are controlled before they surface in the form of the medical ailments of individuals. A group (usually the government) again appropriates the technologies to ultimately assist individuals. In a sense, the technology and structure of public health are organized to fit the needs and wishes of communities into the procedures and regimes of the public health system, rather than vice versa.

Heretical Models   The orthodoxy of the medical and public health models reverberates in the ways in which health and health policy are defined, discussed, and organized in the United States. As we have seen, the medical model is very good at handling the post hoc ailments of individuals within the context of short-term organic pathogens or physical trauma. The public health model monitors and manages organic materials that might infiltrate the shared resources of communities. Both have enhanced the physical health of the aggregate population.

What if, however, one's health concerns reach beyond physical health? Where does one turn? Often one must go beyond the orthodoxy and venture into the realm of heretical models.

Heresy refers to opinions or doctrines that are at variance with the established orthodoxy of beliefs and procedures. Heresy comes in many forms. It can share the mainstream orientation, but differ in methodology. It can differ in terms of ideas, but employ the same methodology as the orthodoxy. It may differ in both ideas and procedures. It may pick and choose from within and without the orthodoxy. Or it may even agree with the orthodoxy in both ideas and methods, but not be accepted as part of the orthodoxy.

The orthodoxy can select from existing heresies in order to revitalize or alter itself, or it can purge itself of heresies discovered in its realm of practices (Starr 1982). From the point of view of health policy, there are many seemingly hopeless heresies (e.g., faith healing, and psychic surgery). Other former heresies have become legitimate (e.g., chiropractics, acupuncture, and hypnosis). Sometimes practices are moved from the orthodoxy into heresy (e.g., bloodletting). In short, there is a permeable layer that exists between orthodoxy and heresy.

The Right to Die movement promotes a heresy. While embracing an overwhelming number of the ideas and procedures of the orthodoxy, it differs in at least two significant ways. First, the right to die model incorporates the notion that each individual should have a direct gateway to medical technology and information. Second, it emphasizes the preeminence of the individual's definition of health via their subjective quality of life.

The Right to Die Model

As noted previously, the medical model emerged triumphant in the era of infectious diseases, and the public health model became a powerful force as the urbanization and resource sharing of contemporary societies necessitated coordinated effort. These two models are still very useful. But they ushered in a context in which chronic ailments are now our major foci. As the limits of practical life spans are being approached, a new concern is being voiced regarding living out one's life in a dignified and healthy manner. This new era of chronic ailments has given rise to a greater examination of how one wants to live out one's life rather than what disease or injury one fears dying from. The limits of life span are halting the promise of immortality via medical technology.

Assuming that medical technology is reaching its limit in that regard, the right to die model asks two questions: How can medical technology be used for individual empowerment rather than the empowerment of medical practitioners, and why should medical practitioners and government bureaucrats have greater say in what constitutes my quality of life than I do? The first issue involves individual empowerment; the second concerns subjective quality of life.

Power/Knowledge versus Power/Freedom   The rise of medical technology was associated with a rise in the political and social power of medical practitioners—especially physicians. The medical establishment has thus wedged itself in as the primary gatekeeper (middleman) between the population at large and medical services. Through its exclusive claim to medical knowledge, it has persuaded the powers that be that it must remain the final arbiter of health via medical technology.

The medical profession has bolstered its position as the possessor of sacred knowledge. This knowledge, inaccessible to others, is tied to the exclusive access to medical technology. This appropriation of medical technology embodies what French social philosopher Michel Foucault called "power/knowledge." Power/knowledge refers to the inextricable importance of sacred languages in controlling access to valued resources for the benefit of societal elites. In religious institutions, certain individuals (shamans or priests) train in the sacred lore and possess the technology for access to the gods. In legal institutions (courts, tribunals, judges), practitioners learn the esoteric processes of laws and serve as gatekeepers between the general population and the political economy. In medicine, medical practitioners are steeped in organic knowledge of the body and serve as arbiters deciding who, what, when, where, and how medical technology is brought into play. Foucault recognized that the common threads connecting these groups were that (1) they were legitimized by the political machinery, (2) they possessed a special knowledge with its own esoteric language, (3) they controlled access to valued resources, and (4) they attempted to maintain and/or increase the scope of their authority (Foucault 1973, 1980).

Once groups are entrenched within the organization of power in society, it is very difficult to extricate them. In organizing for power, they have intensified access to knowledge (prolonged education), limited access to that knowledge (e.g., medical school requirements), linked with other powerful groups (e.g., the American Medical Association), and permeated the public awareness of their existence and the need for professional autonomy. The medical and public health orthodoxies have power/knowledge.

An alternative conception might be called "power/freedom." Within the power/freedom paradigm, access to information, technology, and other resources would be wrested from power/knowledge groups and institutions and given to individuals. Technology, once created, would be directly accessible to all. Power/freedom is essentially a democratizing orientation.

The power/freedom orientation calls for a few changes in current medical care. It accepts that the complexities of sacred knowledge need to remain with the medical profession—since such training is long and involved. However, it seeks to remove the medical profession from its role as gatekeeper of medical technology: that is, it seeks to change the authoritarian and paternalistic doctor/patient relationship into an egalitarian and contractual consultant/employer relationship. In the former, a treatment is prescribed; in the latter, treatments are described. In the latter relationship, the "employer's," or patient's, goals and ethical predilections are the primary consideration. The employer decides what is best for him or her—not someone else. And the "consultant" provides recommendations without having to struggle over whether "they are doing the right thing"—it relieves them from that ominous burden.

The power/freedom paradigm calls for each individual to be the arbiter of his or her own health. It attempts to alter the orientations of the medical model (which treats diseases) and the public health model (which treats communities) to an orientation in which whole individuals are treated—situations in which technology is responsive to individuals rather than in which individuals are responding to technology. In order for this transformation to take place, the "clinical gaze" must be controlled and the "locus of control" must be shifted.

The Clinical Gaze The clinical gaze in medical practice refers to the dispassionate, analytical treatment of individuals as specimen objects. Individuals are "hosts" to deficits; the person is of secondary concern (Foucault 1973; B. Turner and Samson 1995).

The clinical gaze is alienating because it analyzes people as though they were inanimate objects. It has its place in diagnosis, but it is not integral to the treatment of deficit or the curing stages of the orthodox medical and public health models.

However, the orthodoxy has established the clinical gaze as the paragon par excellence of medical practice. In the realm of power/ knowledge, the clinical gaze establishes social and interactive "distance" between doctor/patient—and presumes that all issues of relevance to medical practice have been answered a priori within the scope of medical power/knowledge. The focus is on the medical practitioner's definition of ethics and goals because the orthodoxy revolves around its vested interests. The goals and ethics of patients are irrelevant.

Although the clinical gaze has its place, it has been used by the orthodoxy to override the preferences that individuals might have with regard to their self-empowerment. The clinical gaze has been used to superimpose the goals and ethics of medical practice on the use of medical technology and subjugate the wishes of individual patients.

The right to die model, instead, views technology as a tool and not as an independent value system. Technology is a tool that can be employed to achieve various outcomes. And those outcomes, as they relate to health, do not necessarily coincide with those of the current medical orthodoxy. The scope of the clinical gaze in the right to die model would be limited to diagnosis and suggested treatment; the orthodoxy would be removed as the gateway to actual treatment.

Locus of Control Locus of control has to do with the question, Who makes the crucial decisions? In the medical model, the crucial decisions reside with the medical practitioner. He or she decides (unilaterally) what the goals are, what tests are to be run, what treatment is to follow, when a condition has been cured, or when to "pull the plug." Metaphorically, the physician has adopted the "white (frocked) man's burden" role with regard to their patients. They can claim this because they have essentially blocked all other avenues of access to medical technology for the general population. If someone wants a medical excuse from work, prescription drugs, and reimbursement by health insurance, and so on, for example, he or she must first have permission from medical practitioners. There are times when the medical practitioner's wishes supersede that of the patient. Medical practitioners have routinely ignored patients' rights initiatives under the guise that they interfere with the autonomy of the medical profession. Calls for increased medication for terminally ill patients were opposed because of fears that the patients might become addicted to the painkillers (Humphry and Wickett 1986). Living wills are viewed only as "recommendations." Ultimately, then, in matters of life and death, the locus of control lies with the medical practitioner rather than the individual patient. Furthermore, the political machinery that exists in society supports this arrangement.

The right to die model asks these questions: Whose life is it, anyway? Doesn't it make more sense for an individual to decide what is right for himself or herself? Whose ethical and moral principles are more important—the individual's or their medical practitioner's? After all, we are not talking about situations in which the individual's decision will directly affect the health of others. We are referring to decisions the consequences of which will affect only the health of the individuals themselves. Within the context of relatively democratic, urbanized market societies in which individuals must constantly make important decisions regarding every aspect of their lives, they are suddenly prohibited from doing so when it comes to their health—especially, their final life decision: when they want to die.

From the point of view of the right to die model, the medical model has the following biases. The medical model says, (1) you must endure pain, indignity, alienation, and loss of liberty in order to physically exist as long as possible, (2) you must not give up (die), because others want you to physically exist, and (3) you must use up all of your financial resources in order to maximize that existence. On the other side, the right to die model asks, (1) Are we so afraid of death that we refuse to allow others to die?, (2) Do we fear that individuals are so irrational that they are not capable of making their own end of life decision?, and (3) Are we willing to ignore the moral and ethical standards of individuals?

The right to die model suggests that the present forms of the medical model work for the vested interests and ideologies of medical practitioners. It suggests that an orientation more in consonance with our era will switch the locus of control in health, as in all other aspects of our lives, to the responsible individual. As the medical model is presently organized, the individual must submit to the wishes of medical practice. The ideal would be for medical practice to serve individuals and, through individuals, their communities. The right to die model demands empowerment of individuals and communities.

Quality of Life

The medical and public health models are part of the orthodoxy. They have essentially equated quality of life with longevity and the decrease in morbidity (ailments). These measurements are "objective" measures and remain useful information.

The right to die model argues that, although longevity is important, the essential hallmark of humanity dwells in our subjectivity. The quality of life, it is argued, does not reside in the human body; it resides in the human mind. And each individual, within his or her own mind, must ultimately grapple with the ethical correctness and moral acceptability of his or her decisions. This individual action also takes place within the context of communities, families, friends, and others.

The following two sections compare the orthodoxy and heresy with respect to the issue of the quality of life.

Vital Statistics: Orthodoxy   The panoply of mortality and morbidity statistics referred to as vital statistics provides general aggregate information about populations and subpopulations. Infant mortality rates measure the number of infants (those under one year of age) who died during their first year with the total number born. This is indicative of many things: the hazards of early youth, the availability of medical technology, the safety of the environment, and so on (U.S. Bureau of the Census 1975, 1994). Life expectancy measures the number of years an individual born within a particular place and time can be expected to live on average. It can tell us much about hazards throughout the life course. Any deficit that can be counted can also be used to create a vital statistic, for example, cancer rates or rates of heart attacks. "Body counts" are the stuff of medical practice, and the aggregate measures constitute important data for the public health model. By comparing the vital statistics of one area or group to another, or by comparing a group to itself over time, much about objective, relative health status can be surmised. Are the infant mortality rates of the poor significantly different from those of the nonpoor? Is the increase in life expectancy in the United States reaching a plateau? Are the rates of leukemia greater in areas surrounding nuclear reactors?

There is no doubt that vital statistics represent important information for society. There is also no doubt that this information is a direct by-product of the medical and public health models. The right to die model wants the practitioners and technology of medical and public health practice to remain, but it does not want them to dictate their agendas to individuals in one very specific circumstance.

Vital Statistics: The Right to Die Model   The orthodoxy compiles and constructs vital statistics by measuring objective conditions that exist within and beyond individuals. The right to die model sees the beliefs of individuals as "vital." Although existing longer is often desirable, living in consonance with the dictates of one's own convictions and wishes takes precedence. The vital statistics of import to this model have not been gathered—in fact, they are currently beyond the scope of the orthodoxy.

Living wills and "Do Not Resuscitate" bracelets are one step in this direction. They ask for the removal or refusal of interventionist medical practice and technology for prolonging life. But the right to die goes even further than that. It posits that individuals should be able to direct medical technology to terminate their own lives under certain conditions. It asks for direct access to technology, active intervention, and/or the cooperation of medical practitioners in carrying out the wishes of individuals. It rests on the notion that only individuals operating within a liberating context can determine the quality of their own lives and that this assessment should be respected and carried out.

How Heretical Is the Right to Die Model?

It has been pointed out that the right to die model is a form of heresy. It lies beyond the accepted modus operandi of health practice. Yet it actually accepts and embraces the technological and practical aspects of the orthodoxy.

The right to die model wants to change the focus of medical practice from its supporting place in the political-legal hierarchy. It views medical knowledge not as sacred but as useful technology. Physicians, strictly speaking, are useful technicians.

The right to die model also wants to supplant the modus operandi of the medical orthodoxy with the subjective decisions of individuals, especially with regard to end-of-life decisions. It wants to use medical technology to allow empowered individuals to determine how and under what circumstances they want to die. And it calls for proactive medical interventions to assist in that process.

The heresy of the right to die, then, is primarily one in which medical and public health models are transformed into partners in the emancipation of individuals rather than as simply purveyors of prolonging physical existence.

Conclusion

This chapter began by discussing the love/hate relationship humankind has had with technology. The rise of the medical profession accompanied the efficacy of medical technology in combating acute, infectious diseases. It rode this wave of success into political power—based on the power/knowledge of medicine and controlling access to medical technology—and continues to play an essential role.

As populations began to share resources, the management and control of those resources became paramount. In using the medical model to treat communities, the public health model was born. Its role was to maintain the safety of the resource base through interventionist measures. In the form of regulations and public policy, public health practitioners monitor the environment and the health of the aggregate population vital statistics.

The era of epidemics and infectious diseases has—for the most part—passed. The institutionalization of public health is well in place. Medical and public health practitioners have shown their worth, for we have reached the era of chronic ailments and the threshold of biological life spans. The focus of the orthodoxy was on extending physical existence. The concern now is not longevity per se but quality of life.

The right to die model embraces the technologies and successes of the other two models. It is interested in keeping the knowledge and technology in place, but it also wants to extricate the mind-set of medical practitioners from the authoritarian paternalism of the doctor/patient relationship and change it to a partnership in a consultant/employer relationship. The individual (patient, employer) would determine how and under what circumstances medical technology would be called upon to assist in his or her life and death. The question is, after all, not whether one will die, but how well one lives until death, and how one dies.

How does heresy become part of the orthodoxy? How do heretical individuals dispersed in space and time organize themselves to challenge the power/knowledge and powers that be? The following chapters discuss how the right to die model is being instantiated into a Right to Die movement.

Addendum: The Hippocratic Oath

The Hippocratic Oath is commonly cited as a sacred document in the medical orthodoxy's opposition to the right to die and voluntary suicide. Although attributed to Hippocrates, the oath is of a much later vintage. Because of its seeming importance to this issue, the text is reproduced here:

I swear by Apollo the physician, and Aesculapius, and Health, and All-heal, and all the gods and goddesses, that, according to my ability and judgment, I will keep this Oath and this stipulation—to reckon him who taught me this Art equally dear to me as my parents, to share my substance with him, and relieve his necessities if required; to look upon his offspring in the same footing as my own brothers, and to teach them this art, if they shall wish to learn it, without fee or stipulation; and that by precept, lecture, and every other mode of instruction, I will impart a knowledge of the Art to my own sons, and those of my teachers, and to disciples bound by a stipulation and oath according to the law of medicine, but to none others. I will follow that system of regimen which, according to my ability and judgment, I consider for the benefit of my patients, and abstain from whatever is deleterious and mischievous. I will give no deadly medicine to any one if asked, nor suggest any such counsel; and in like manner I will not give to a woman a pessary to produce abortion. With purity and with holiness I will pass my life and practice my Art. I will not cut persons laboring under the stone, but will leave this to be done by men who are practitioners of this work. Into whatever houses I enter, I will go into them for the benefit of the sick, and will abstain from every voluntary act of mischief and corruption; and, further from the seduction of females or males, of freemen and slaves. Whatever, in connection with my professional practice or not, in connection with it, I see or hear, in the life of men, which ought not to be spoken of abroad, I will not divulge, as reckoning that all such should be kept secret. While I continue to keep this Oath unviolated, may it be granted to me to enjoy life and the practice of the art, respected by all men, in all times! But should I trespass and violate this Oath, may the reverse be my lot! (source: http://doyle.ibme.utoronto.ca/wwwbooks/hippo/oath.htm)

After reading over the text of the Hippocratic Oath, and realizing that not all physicians actually swear to it, it seems to us an enigma that it is referred to with such frequency by the medical orthodoxy. Although, admittedly, physician-assisted suicide is deemed inappropriate, so is surgery. Historically, physicians are the progeny of apothecaries or druggists, whereas surgeons are descended from barbers. The use of "deadly medicine," interestingly, is not the same as the use of medicine for the hastening of death; most medicines are "deadly" in many circumstances. Presumably, the oath is referring primarily to only herbal (i.e., "natural") potions.

The Hippocratic Oath assumes the continuance of a patriarchal structure in which medical practice is apprenticed only to males. Note its link to the quote by Jean-Paul Sartre at the beginning of this chapter.

Notice also that the physician's rather than the patient's interests are highlighted. What is the "law of medicine" that is referred to? Is it really superior to other laws? Who determines what is to the patient's benefit? In the oath, the physician is claiming "professional privilege" and full autonomy to make such decisions.

Likewise, the worship of Greco-Roman deities, as suggested in the oath, is not currently a requirement for the profession. On this basis alone, it can be seen that it is more of a traditional rite of passage than a pledge to be taken seriously.

The world has obviously changed since the formalization of the Hippocratic Oath. Surgery is performed routinely—often on an outpatient basis. Medical education is centralized and regulated under the auspices of the federal government. Females are not prohibited from becoming physicians. Chronic ailments, rather than infectious diseases, predominate—and cannot be cured. The democratization of society has shifted the burden of choice from oligarchies to individuals. The training and reimbursements that physicians receive are obtained primarily from community resources (e.g., tax dollars and third-party insurers). The world has changed.

As a "binding pledge" on which to base current medical practice, the Hippocratic Oath certainly lacks validity. If that part of the oath is inviolate, physicians could simply remove themselves as gatekeepers to medical technology in this special case. Of course, this would mean a tremendous loss of power for the orthodoxy. Another option would be to allow physicians to choose, individually, whether they would participate in such procedures. A third option would be for them to subjugate their interests to those of the patient—and adopt the "heretical" right to die model into the orthodoxy.

References to the document do, however, reveal something about the right to die debate. Specifically, it focuses on how the themes of the right to die are constantly being rhetorically attached to more basic, historical themes. The framing of the issues and the historical development of the Right to Die movement in the United States are discussed in greater detail in chapter 4.

Chapter Four

The Hemlock Society in Transition: A Qualitative Analysis

Given the controversy surrounding right to die issues and physician-assisted suicide (PAS) in the United States, how has the Hemlock Society expanded, challenged, and been challenged by the Right to Die movement? In chapter 2, we suggested the usefulness of a framework that draws on resource mobilization, framing, and new social movement theories for generating insights into this complex and controversial movement. In this chapter, we use this framework to explore some of the key dimensions of the Right to Die movement as reflected in the evolving role of the Hemlock Society. We also open an ethnographic window onto an important moment of transition and goal reorientation in the HS, drawing on documents, interviews, and observations of the society's Arkansas chapter to elicit the voices of HS participants themselves. We conclude by summarizing insights gained from a triangulated perspective on the movement.

The Hemlock Society and the Right to Die Movement: An Organizational Perspective

An organizational approach to social movements focuses on issues such as leadership, organizing skills, fund-raising, ability to attract and sustain membership, and cooperative and competitive relationships with other SMOs. In their pioneering work on resource mobilization, theorists Mayer Zald and John McCarthy (1980) used the market-based imagery of a "social movement industry" to capture the reality of the shifting dynamics between SMOs within the same movement field. In order for an SMO to be successful, it must ward off competitors and negotiate coalitions, mergers, and new organizational identities as movements adapt to changing social circumstances (Zald and Ash 1966). As illustrated in our background sketch of the early phases of the Right to Die movement (chapter 2), there were many examples of such organizational maneuvering, including the division of labor between Concern for Dying and the Society for the Right to Die, predecessors of the HS. As a Right to Die movement emerged, the many organizational name changes, splits, and cooperative arrangements (shown in Figure 2.1) reflected the struggle for a more advantageous position and a more efficient use of limited resources.

When the HS was formed, it entered as a new competitor in the field. Organizationally, it was well equipped to succeed. Derek Humphry's energetic leadership, writing skills, and biographical experience helped create effective resources for the organization in terms of membership loyalty and public visibility. There was a readily available constituency made up of those who viewed passive euthanasia—the strategy advocated by all other right to die organizations—as too limited and unable to sufficiently alleviate suffering and promote dying with dignity. Insights into this constituency can be gained by examining Ellen's story (chapter 1), as well as the medical issues considered in chapter 3.

Despite Humphry's strong leadership, the HS organization had a strongly grassroots quality; organized into federated chapters at the state level, it permitted social interaction and the development of locally suitable agendas. By contrast, Choice in Dying (the recombination of Concern for Dying and the Society for the Right to Die) dealt with constituents individually through direct mail, creating what McCarthy and Zald (1977, 1230) have called an "isolated adherent membership." Although both strategies can be successful in different ways, there is reason to believe that the federated structure worked to the advantage of the HS.[1] In particular, face-to-face contact in local chapters encouraged the development of a valued support community. Overall, HS mobilization strategies were successful despite the efforts of other right to die organizations to characterize it as a radical fringe group. Such success is reflected in HS membership figures as well as electoral victories and near-victories that show strong public support for the "right to die." As we will demonstrate later in this chapter and in chapter 6, the HS has periodically worked to foster mutually advantageous cooperative relationships within the Right to Die movement, an important strategy that maximizes limited resources.

Another important organizational dimension relates to the political environment in which SMOs function. The broader political structure at times constrains and at other times facilitates the agendas and actions of SMOs. This suggests a symbiotic relationship between "political opportunity structures" and SMOs (Tilly 1978; McAdam 1982; Tarrow 1991; Kriesi et al. 1992). For example, with the exception of a vote supporting the right to die in Oregon in both 1994 and 1997, the political and legal reality in the United States defines active euthanasia and PAS as illegal acts. Influential political elites may be sympathetic or unsympathetic to the movement, or they may be divided among themselves. Likewise, the climate of the federal courts is an important element of the political opportunity structure.

Periodically, SMOs are able to alter the political opportunity structure through mass mobilization or other successful movement strategies. The U.S. Supreme Court would not have taken up the right to die issue in the first place had the movement not pressured the government through the courts, political initiatives, and individual "mercy killings" (see chapter 6). In a 1997 decision anxiously awaited by both the Right to Die movement and the countermovement, the Supreme Court did not uphold a constitutional right to die in the United States; however, it invited states to decide the legality of right to die issues, opening the door to more political initiatives such as those in Oregon.

The political environment has other important consequences for movements. For example, constraints are placed on SMOs by the U.S. Internal Revenue Service tax code, which regulates incorporated organizations (McCarthy, Britt, and Wolfson 1991). The HS (as well as most of its predecessors) was set up as a nonprofit, tax-exempt educational organization. Designated 501(c)(3) by the IRS, such organizations have a significant advantage in fund-raising because they are tax-exempt and contributions are tax-free. This provides money to pay salaried professionals and support the infrastructure of an SMO. An organization wishing to engage in direct political lobbying must apply for 501(c)(4) status. Although this frees it to operate politically, the organization is more hampered in fund-raising. McCarthy, Britt, and Wolfson (1991) have suggested that these constraints represent a deliberate effort by the government to "channel" organizations toward more innocuous educational activities instead of those promoting more fundamental structural political change.

Such politically motivated channeling efforts are historically variable; for example, hostility toward "progressive" grassroots groups was evident in the scrutiny and regulation directed at them during the Reagan-Bush era. In a more recent example, 1997 congressional budget-cutting initiatives with a strongly partisan flavor attacked the nonprofit mailing status of grassroots groups, a move that would greatly hamper their outreach and funding efforts. In the 1980s and the 1990s, particularly during periods of economic downturn that affect donations, many SMOs have consumed valuable energy debating the fine line between 501(c)(3) and 501(c)(4) activities. Some have divided themselves into two complementary components in order "to take the best advantage of the evolving rights associated with each legitimate status" (McCarthy, Britt, and Wolfson 1991, 56). The HS has not escaped such debates, which, as we will see when we take an ethnographic look at the organization, can be perilous.

Of course, the social movement field is influenced not only by the protagonists of a movement but also by the antagonists, or counter-movement organizations (Hunt, Benford, and Snow 1994; Klandermans 1992; Zald and Useem 1987). Active euthanasia in the United States has been opposed steadfastly by the Catholic Church and more recently by an increasingly well-organized and highly active "right to life" movement. One of its militant SMOs, Operation Rescue, has vowed to oppose active euthanasia and thus, the HS. Right to life organizations have poured money into local campaigns around the nation (see chapter 6). Even more recently, disability rights groups such as Not Dead Yet have opposed right to die organizations on the grounds that disabled patients, who are already treated with great insensitivity by the medical system, will be more likely to be euthanized if the right to die becomes institutionalized. Such groups treat the HS concept of voluntary active euthanasia with suspicion, emphasizing the likelihood of involuntary outcomes. The presence of these various players has an important impact on the social movement field as a whole.

We can see, then, how an organizational perspective provides important insights into how SMOs such as the HS acquire resources and at the same time are constrained by a range of organized actors in the social movement field. Likewise, resource mobilization strategies of SMOs are dramatically affected by existing political opportunity structures and in turn affect those larger structures through periodic challenges (more detailed attention to such recent challenges is given in chapters 6 and 7).

"Framing" the Right to Die Movement

Beyond competing for material resources and members with other organizations, SMOs vie for a legitimate symbolic identity in the eyes of the American public (R. Turner 1983; R. Turner and Killian 1972). Divided cultural sentiments about artificial control over life and death—such as those presented in the previous chapters—guarantee that framing concerns will be salient in the Right to Die movement, both at a personal and at an organizational level (Gamson 1988; Snow et al. 1986; Snow and Benford 1988, 1992). With its commitment to active euthanasia, the HS has been at high risk of being cast in the role of villain because active intervention in death is, to some, equivalent to murder. This has meant that HS leaders and grassroots participants have had to be very careful about framing issues in general and about presentation of information to the public in particular.

Participants in the local Arkansas HS chapter that we observed were well aware of this problem. For example, some professionals in the organization were concerned about what could happen to their practices if they were publicly defined as euthanasia activists. One of the authors (Fox) initially became chapter president in part because, as a tenured full professor (who taught Medical Sociology and Death and Dying courses), she was "biographically available" (McAdam 1986) and politically in the most well protected position to become public spokesperson for the group. The group carefully constructed its public identity to maintain confidentiality concerning its members. As discussed in chapter 5, our survey indicates that such privacy continues to be extremely important to HS members.

As seen in chapter 2, frames can function at a number of levels: they help individuals make sense of their experiences; they help groups and SMOs work out their strategies for social change; and they are consciously used to persuade the public of the value of particular issues, foster the legitimate identity of particular SMOs, and manipulate countermovement agendas (Benford 1993a; Hunt, Benford, and Snow 1994; Klandermans 1992; Mueller 1994; Snow et al. 1986). Hunt, Benford, and Snow (1994) suggest that frames have diagnostic, prognostic, and motivational functions. In the first case, a frame, or interpretation of reality, is developed to identify the source of a problem. Typically, it also suggests a strategy for change (the prognostic function), which in turn energizes movement participants (the motivational function). The mark of a successful frame is that it resonates with the experiences of those who adopt it; this authenticity gives it the power to attract new members to SMOs and to influence public policy. Just as the successes and failures of the HS are linked to organizational know-how, they are also linked to symbolic "framing" battles.

In our historical overview in chapter 2, the names of the SMOs themselves reveal framing concerns, beginning with the "Euthanasia Society of America" (evoking an image of professionalism) and evolving through "The Society for the Right to Die," "Concern for Dying," "Choice in Dying," the "Hemlock Society," and more recently, "Compassion in Dying," "Patients' Rights Organization," and "Euthanasia Research and Guidance Organization" (ERGO). Along with an emphasis on professionalism and compassion, the language of human/civil rights has become increasingly visible in these organizations, as it has in many SMOs that have adopted the template, or "master frame," of the civil rights movement. This frame's prognostic dimension calls on the government to guarantee basic human rights. Exactly what these rights are and should be is the disputed terrain of social movements.

As noted previously, Derek Humphry's understanding of the media and the symbolic presentation of public issues was a crucial resource to the HS organization. An examination of the HS literature shows that Humphry was masterful in "packaging" HS identity, both for participants and for the public at large. First, the HS made it clear that any assistance with death was intended to be indirect, and the organization's literature was careful to state that it "does not encourage suicide for any primary emotional, traumatic, or financial reasons in the absence of terminal illness ... [and] ... approves of the work of those involved in suicide prevention" (HS n.d.a). Humphry's careful issue framing helped the HS craft a legitimate public identity; it affirmed the need for active euthanasia in the Right to Die movement yet distanced itself from direct assistance that could lead to charges of murder and a lack of respect for life. Humphry has made it clear that euthanasia would be voluntary, legal, and rare. Although this framing did not reassure the most hardened critics of active euthanasia, it did create a middle ground that was appealing to many.

Moreover, Humphry supplied a frame that elevated a *rhetoric of compassion* to prominence in the organization's definition of purpose, or "vocabulary of motive" (Benford 1993b; Mills 1940). As we saw in

Ellen's case, individuals who engage in active euthanasia often face a moral conflict and need to remind *themselves* (as well as others) that they are forced to take action to alleviate suffering in the face of an unresponsive medical system. A frame of compassion assists them in doing so. By joining together with others similarly motivated, they experience group solidarity and individual validation, sharing common definitions of what the source of the problem is (technology gone awry, a medical system that lacks compassion, the intrusion of regulations into private lives) and what to do about it (to work for social acceptance of the right to die with dignity).

A frame that highlights compassion has additional strategic value when presented to the public. Opposing active euthanasia is on the agenda for the "prolife" movement, which attempts to frame "choice" organizations—be they about birth or death—to be sinful and, worse, murderous. In response, right to die SMOs underscore the moral value of compassion and the need to redefine assisted suicide in more positive terms. For example, the HS claims that active euthanasia—giving a patient a chance to plan and choose the moment of death, painlessly and with dignity—is more humane than disconnecting a life-support system (passive euthanasia) and letting a patient die slowly. The HS prescription for justice, therefore, depends on an "injustice frame" (Gamson, Fireman, and Rytina 1982) that diagnoses the existing medical system—with its detached "clinical gaze" and its orthodoxy—as inhumane. It also depends on a prognosis defining active euthanasia (a heretical model) as a solution and on a motivational rhetoric based on solidarity through compassionate action. Interestingly, as we will see later in this chapter and in subsequent chapters, this emphasis on compassion has opened the door to a major competitor to the HS: Compassion in Dying, an SMO that frames its actions as more compassionate than those of the HS.

Other elements of the HS frame—rationality, responsibility, cooperation with professionals, a disassociation with directly assisted suicide, and an emphasis on legal change—can be gleaned from HS organizational goals (see chapter 2) and even from the hemlock symbolism itself. These carefully chosen symbolic elements of the frame again function on several levels, reassuring individual participants about their culturally problematic actions and enabling the HS to publicly lay claim to a mainstream identity. SMOs in the Right to Die movement continue to compete for such an identity, each claiming that it most truly represents the wishes of the American public.[2]

Indeed, with more competitors in the field, with individuals such as Dr. Jack Kevorkian galvanizing the debate, and with an actively mobilized prolife movement, each organization must work harder to draw adherents on the one hand and resist negative labeling on the other. Even legal concerns over 501(c)(3) and 501(c)(4) tax code status contain a symbolic element because grassroots groups use these designations to claim a viable public identity that will legitimate their work for social change. On the countermovement side, the American Medical Association (AMA) has increasingly felt compelled to enter the framing debate, formulating a statement on patients' rights, pursuing the debate in medical journals, and challenging dissenters among its ranks who support active euthanasia (see chapters 6 and 7 for the development of the AMA response).

We can see from the examples above, then, that strategic maneuvers by the HS and others in the organizational field are permeated by symbolic contests over framing. A framing analysis helps contextualize the Right to Die movement and better tell its story. Below we will see that the NSM perspective provides an even broader context for the movement—both its organizational and symbolic dimensions.

Individual and Collective Identity in the Hemlock Society

Derek Humphry's framing and organizational skills were not solely responsible for the HS success, although his shaping of the organization's mission and style was crucial in attracting a particular constituency. As we saw in chapters 2 and 3, both macro- and microlevel social changes laid the groundwork for the growth of a Right to Die movement that increasingly embraces voluntary active euthanasia. NSM theory encourages us to look at these broad changes and consider how they are linked to constructions of personal and collective identity. For example, (macrolevel) changes in medical technology and (microlevel) dramas personally experienced by people as a result of the artificial prolongation of life create a kind of "infrastructural conduciveness" for a social movement.[3] Without this sociological context, the demand for a "right to die" would not make cultural sense. Also important is the broad demographic shift toward an older population; there is strong evidence that euthanasia organizations are typically sustained by older individuals for whom prolongation concerns are at their greatest. Our observations of a local HS chapter verified that membership consisted mostly of retired people who have experienced the death of a spouse or child and/or who have thought about their own imminent deaths. Our survey of the HS (discussed in chapter 5) supports these findings.

Far from being merely a demographic response, however, membership participation is also linked to microlevel issues such as identity negotiation. Identity negotiation comes into play when one is forced to question one's established sense of self. An illness or impending death forces an individual into new and often troubling roles. An organization or social network that offers effective assistance with such identity shifts is a valuable resource, particularly in a society that frequently falls short of providing such support. As we saw in chapter 1, the absence of social support increases the stress of individuals such as Ellen who are attempting to cope with life and death decisions.

In the Arkansas chapter of the HS, we found that physicians, pharmacists, medical administrators, social workers, and others were drawn to the organization because they increasingly had to confront ethical and legal questions relating to euthanasia in their workplace. This forced them to redefine their roles and venture outside of an established definition of their "work." Moreover, because of the demographic and epidemiological changes discussed in chapter 3, there is a growing likelihood that individuals experiencing dilemmas about euthanasia in their professional lives will have a family member or loved one whose situation brings these issues into a more intimate sphere. This personal dimension was also a powerful motivation for members to join the local HS chapter.

What all of the groups that we studied shared in common—apart from a tendency to be upper middle class, white, highly educated, and aware of the infringements of medical technology on their lives (see chapter 5 for data on the national HS)—was a need to respond to powerful symbolic changes in their everyday environments that called their previous identity into question. All of them had to engage in an act of reframing—of the self, and of the relationship between self and society. In fact, the HS organization grew and became successful because it translated problematic individual identity into a viable *collective* identity, with relatively "agreed upon definition of membership, boundaries and activities for the group" (H. Johnston, Larana, and Gusfield 1994, 15). This new collective identity then strengthened both individual identity and the public identity presented to a broader audience (H. Johnston, Larana, and Gusfield 1994).

NSM theorists claim that certain movements are "new" because they depart from traditional class-based mobilizations and instead react to a postindustrial information-based society in which "administrative colonization" has increasingly invaded people's lives (Habermas 1975; Luke 1989). People resist by claiming the right to define their identity free of outside control. This notion of resistance fits in well with what we have observed of the Right to Die movement. In an age in which bureaucratic control of medical technology and the "clinical gaze" have spilled over into the most private aspects of human experience, including life and death, movements that emphasize dignity and control of one's identity—in other words, choice—make cultural sense. This helps explain why a particular identity issue—the embrace of the heretical model of active euthanasia—has become a rallying point for activists at this point in time. The self-production of identity even at the moment of death, or, to borrow a term from the Right to Die movement, "self-deliverance," is a key act of resistance that on the one hand reprivatizes the intimate sphere of death and on the other "socializes" it as the movement constructs a strong collective identity.

It has been claimed that new social movements are particularly likely to bypass the established political arena, operating through "submerged networks" (not very visible to the public or to the media) that may have only a very loose organizational structure. It is in these submerged networks of grassroots participants that identity is collectively negotiated and frames are constructed and refined. Often they represent a kind of cultural rather than a political rebellion (although the two are not always separable). As Carol Mueller (1994) points out, this less public phase often precedes a more visible movement, providing the space in which "challenging constructions are created" and individuals come to share "injustice frames" (Gamson, Fireman, and Rytina 1982) and experience "cognitive liberation" (McAdam 1982). This later makes sustained participation possible in the more public phase of a movement, based on a shared collective identity.

Does this apply to the HS? Among the organizationally active "early joiners" in the movement (see chapter 5), a rehearsal for the more public phase of the movement did take place; individuals such as Ellen took action secretly and eventually came together in supportive networks; the federated chapter structure of the HS facilitated this kind of community building. In many cases, these communities remained "submerged networks" and operated at a subpolitical level. That such networks are not highly formalized has several implications. First, we need to look more carefully to find movement actors themselves. Second, we might expect to find tension between organized and unorganized actors in the Right to Die movement. Likewise, we may anticipate factionalization *within* SMOs such as the HS, whose members may be linked to submerged networks while also belonging to the more formal organization. As illustrated below, this is indeed what we find. For example, Dr. Kevorkian with his "direct action" approach represents a more radical stance on active euthanasia than does the official position of the HS. Within the HS, many members support Kevorkian's tactics, while some do not. This creates a potential fissure in the HS that can lead to a split, depending on such things as political opportunity structures and shifts in the social movement field.

The HS has not avoided political action, although this tactic has been controversial. The ambivalence of HS members, who were split over the issue of direct political involvement versus educating the public, may be related to an inherent ambiguity in the so-called new social movements—they are assumed to transcend social class, yet they often consist of a middle- to upper-middle-class membership that may be both surprisingly radical by present cultural standards (active euthanasia) yet constrained in its political radicalism due to its relatively privileged social position. Some have questioned whether such movements lack the radical edge found in more traditional class-based resistance movements (Eder 1993). This is a point worth raising; the Right to Die movement does not focus, for example, on the important role of capitalist corporate medicine in structuring people's choices, and its rhetoric is not class based or anticorporate (such rhetoric is in any case rare in U.S. movements). The unclear nature of many NSMs heightens disagreements over identity and framing and suggests that debates are likely to take the form, as articulated by one of our local members, of arguments about what is "okay radical" versus "too radical."

NSM theory offers insights into identity issues that help make sense of the Right to Die movement, but this is of course not enough to explain a movement. For this, one must look at the "actual operation of specific social structures" (Klandermans 1992, 78). In our local observations, we were able to take advantage of a rare window that opened onto the negotiation of organizational identity in the HS following the departure of Derek Humphry in 1992. Prior to this time, Humphry's voice dominated the "presentation of self" of the HS through public pronouncements and official literature. The organizational turmoil in the HS brought to the surface a number of previously submerged voices reflecting on the history and present dilemmas of the organization. To us, this offered an extraordinary opportunity to gain insight into the movement and to observe how RM, framing, and NSM issues converge as an organization struggles to redefine itself through internal social control efforts and through interactions with the broader movement field (Benford 1993a).

The Hemlock Society in Transition: An Ethnographic Window onto the Right to Die Movement

Internal Tensions in the Hemlock Society   A good deal of the tension within the HS only became visible to selected individuals following the May 1992 departure of Derek Humphry from the organization. In 1991 Humphry authored a best-seller, *Final Exit,* a "how-to" book about active euthanasia. Ironically, the book also facilitated his formal "final exit" from the organization. Its publication brought widespread publicity and an expanded financial base to the HS. In an interview with one of the authors in March 1992, Humphry stated that his financial situation was such that he could afford to resign from the paid position of executive director and spend his time dedicated to law reform (Humphry 1992). It is possible that there was at this time tension growing between Humphry and the HS board of directors. Humphry's 1989 divorce from Ann Wickett, his second wife and cofounder of Hemlock, had brought negative media publicity to the organization. This was aggravated by Wickett's public denigration of Humphry's character, as well as her death due to noneuthanasic suicide some time later. In essence, the "nice guy" of the active euthanasia movement was suspect. The HS weathered this negative publicity, although it experienced considerable organizational stress.

Another emerging problem reflected a characteristic tension between a charismatic leader and staff as an organization becomes more formalized. Although, as executive director of a 501(c)(3) organization, Humphry was responsible to a board of directors, interviews with several current and former members of the board suggest otherwise. As board member John Westover remarked, "Hemlock was a one-man show. Sure, we had a board, but if Derek didn't agree with the board, he just did what he wanted and the board had to accept it" (Westover 1993).

Humphry was in fact becoming far more interested in law reform than in the educational goals mandated by the 501(c)(3) status of the HS, with his board apparently trying to hold the reins tight. Humphry's shift in interest is documented in a 1992 interview regarding plans to formalize the structure of a new local chapter. Humphry gave the following advice: "It would be far better if you would consider going for a (c)(4) rather than a (c)(3). The public is educated and aware of the issues at stake now. I think it would be better for your chapter to be poised to push law reform rather than education. You may handicap yourself by a (c)(3) status. I am trying to make the board understand this position about Hemlock" (Humphry 1992). Humphry's priority at this time was clearly legislative reform, more in keeping with the parameters of a 501(c)(4) status. Thus, it was a combination of negative publicity, Humphry's personal decision to engage in active law reform, the securing of a solid financial base for both the HS and Humphry, and growing tension between a "one-man show" and the board that combined to produce the resignation of the founder of the HS as executive director.

Some understanding of the problems being experienced between Humphry and his board may be obliquely glimpsed through interactions at the local level. For example, the Arkansas board of directors resoundingly rejected Humphry's advice to pursue a 501(c)(4) rather than a 501(c)(3) status. At a meeting attended by one of the authors, the following comments were made:

No, we don't want to go that way. We want to educate, not do political reform. The rest of the country may not need educating, but Arkansas still does. Arkansas isn't ready for that [death with dignity law] yet.

That's too far for us. Look, we have enough trouble just being Hemlockers. We are already suspect. Some of my friends who know I am in Hemlock think I want to go around killing people as it is. We just need to focus on educating the public now as to what we stand for.

Summing up the issue, another person said, "[That's] right. Being (c)(3) is *okay radical,* being (c)(4) is *too radical.*" Humphry's efforts to reframe the organization's goals clearly did not resonate with the experience of this local chapter.

Humphry's new priorities had some serious consequences—both material and symbolic—for the HS organization. The national HS ran into trouble when, at the behest of Humphry, it helped sponsor and organize 501(c)(4) organizations in the states of Washington and California for initiative drives to legalize active euthanasia in 1991 and 1992, respectively. For example, the HS made a "loan" to the California political organization Americans against Human Suffering. There is clear evidence of national HS sponsorship; direct mail solicitations by the organization were done using Hemlock's membership mailing list as well as solicitations printed in HS quarterly newsletters to its membership. Humphry secured the advice of two attorneys prior to the action, but the attorneys proved to be wrong. So overt was the relationship between the California 501(c)(4) group and the national HS that in 1993 the IRS revoked its 501(c)(3) status for excessive financial contributions to a political action organization (Humphry 1993). Although a 501(c)(3) was granted when the HS reapplied after a year, this was still an embarrassing episode for the organization, and some of Humphry's critics accused him of behaving nonprofessionally and running the HS "like a family organization" (HS 1993, 1). It is worth noting that attempts to legalize active euthanasia failed marginally by very small voting percentages in California and in Washington State, ultimately proving successful in Oregon in 1994. Although remaining a HS member, Humphry separated himself from the organization to pursue the legislative reform avenue.

Factionalization and Professionalization   Following the death (or in this case, departure) of a charismatic leader, a range of possible changes in an SMO can be expected, including a decline in membership, increased professionalization of the executive core, and factionalization (Zald and Ash 1966). At the time of Humphry's departure, the HS was claiming a membership of up to 50,000. By 1998 membership claims dropped to 25,000. Internal factionalization in the HS also became quickly evident. At the same time, the board made efforts to stabilize the organization by professionalizing its leadership, conducting a national search for a new executive director. The board's choice, although not unanimous, was Dr. John Pridonoff, whose background was in psychology and theology. Pridonoff had been the administrator since 1968 of The Counseling Center in San Diego, California, a "nonprofit organization providing trauma, grief, pastoral and crisis intervention counseling to medical professionals and other caregivers" (HS 1992, 1). He also came from a background of AIDS work, a connection that the euthanasia movement has made in some other countries but which has not been embraced in the United States. Pridonoff, who was in place by the fall of 1992, upheld the 501(c)(3) priority of educating the public as well as revitalizing the grassroots chapters of the HS.

Humphry's stepping down did not mean that his voice was no longer heard in the organization. In the first week of January 1993, Humphry sent a letter to all chapter leaders denouncing the leadership of the HS and calling for a resignation of the new executive director and the president of the board of directors. Humphry charged them with engaging in "retrograde policies." In particular, he charged that Pridonoff did not understand the mission of the HS and was withdrawing crucial resources such as advertising the organization in national magazines and newspapers just as the Right to Die movement was poised to gain major victories. He also claimed that there was a bad morale problem in the ranks. Attempting to use the federated chapters as a power base, he called on each chapter to take a position and make it known to the board of directors.

Humphry's letter spurred a rather frenzied series of communications from various national leaders in the HS to all chapter leaders as well as rebuttal from Humphry, each taking a position of support or rejection of Humphry's charges. High emotions characterized the majority of the communications, many of them containing little more than thinly disguised character assaults on the various individuals. A story about the disagreement was carried in the *Oregonian* in January (Timms 1993), including Humphry's threat to form a rival organization if changes were not made.

All of this created great dismay among those in the HS who knew of the transformations. The process of the renegotiation of the HS's identity is well captured in a special "crisis" issue of a newsletter mailed out to chapter leaders in January 1993. A member of the board who opposed Humphry's position wrote: "Will Derek establish a rival euthanasia society, split Hemlock and shatter our resources? I hope not. It certainly won't happen unless Hemlock members prefer a personality to a cause" (HS 1993, 4). At the height of the conflict, the Arkansas Chapter Board of Directors sent letters to all key players at the national level. An excerpt illustrates the sense of dismay that was being experienced in one local chapter:

We write this letter with a sense of despair, alienation, betrayal and anger that we who have given of our talents, experience and time to enhance and put forth the principles of the Hemlock Society should have that effort potentially wasted by the continuing crisis in Hemlock management. . . . Set aside personal grievances and deal with this issue effectively now. The future of this movement and the goals of this movement lie in trust with you. Do not betray that trust. (Fox 1993)

Telephone conversations with other chapter leaders during this time period indicated that similar feelings surfaced all over the country. As one chapter leader in a northwestern state noted: "Who do they think they are to do this to us? *We* are the organization and they are allowing petty differences to screw it up."

These voices, although responding to a perceived personality conflict, also reveal a sense of the volatility of the euthanasia issue. HS leaders and members were especially concerned about public "framing" issues. Legislative reform attempts to legalize active euthanasia failed marginally by very small percentages in California and Washington after being predicted to win prior to voting. Conservative opponents who threw their weight against the reform propositions were the Catholic Church, the AMA, and right to life groups. Worried that the Right to Life countermovement could take advantage of the organization's disarray, Gerald Larue, a former HS president, suggested mediation efforts:

I am terribly disturbed, and I am sure you are too, by the correspondence, the news items, the accusations and the charges that indicate disharmony within the Hemlock family. The fact that such disruption occurs at a time when there is mounting hope that, in the near future, efforts to legalize active euthanasia could be successful, adds to my dismay. The excellent campaigns waged by local Hemlock leadership in Washington and California demonstrated that there are thousands upon thousands of individuals who agree that the time has come when persons suffering from terminal illness must have the right to choose the time and place of their dying. President Clinton is prepared to support a woman's right to choice. This action weakens the challenge from the right-to-life groups that link abortion and euthanasia in their attacks on Hemlock and the Initiatives. . . . This is no time for in-house quarrels. (Larue 1993)

In a similar vein, a chapter leader of Hemlock of Central Oregon worried about the diminished emphasis on advertising, noting that "Hemlock's involvement in this highly sensitive political movement must stay clearly focused in the public's eye" (P. Rosen 1993).

Other letters supported Pridonoff's strategy. Unlike Humphry, who felt that the public was educated and ready to be mobilized electorally, Pridonoff saw the need to increase education and garner the support of local medical societies to help the HS claim a more mainstream identity. As one chapter leader wrote: "Certainly no more money should be poured into future attempts to legalize medically assisted suicide until the backing and endorsement from these important groups has been received. Every failed initiative gives the right to life groups another chance to polarize the public" (Voorhis et al. 1993).

A point of contention was Pridonoff's strong interest in AIDS. Humphry and some others clearly opposed making this a highly visible issue for the HS, particularly if it took resources away from other priorities. Luis Gallop, chair of New Hampshire Hemlock and advertising consultant to the HS, wrote:

I explained to him [Pridonoff] that it would be inefficient from a media selection aspect to attempt to isolate this audience specifically; but it also appeared to me that AIDS patients, who are usually younger, fight for their lives whereas Hemlock people tend to be older and attempting to escape from the pain and lack of meaning of untenable lives. I understand that other chapters he had addressed directly find he does not have a deep understanding of the Hemlock "ethic" which brought me into the movement when Derek Humphry headed it. (Gallop 1993)

The larger issue was a fear of attaching the stigmatized AIDS identity to the HS. Combining concerns over symbolic identity with RM issues, the AIDS connection was seen by many as a liability for any organization trying to claim a mainstream identity in the United States.

Humphry's attempt to regain control of the HS failed. Denied easy access to speak at the February 1993 meeting of the board of directors, Humphry disengaged from battle and turned his attention elsewhere. Shortly thereafter, he was publicly aligned with Americans against Human Suffering and ERGO, the new organization that he founded. He focused on a potential new initiative drive for 1996. The board issued no new communications with chapter leaders regarding the Humphry/ board conflict. The window that briefly opened onto the turmoil within the organization was closed. Solid denials of any continuing problems were the responses of the leadership to any inquiries regarding the conflict. Subsequent communication from Humphry to chapter leaders referred only to the newly reorganized California group. This communication did not attempt to solicit membership away from the HS.

In the meantime, there was evidence of a new professionalization of the executive core of HS. For example, the following statement sent to HS chapter leaders from the new executive director, Pridonoff, reflects a great deal of political and organizational astuteness: "When an organization makes a shift from being around a 'personality' to 'issues' there are significant changes and a period of ebbs and flows. We have seen this with other major non-profit organizations (such as the National Organization for Women, Planned Parenthood, and—in the early years after the retirement of its founder—Lord Robert S. Baden-Powell, the Boy Scouts)" (HS 1993, 4). This new professional attitude was extended toward the next wave of dissension in the HS, when a local chapter decided to undergo what RM theorists McCarthy and Zald (1977) refer to as "goal reorientation."

Goal Reorientation within a Hemlock Chapter

Despite the presentation of the HS by its official spokespersons as a unified, rational organization, "Hemlockers" do not all agree on goals and priorities, and particular chapters continue to disagree over tactics necessary to make active euthanasia a social reality. Moreover, organizations such as the HS move in a broader social movement field that includes individuals not necessarily affiliated with a particular organization (Marwell and Oliver 1984). This set of alignments in turn contributes to the uncertain boundaries of collective identity in the HS. For example, in the Right to Die movement, the most notable outside player has been Dr. Jack Kevorkian. His direct action approach has been to assist terminally or hopelessly ill individuals with their requested deaths by using the technology at his disposal. He has drawn tremendous publicity, both positive and negative, and has been the recipient of failed social control mechanisms by the state of Michigan (as evidenced by the state's inability until recently to successfully charge him with murder). His "death machine" has attracted the ire of prolife groups such as Operation Rescue, and his activism has affected the legal environment within which the movement operates.

Not surprisingly, Kevorkian's polarizing presence has led to organizational efforts at social control of deviant views in the HS. Until recently, Kevorkian was seen by the leadership core of the HS as a threat to the movement because an association between the HS and Kevorkian in the public's mind could threaten its carefully constructed public identity and limit its resource mobilization efforts. In a newspaper article in March 1992, Humphry referred to Kevorkian as the "loose cannon" of the euthanasia movement (Dungan 1992). During an interview with one of the authors, he explained his statement:

He doesn't cooperate. Before the election in Washington, I called him and asked him to not assist anyone [to die] until after the election. The polls predicted we were likely to pass Proposition 119. Every time he assists in someone's death, he scares a lot of people. All I was asking for was a few weeks of reprieve, long enough to get past the election. He wouldn't do it. I believe that he hurts legislative reform possibilities when he assists in deaths.

Humphry's efforts at "damage control" were unsuccessful. Interestingly, Humphry's condemnation of Kevorkian drew protests from a number of federated chapters. Letters supporting Kevorkian were published in the HS newsletter, prompting Humphry to restate the goals of the HS in the same newsletter, noting that such direct action is contrary to the educational function of a 501(c)(3) organization. Ironically, Humphry's own agenda of political action was also technically not permitted by a 501(c)(3) status.

In April 1993, a more radical splinter group provided a challenge to the HS. Calling itself Compassion in Dying, the group was formed from the core of the Washington State HS chapter. It consisted of individuals who did not resign from HS but who in addition formed a new direct action group. They publicly stated that their purpose was to personally assist in the suicides of terminally ill people who requested their help (later, however, the group officially stated that members did not "personally" assist with deaths except by being present). They believed their actions would help educate the public and energize the Right to Die movement. An interview with Ralph Mero, at that time the president of Compassion in Dying, revealed the frustration that prompted the new line of action:

We decided, after examining our consciences, that we needed to take more direct action. We spent over three million dollars on the initiative effort here in Washington and it failed. We are not willing to put out that much money and effort again to see it fail. We believe in what we are planning to do, so we will simply go on and do it and not waste any more time and money. We feel that if physicians see responsible people approaching assisted suicide with control and dignity they will begin to support our position. (Mero 1993)

Like the HS, but with a more radical agenda, Compassion in Dying wanted to use its limited resources in the most effective way. The HS organizational leadership under Pridonoff responded differently to this situation than did Humphry. Rather than condemning the direct action approach assumed by Compassion in Dying and risk losing the Washington State chapter, as well as other grassroots chapters that might support such direct action, the new leadership attempted to create linkage. In a *Hemlock Chapter Leaders' Newsletter,* guidance was given to members for responding to media questions concerning Hemlock's position regarding Compassion in Dying. Chapters were told to be supportive in terms of philosophy, if indeed chapters so supported such direct action, but to designate the HS as an educational 501(c)(3) organization whose goals and aims do not include direct action. While not condoning Compassion in Dying's intent, the condemnation of such direct action as a "loose cannon" disappeared under the new leadership.

Conclusions from a Triangulated Perspective

Our project in this chapter has been to tell the evolving story of the HS, using RM theory, framing theory, and NSM theory to gain insight into the organization and into the Right to Die movement as a whole. By paying close attention to the voices emerging from our local research and from national newsletters and interviews, we find that each time an issue is raised that is significant from the perspective of one theory (framing, for example), it is closely intertwined with and contingent upon issues that are identified by the other two perspectives (RM and NSM theories). A triangulated perspective thus forces us to push our analysis further and to think more holistically. What can we conclude from such a perspective?

Our examination of the Right to Die movement suggests that it is a classic example of the emergence of a shifting field of organizations that represent a "social movement industry," with attendant divisions of labor, competition, and cooperation (Zald and McCarthy 1980). Within this field, the HS, although successful, has been in a state of dramatic flux, negotiating the change from charismatic to professionalized leadership while struggling to maintain social control in the face of internal conflict (goal reorientation) and external pressures (competition and institutional "channeling"). Tension between a charismatic founding leader and the process of organizational institutionalization is a well-known sociological phenomenon (Weber 1968). At such times, RM theorists McCarthy and Zald remind us that "tactical dilemmas and disagreements with social movement leadership can result in switching goals or the formation of more radical groups" (1977, 1232).

Moreover, they suggest that tension and conflict are likely to be present in organizations wherein "conscience" constituents (those who support an SMO for moral reasons rather than deriving a direct benefit) and "beneficiary" constituents are linked together by a federated chapter structure.

One response to organizational tensions is goal transformation, in which an overriding goal for the SMO becomes "maintenance of membership funds and other requirements of organizational existence" (Zald and Ash 1966, 328). This approach is somewhat apparent in the HS's response to the formation of Compassion in Dying. Although it still represents an effort at social control, it has been less heavy-handed than the earlier approach of condemnation of "deviants." The HS has responded by establishing rudimentary linkages with other organizations as well as by redefining ideological positions. Drawing on an RM perspective, we have been able to map this changing organizational field and observe its relationship to a shifting political opportunity structure.

Organizational tactics are inseparable from the broader symbolic universe within which they operate. We therefore considered why this movement has taken on a particular shape for reasons other than RM skills on the part of a leadership cadre. NSM theories suggested both the source of the growing power of the Right to Die movement and a reason for its limited critique. Regarding the former, we observed how the movement has been fueled by a growing impatience with technical and administrative forces characteristic of complex modern societies such as the United States (and embodied more particularly in current medical practices addressed in chapter 3). Dying with dignity not only puts an end to physical pain but preserves a certain notion of self, which puts "identity negotiation" close to the heart of the movement. Deep social concern over this issue helps explain how the HS successfully competed with other SMOs by espousing active euthanasia, and also why the HS itself experienced goal reorientation when some rank-and-file members formed Compassion in Dying. Impatient with human suffering in the face of bureaucratic and organizational constraints (embodied in the HS itself), Compassion in Dying members acted to claim symbolic territory that the larger organization was unwilling to appropriate. In doing so, they began to construct their own community of support, with a collective identity linked to direct action. (Chapter 6 discusses recent developments affecting the relationship between HS and Compassion in Dying.)

We have observed that the class composition and identity issues of the Right to Die movement may limit its critique. As documented in chapter 5, most HS members have a relatively privileged social status. The movement is radical in advocating active euthanasia, but by focusing on education and limited political activity, its message is, as one would expect, a reformist one. The rift in the HS over 501(c)(3) and 501(c)(4) status revealed strong ambivalence about direct political action. It can be debated whether changing the nation's laws through political action is truly radical; what is important is that many participants perceived that this, in conjunction with negative labels already attached to active euthanasia, would "stir things up" too much. When Compassion in Dying was formed, it strove to capture the moral energy of protest against inhumane social structures while remaining in the category of "okay radical." Ralph Mero (1993), for example, was careful to point out that "our organization consists of health care people, religious leaders, social workers and teachers. We are not a bunch of crazy radicals."

Perhaps most strikingly absent from HS documents and interactions is a political economic critique of capitalism and its structuring of for-profit medicine. Although it is acknowledged that part of the indignity of being kept alive against one's wishes is the resulting economic price tag, and although it is acknowledged that structures such as HMOs put economic pressures on the doctor-patient relationship, an economic critique of capitalist medicine is at best a subtext in the movement. What seems to make sense to HS and Compassion in Dying members is an agenda of creating more compassion *within* the existing system. Our triangulated theoretical perspective suggests that, in this movement and in many others potentially in the NSM category, there is likely to be an ongoing and often uncomfortable negotiation of identity (at personal, organizational, and public levels) relating to the categories of "okay radical" versus "too radical."

This in turn points to the central importance of symbolic framing in social movements. The HS took great pains to frame its interpretation of the "right to die" in a way that would resonate with mainstream cultural values such as professionalism and compassion. This is a function not only of its class composition but of its embeddedness in a social movements field that contains militantly critical countermovements (such as conservative religious organizations that are characteristic of the U.S. social landscape). By creating a frame centered around "safe" values such as compassion, the HS has both hedged its bets in a competitive movement field and provided reassuring "frame resonance" for its own members. Internal challengers to the HS, such as Compassion in Dying, stretched the original frame by espousing direct assistance to patients yet continuing to use HS language of rationality, professionalism, and compassion. By maintaining ties with Compassion in Dying, the HS showed that it was able to negotiate not only organizational fields, but also shifting "identity fields" (Hunt, Benford, and Snow 1994) that demanded a creative response from organizational leadership. By focusing on a language of rights, the HS and the Right to Die movement established their place in the lineage of movements that have drawn on the culturally familiar (although not uncontested) "master frame" of the civil rights movement (Snow and Benford 1992). Some rights are still too controversial, however, as illustrated by the ambivalent status of AIDS in the U.S. Right to Die movement.

The closer look taken at the HS in this chapter, based on ethnographic observations and use of documents, yields the conclusion that RM, symbolic framing, and NSM issues are interwoven into a seamless web. Theoretical triangulation helps us to notice that identity construction in the HS was partly a resource mobilization task, underlined by a resonant frame that included active euthanasia and brought together the organization's goals with individual life experiences.[4] By now, we have answered some of the sociological questions that Ellen's story first suggested; we have discussed sociocultural circumstances that produce situations such as hers, and we have seen how the Right to Die movement responded to such painful situations through community building and identity negotiation. We have also seen why the HS had such a key role in the emergence of the movement and why, more recently, it has been challenged by groups such as Compassion in Dying. In chapter 5, we answer some of our other questions: What kinds of people join the HS, and why? How different are they from other members of society in their social characteristics and beliefs? We will then return to a broader discussion of the changing shape of the Right to Die movement and its social implications.

Chapter Five

Survey of the Hemlock Society USA

The evolution of the Hemlock Society as an SMO was discussed in the previous chapter. The qualitative analysis highlighted events that involved the upper echelons of the organization and the contexts within which they operated. Grassroots supporters and potential supporters also influence SMOs. An important constituency of any voluntary organization is its membership; this provides the base for financial and social support. Our goal in this chapter is to create a sketch of HS membership from recent survey data. The authors were intimately involved in the creation, distribution, and analysis of this nationwide membership survey (Fox and Kamakahi 1995).

Creation of the Questionnaire

Although there had been previous small-scale profiles of the HS membership (Holden 1993; Suber and Quinn 1983), the HS decided that it wanted a more complete nationwide profile of its membership. Was the organization in tune with the membership, and had the membership's character been changing over time? What kind of involvement and commitment characterized the membership? Where did the membership stand on various right to die issues? Were they activists or closet supporters? Were members personally involved in situations where a right to die choice was salient? Were members generally healthy? How did they feel about Dr. Jack Kevorkian? In surveying its members, Hemlock was taking a step to empirically assess its primary resource base in order to see whom it was (and was not) attracting.

It was at this point that the HS and the authors began to collaborate on a questionnaire. The project involved both HS organizational resources and the authors' skills and experience in questionnaire construction, data collection, theoretical interpretation, and statistical analysis. Thus, applied and scholarly interests were melded together. On the applied side, the HS was interested in obtaining information regarding various characteristics, attitudes, and opinions of its membership. On the scholarly side, the researchers were interested in how specific theoretical issues could be related to the resulting data. The applied and the scholarly foci were by no means mutually exclusive.

A mail-in questionnaire, to be disseminated through the HS membership newsletter, was decided upon as the survey instrument (see "Data Collection" at the end of this chapter). This method allowed a variety of questions to be asked, it provided for the largest potential sample, and it gave respondents a chance to use their own time frame in thinking about items. Apart from demographic items, virtually all the items being discussed for possible inclusion on the questionnaire were related to the right to die issue (see "Formulating the Questions" at the end of this chapter).

When finished, the Hemlock survey contained 54 numbered items, although many items had subitems nested within them. It was divided into four separate sections. The first section probed for demographic information such as age, sex, race, socioeconomic status, and formal education. The second asked respondents various questions concerning their relationship to the HS: Was the organization reflective of the membership's interests? The third section of the questionnaire asked respondents about their attitudes toward right to die issues in general. The final section included miscellaneous items that were deemed important but did not seem to fit into the other three headings. The questionnaire was thus a blend of pragmatic concerns for HS and theoretical concerns for us as researchers (appendix 3 reproduces the survey).

Initial Analysis of Results

We examined the previous research literature on the HS to see how our data compared with earlier findings. We were especially interested in comparing our demographic data with the few previous studies done on the organization (Holden 1993; Suber and Quinn 1983). In addition, we sought a range of information never previously gathered on the HS.

Eventually, 6,398 questionnaires were returned—a response rate of about 25 percent. We expected a higher response rate given that we were addressing a motivated group. But because we mailed the survey to all members, our sample size exceeded that for the overwhelming majority of studies, giving us a very large national sample of the flagship SMO in the Right to Die movement (see "Sampling and Return Rate" at the end of this chapter). See Table 5.1 for a summary of the demographic data for HS members compared to the U.S. population as a whole.

Sex   We were able to closely match the demographic results of a previous, small survey of the HS (Holden 1993) with our findings concerning a group that we refer to as the "early joiners" (those who became HS members in the first five years of the organization's existence). This gave us confidence that there was no sampling bias.

Again replicating previous findings, we found that females constituted the majority of Hemlock members (Holden 1993; Humphry and Wickett 1986). We had originally suspected that this might be an artifact of women on average living longer than their male counterparts. However, we found that women outnumbered male members in all age categories. This suggested to us that the preponderance of females was not an artifact but was perhaps a direct result of women taking proactive measures to prevent a probable dilemma—to be terminally ill, without a spouse or caregiver, and under the auspices of an authoritarian medical regime that dictates "longevity at all costs." Given the current disparities in male and female life expectancies and that women have a greater likelihood, on average, of being younger than their spouses, adopting the caregiver role, and outliving their spouses, the right to die issue can be construed, in part, as more of a woman's issue than a man's issue. Interestingly, in the general population, females have been consistently more opposed to physician-assisted suicide and euthanasia than have males (Kamakahi 1997; Wood 1990).

Age   We found HS members to be much older, on average, than the general adult population in the United States. Slightly more than 68 percent of the respondents were 65 years old or older; this compares with the 12.6 percent over 65 years of age in the general population. This was consistent with previous information available to us. These members are also very atypical for their age cohorts; in the general population, these age cohorts (65 years old or greater) have been most opposed to right to die issues (Wood 1990).

TABLE 5.1.

Comparison of the Demographic Characteristics of HS Members and the U.S. Population.

	Hemlock Members (%)	*U.S. Population (%)*
Sex		
Female	60.70	51.30
Male	39.30	48.70
Age		
65 years or more	68.00	12.60
64 years or less	32.00	87.40
Income		
$60,000 or more	41.90	20.00
Less than $60,000	58.10	80.00
Education		
College Graduate	70.50	21.40
Non-college Graduate	29.50	78.60
Religious affiliation		
Catholic	3.00	34.70
Jewish	11.10	2.50
Protestant	31.40	34.40
None	37.90	0.50
Other	16.50	27.90
Marital status		
Married	54.50	78.00
Other	45.50	22.00
Geographic dispersion		
Midwest	13.44	23.70
Northeast	14.25	19.90
South	20.32	34.64
West	51.99	21.76
Race/ethnicity		
African American	0.20	12.10
Asian/Pacific Islander	0.50	2.90
Caucasian	95.10	80.30
Hispanic	0.30	9.00
Native American	2.10	0.80
Other	1.80	3.90

Notes: The U.S. population figures represent those reported by the U.S. Bureau of the Census (1997) for the year 1996. For the education and marital status variables, only the U.S. adult population was used for comparison purposes.

Source: Kamakahi 1997.

It has been found that the aggregate change in acceptance of the right to die was a function of attrition (Kamakahi 1997) (but see our discussion in chapter 8). Older segments of the population are generally more opposed than younger segments. Over time, the same age cohorts have displayed consistent responses to right to die issues. However, as older cohorts die off, younger groups that are more accepting of the right to die replace them. The aggregate outcome is a greater societal acceptance of the right to die.

One explanation for this phenomenon is that death and dying issues are more salient to older sectors of the population. But this would also be the case in the general population. So what is the difference between the two? Obviously, there must be a cultural difference between HS members and the general population. By culture, we refer to the influences of social relations and ideas that we incorporate into our worldview (either voluntarily or involuntarily). Cultural differences are primarily the result of disparities in the social context and relations within which one is or has been immersed. Thus, we became more sensitized to look for more such differences between HS members and the general population.

Socioeconomic Status (SES)   Socioeconomic status (SES) is often measured in terms of income, educational attainment, and occupational prestige. We obtained direct information on the first two criteria. The household income of HS members in the $60,000-or-higher range was two times greater than that of the general population (41.9 percent versus 20 percent). In terms of educational status, three times as many Hemlock members had attained at least a baccalaureate degree than would be predicted by the general population figures. Also, most of the members were retired, and two-thirds owned their own home. It would be safe to say that HS members were societal elites.

The fact that the HS membership was primarily female suggests that these women were extraordinary achievers in the educational arena—at a time when such opportunities were not in abundance.

Religious Affiliation   We found that those respondents reporting no religious affiliation (i.e., agnostics, atheists) were present in the HS membership 76 times more than would have been expected by their presence in the general adult U.S. population. Those reporting Jewish affiliation were 4.5 times greater among HS members. On the other end of the spectrum, Catholics were present in only 1/12 the numbers that would be expected by their presence in the U.S. population. The membership and population percentages for Protestants were very similar. (Two-thirds of all respondents, however, indicated later in the questionnaire that they did not believe in an afterlife.) On the whole, the religious affiliation of HS members, then, differed markedly from that in the general population.

Family Characteristics   The family characteristics revealed that the majority of HS members were married, and they reported having fewer children, on average, than is reported for the same age cohorts in the general population. Spouses, rather than children, were cited as the ones who "would most likely serve as your primary caregiver in case of terminal illness." The fewer offspring may very well be a function of the shortening of the childbearing years due to either the lengthened educational career and/or the continual presence of HS (female) members in the workforce. Having fewer children would also mean having fewer potential filial caregivers in the future.

Geographical Dispersion   New England, the Pacific, and the Mountain states (except for Utah) displayed higher proportions of HS members per population size than other areas of the United States. The South (i.e., West South Central, East South Central, and South Atlantic) had the lowest number of HS members per population ratios. The East North Central and Middle Atlantic states had intermediary values. In other words, regional patterns were exhibited. These regional differences mirror those reported in national polls on right to die issues. It is interesting to note that the physician-assisted suicide voter initiatives have primarily been launched on the West Coast.

Race/Ethnicity   With regard to race (actually a misnomer for ethnic identity), both Whites (Caucasians) and Native Americans were over-represented in the HS membership. The former was an expected result, as it is consistent with previous research and fits in with the "societal elite" interpretation: Whites are both the numerical and the power majorities in the United States. The high percentage of Native Americans was somewhat of an enigma. An ad hoc interpretation is that the right to die within Native American cultures is seen as a part of the cycle of life (rather than as antithetical to life), and therefore the right to die does not conflict with the cultural ethos.

Summary of Demographic Information   We found the demographic information from our survey meshed quite well with previous
information and impressions of the Hemlock Society (see Table 5.1). In
general, we could say that HS members are relatively privileged members of society. This avant-garde in the Right to Die movement is overwhelmingly female and older than the U.S. population. HS members
have above-average incomes and much higher levels of educational
attainment. They report lower religious affiliations with dominant
churches. HS members are also concentrated in certain regions of the
country. The identification of HS members as societal elites provides
some grounding for our contention that they are culturally different
from the general population. As the national ethos changes, there may
be some movement toward the greater acceptance of the right to die.
This would be reflected, demographically, in the HS membership mir-
roring that of the general population.

The rigor of our findings exceeded that of other studies of the HS.
This detailed demographic information served as a foundation for investigating many of the other issues addressed in the survey instrument.

Trends in Hemlock's Membership   Having presented an overview of membership demographics, we were interested in looking at
any possible trends in membership characteristics. This longitudinal
examination of HS provided a means by which we could look at social
change within the organization in a quantitative manner, something
that had not been done before our study. Included in the survey was an
item that asked respondents how long they had been HS members.
This question allowed us to sort the early joiners (members for 11 to 15
years) from the middle joiners (members for 6 to 10 years) from the
late joiners (members for 5 years or fewer). The percentages of
respondents who fell into these groups were 12.9 percent, 34.1 percent,
and 53.0 percent, respectively.

Demographically, females are still in the majority, but the proportion
of the male membership has increased over time (33 percent to 38 percent). The members in each cohort are younger (from 68 years of age to
about 60 years of age); but this is probably happenstance, as the ages at
which they joined the HS would be similar among the cohorts. In terms
of religious affiliation, perhaps as a function of "regression to the mean"
(because the initial values were so extreme, the expected movement is
toward less-extreme values), there are slightly more Catholics and fewer
nonaffiliated members in more recent cohorts (see Table 5.2).

TABLE 5.2.

Hemlock Cohorts.

Variable	Early Joiners (%)	Middle Joiners (%)	Late Joiners (%)
Demographics			
Female	67	62	62
Catholic	2	3	4
No religion	40	37	34
Belief in an afterlife	27	28	37
Occupation in health field	11	13	15
Organizational			
Discuss Hemlock membership with:			
Family	40	36	33
Casual acquaintances	28	25	20
Family doctor	48	46	40
Family lawyer	36	35	29
Anyone	63	57	51

Our findings suggest a trend in the direction of a more general acceptance of the right to die. This is consistent with national poll data, which reveals that each younger age cohort has been more accepting of right to die issues (see Table 5.3). If so, greater acceptance for HS and its agenda may be imminent.

TABLE 5.3.

Gallup Polls of the U.S. Population.

Group	Late 1970s	Early 1980s	Late 1980s
Approval of physician-assisted suicide for terminally ill			
Total population	61.01%	65.36%	68.56%
Approval of suicide for terminally ill			
Total population	39.49%	47.70%	51.58%

Source: Kamakahi, 1997.

Hemlock Society Items   Prior to our survey, no one had investigated how the HS membership viewed the various aspects of the organization. We thus had a unique opportunity to explore this. The section of our questionnaire on the HS was, of course, of great practical interest to the organization and great scholarly interest to us. How did the membership regard the SMO itself? Was there general agreement about the organization's mission? Were there differences in political strategies? Did people join for the same reasons?

We found that there was almost unanimous agreement by the membership regarding HS goals.[1] The responses provided information regarding the relative importance of members' goals. The four highest-rated responses were (1) to educate the public about physician-assisted suicide (98.0 percent), (2) to empower patients regarding options for the terminally ill (98.0 percent), (3) to disseminate information to the medical community about aid-in-dying (96.4 percent), (4) and to provide direct information about euthanasia techniques (93.7 percent). In other words, there was vast agreement upon the HS's mission to educate and advocate for right to die issues.

Interestingly, most of the members were not active in their local HS chapters, nor did they show much interest in becoming active at the grassroots level. There was a trend away from grassroots involvement and toward political solutions in more recent member cohorts. In general, newer members were less fervent about their motivations for joining and reported less attachment to the organization per se. More recent members were also more interested in supporting the right to die idea but were less directly involved in the actual operation of the movement. More recent members were also less likely to disclose their membership in the HS to their social relations (e.g., family, friends, lawyers, doctors). Nevertheless, the most prominent reasons for joining for all members were the belief that the government does not have the right to legislate certain personal choices (96.4 percent) and support of right to die legislation (92.7 percent). We can conclude from our survey that the membership was unified and supportive of the HS's overall goals. Our data demonstrate that the HS's position as an educational and political advocacy group was secure.

It would seem, then, that those who joined the HS in its early stages were more adamant about the right to die issue and more involved in Hemlock's grassroots activities. Newer members are, in general, more tangentially (perhaps abstractly) committed to the issue. This type of development would be expected of an SMO that is drawing greater mainstream support from the general population.

Right to Die Issues   Prior to our survey, no one knew precisely how HS members viewed or framed the right to die issue. Our instrument allowed us to explore this realm. In this section of our questionnaire, we investigated how Hemlock members were positioned with regard to the Right to Die movement in general. What were their reasons for defending a right to die?

Overall, there was very strong agreement that the right to die was an undeniable human right (95.9 percent), a matter of personal choice for one's own future (92.2 percent), and a question of civil rights (91.7 percent). As with our previous findings, later members, although still overwhelmingly supportive, were less fervent in their views than their predecessors. The data indicate most clearly that the foundation of the membership's advocacy for the right to die rests on issues of rights and individual choice.

There are some interesting implications to these findings. A "right" refers to the legitimized ability to follow a course of action without external interference. With regard to human rights, these presumably are endowed as a "birthright" and therefore take precedence over any constraining action by any social or political entity. To say, therefore, that the right to die is a human right is to establish it as more fundamental than any governmental or religious body's rules. A civil right, on the other hand, is a privilege that can legitimately be regulated under the auspices of political institutions. A "personal choice" interpretation upholds the individual's sphere of discretion to act without external compulsion. That the human rights interpretation received the most support suggests that members see the right to die as a birthright. This political stance emerges from a group that considers its own political views to be "slightly left of center" (36.6 percent liberal; 33.8 percent middle-of-the-road; 15.1 percent conservative—also 49.4 percent Democrat, 23.5 percent independent, and 21.7 percent Republican).

Our results for the right to die issues mirror those of the HS items. Those who joined nearer the organization's inception were more likely to report stronger overall commitments and sentiments regarding issues. Early joiners were more likely to have made practical preparations for their own dying (e.g., living wills, durable powers of attorney) and have much greater confidence in the likelihood of voter initiatives (the former may be a function of their age—as this group was, on average, older).

Interestingly, the question regarding the membership's approval of Dr. Jack Kevorkian revealed that about 75 percent supported him to varying degrees—a total of 65.3 percent did so "wholeheartedly." Kevorkian has been as controversial inside as he has been outside the movement. Although viewed as a maverick, he has galvanized discussion of the Right to Die movement nationwide. About one-quarter of the respondents, however, thought that his actions actually hurt the movement. They may have felt that Kevorkian's actions would produce a backlash of sentiment against the movement. Others might not have appreciated his flaunting the law. Others may think it is not yet time for high-profile actions but rather for political advocacy and public education.

It is clear that the impetus for the social action among HS members revolves around the issue of rights (human and/or civil) and the sovereignty of individuals with regard to their own end-of-life decisions.

Miscellaneous Issues   There were several other issues of interest to us that did not quite fit into the above categories. Many of these issues had not been previously examined. However, they provided a broader context in which we could view HS members beyond the SMO and the Right to Die movement per se (see Table 5.4).

Some questions involved the general health of the respondents. Were HS members generally people at "death's door?" Most respondents indicated that they were in "good" to "excellent" health, both physically (86.9 percent) and mentally (95.4 percent). How did they feel about their standard of living? They rated their subjective standard of living as "good" to "very comfortable" (81.4 percent). Were they active? The vast majority, 95.2 percent, indicated that they had voted in their last state election. It would be safe to characterize this group as healthy and active (only 7 percent indicated that they had been diagnosed with a terminal condition).

We also found that Hemlock members were involved in other social movements besides the Right to Die movement. Among the highest extraorganizational affiliations indicated were the AARP (American Association of Retired Persons) with 67.4 percent; the ACLU (American Civil Liberties Union) with 24.2 percent; Common Cause with 20.6 percent; the Sierra Club with 18.5 percent; NOW (National Organiza-

TABLE 5.4.

Miscellaneous Characteristics of
Hemlock Society Members versus U.S. Population.

	Hemlock Members (%)	*U.S. Population (%)*
Health		
(Rated as good-to-excellent)		
Mental health	95.40	NA*
Physical health	86.90	NA
Other SMO memberships		
AARP	67.40	34.80
ACLU	24.20	0.40
Amnesty International	15.50	0.40
Common Cause	20.60	0.30
Greenpeace	13.50	0.00
League of Women Voters	14.20	0.10
NOW	15.50	2.70
Sierra Club	18.50	0.60
Publications read		
Advocate	2.40	0.10
Atlantic Monthly	9.40	0.60
Harper's	6.70	0.20
Humanist	7.30	0.00
Mother Jones	5.70	0.20
Nation	7.10	0.10
National Review	3.10	0.10
New Republic	4.40	0.10
New Yorker	24.70	0.60
Progressive	3.60	0.10
Spin	0.80	0.20

*NA = not available.

Source: Kamakahi and Fox 1996.

tion for Women) with 15.5 percent; and Amnesty International with
15.5 percent. In a listing of several SMOs, Hemlock members' participation rates were significantly greater than that of the general population (Kamakahi, Fox, and Čapek 1997).

Thus, we have evidence that not only do HS members come predominantly from the societal elite, they are also politically astute and active
and not solely focused on the right to die issue. In terms of trend, our

TABLE 5.5.

Hemlock Cohorts.

Variable	(Early Joiners) Cohort 1 (%)	(Middle Joiners) Cohort 2 (%)	(Late Joiners) Cohort 3 (%)
Memberships in:			
ACLU	33	27	22
Sierra Club	22	19	18
Amnesty International	21	16	15
Greenpeace	18	14	14
AARP	74	72	64
League of Women Voters	18	14	13
Common Cause	30	25	20
NARAL	19	17	14
OWL	7	4	3
Others	32	27	24
None	8	8	13
Reading:			
National Review	2	4	3
Humanist	9	7	5
Nation	9	7	6
New Yorker	27	28	25
Progressive	6	4	3
Atlantic Monthly	10	11	9
general news magazines	52	51	47

Source: Kamakahi and Fox 1996.

results also show that there are fewer extraorganizational memberships and interests in more recent HS cohorts (see Table 5.5). However, the participation rates of each and every cohort are still significantly higher than those of the general adult population.

Discussion

The analysis of our survey instrument has given us much new and
unique information about the HS membership. We were able to repli-
cate the demographic information in previous studies regarding the
early joiners among HS members; the findings indicate that they are
predominantly female, over 65 years old, Caucasian, and with a distinct
pattern of religious affiliation. In addition, we were able to confirm that
members possessed high SES.

Most of what we found, however, covered new ground. We found
that HS members were in good health and overwhelmingly identified
with the HS stated goals. We found, as well, that they were politically
active and intellectually informed regarding a number of movements
and social issues.

Demographically, the membership is moving closer to the mainstream. In terms of commitment, earlier joiners reported a more
activist orientation and identification with the right to die issues, the
HS, and the grassroots political process. Later members still report
strong identification, but to a lesser degree. This may be indicative of
the expansion of the movement into the general population.

The survey results allowed us to look at the membership profile of
the HS, inclusive of their demographic characteristics and their attitudes on various right to die issues. The slow movement of the general
population's attitudes toward greater acceptance of the right to die and
the slow movement of the HS membership profiles toward the mainstream might suggest a long wait for right to die advocates. On the
other hand, this slow movement may instead represent the budding of
a social movement ready to come to fruition.

Our purpose in this chapter is to be descriptive rather than theoretical. However, some of our questions have a bearing on our triangulated interpretation of the Right to Die movement. We will return to a
theoretical discussion in chapter 8. The next chapters look beyond the
HS to gauge the activity in the Right to Die movement in the United
States and around the world. As we will see, national and global events
surrounding the right to die issue provide intriguing food for thought

regarding the future of the movement and the evolving role of the HS in that movement.

Notes Regarding the Survey Instrument

Data Collection   There were a variety of options available, such as focus groups, telephone surveys, or questionnaires. Each method has its advantages and disadvantages. We selected the mail-in option. The bulk of information was weighed against the time frame needed and costs involved (e.g., printing, mailing, return mail). The items could be formatted in ways that facilitated rapid data entry and the use of preferred statistical techniques for data analysis purposes.

Questionnaires are created to gather comparable information from a large number of people in a short span of time. This is a cross-sectional strategy that allows for the gathering of data about a collectivity at a particular point in time. The collectivity of individuals may share membership in the organization in common with others but may be entirely unaware of the actual identities, motivations, and opinions of fellow members (see Babbie 1994). Once these data are gathered, a researcher may construct post hoc a general membership profile from the responses.

In constructing this profile, data (a matrix of symbols) are transformed into information. Information is the meaningful interpretation of data that have been systematically gathered and analyzed. Information can be distinguished from impressions (i.e., haphazardly formulated notions based on one's personal experiences) and raw data (i.e., any array of symbols). Sometimes information and impressions match—but, often they do not. Questionnaires, and surveys in general (e.g., telephone polls, censuses), give researchers and policy makers a means to construct an empirically based "reality check."

Formulating the Questions   As with all good surveys, hours of negotiation, reworking, reevaluating, and revising took place. Many considerations had to be kept in mind. There is a tension in a questionnaire between attempting to get as much information as possible versus the respondent's anticipated motivation to answer and return it. Therefore, the questionnaire had to be relevant to the respondent. This, we felt, would not be a problem because the survey was an official undertaking of the SMO and was to be included as a part of the organization's quarterly newsletter.

The questions needed to be unambiguous. Ideally, items would be clearly understandable to a respondent with an eighth-grade reading level. Complex questions had to be eliminated. Various people were asked to read and review drafts of items looking for these and other potentially confusing aspects of the survey. Could we assume, for example, that members knew the difference between various concepts (e.g., passive and active euthanasia)? Did the response set for each item provide respondents a sufficient spectrum of options? Was the questionnaire too long? This can mean any of a number of things. There may be too many items to respond to. It may take too long to fill out. It may be too complicated to answer reflexively. All of these refer to the subjective states of the respondent. One can never be sure—although pretesting the survey instrument provides a good gauge for assessing what is "too long." Did items gather data on all relevant membership characteristics and concerns? This question gets to the heart of the profile. What information does the organization want and/or need? This is where theory was very important. The theory can be explicit and formal or ad hoc and tacit, but in either case, the sum of items included in the survey reflects the theoretical concerns of those who constructed it. In practice, researchers can search the literature for previous findings of how items empirically correlated with one another, but ultimately, researchers have to decide anew what information is germane to their particular study.

Sampling and Return Rate   Many factors can influence the reception that a survey receives. We were fortunate to have had the sponsorship and endorsement of the HS in our efforts. This inside connection allowed us greater liberty for including probing items and for making the questionnaire slightly longer than would normally be recommended. It also meant that the questionnaire enjoyed the HS's "stamp of approval," removing at least some latent suspicion on the part of our potential respondents. We were confident that we would have a respectable return rate because the instrument was being sent to a motivated population and was of direct relevance to them.

Normally, researchers would be concerned about attaining a sufficient sample. If samples are too small, then findings can be unreliable and/or unstable. Because HS had decided to survey their entire membership, we did not anticipate that sample size would be a problem. Potential sampling bias, however, could be a problem. If the people who return the questionnaire are systematically different from those that did not return the surveys, then sampling bias is said to have occurred. Because the present survey would be able to compare its results with the findings of previous research and other organizational information, we did not see a major problem with sampling bias.

Chapter Six

A Changing Landscape

The 1990s brought dramatic new developments to the frontier of the Right to Die movement. On the political front, statewide ballot initiatives to pass PAS legislation were tried in three states. In Washington State, Proposition 119 in 1991 suffered a loss with 46 percent of the vote favoring PAS. Proposition 161 in California in 1992 also lost with 46 percent in favor of the vote. Oregon voters reaffirmed their 1994 support for the right to die in November 1997 by rejecting Measure 16, a repeal effort (discussed below). Governor Ben Cayetano of Hawaii recently announced plans to put PAS before the state legislature (Omandam 1998; Hofsess 1998k). According to a June 1997 *TimeLines* newsletter, 19 states had introduced physician aid–in–dying bills to their state legislatures (Girsh 1997a). Most bills have died on the floor of the various state legislative bodies, but some were carried over to the next session.

As it currently stands, 35 states, including Texas, explicitly outlaw assisted suicide, and another 9 make the practice illegal through case law or common law. Since January 1998, nine states have introduced measures that would allow assisted suicide, whereas an equal number are considering proposals that would criminalize the practice or increase the penalties under existing law (Bray 1998). Although polls indicate that the majority of Americans support the concept of assisted suicide, that sentiment has not yet been translated into nationwide legislation. The potential for legislative action is strong.

The range of political activity occurring in different states has stimulated the formation of a variety of right to die organizations, most with only state-level ambitions. As one writer notes, "this Right-to-Die movement is fragmented and sometimes at odds. It ranges from Dr. Jack Kevorkian and his 'death machines,' to the court-savvy Seattle-based Compassion in Dying Federation of America" (Hill 1977). The evolving movement might indeed appear to be fragmented. However, students of social movements are more likely to observe this fragmentation as the typical ebb and flow of a growing agent for social change. In the course of many social movements, SMOs rise, face a challenge, and then find their influence slowly sifting away. New groups strengthen and assume territory abdicated by others. In the Right to Die movement, one SMO formed at the state level, Compassion in Dying, has recently extended its reach further into an already well populated social movement field, and it intends to become a major player.

The Rise of Compassion in Dying

As noted previously, Compassion in Dying was formed with a nucleus of activists from the Washington State chapter of the HS. Somewhat disheartened after narrowly losing a right to die state referendum in 1991, this group determined to continue the fight in a new and somewhat more pragmatic way. Deciding to provide more direct support to dying individuals, Compassion in Dying (hereafter referred to as Compassion) created an organizational structure separate from HS (although most members in Compassion continued membership in HS). Compassion defines itself as a "nonprofit organization created to support the right of terminally ill persons to choose to die without pain, suffering, and with personal assistance, if necessary, to intentionally hasten death" (Compassion in Dying 1996).

Unlike the HS, the new group extended its organizational goals to include assisting the terminally ill person with dying. While denying that any members actually administer a lethal dose of medication, Compassion members do counsel the client and family and are present with the person who has chosen to end his or her life.

Under Compassion's guidelines, the client is responsible for securing and administering his or her own fatal dose of medication. In a 1993 telephone interview, Ralph Mero, then executive director of Compassion in Dying, explained the decision to take the next step: "After spending all that money to fail at passing legislation [the Washington

State referendum], here we were still dedicated to the idea that people should not have to die alone and in pain. For people of conscience, who truly believe, personally helping people die is only a natural evolution" (Mero 1993). Compassion, as of this writing, acknowledges that it has been present at the death of a number of people.

It is not clear whether Compassion's original intent was to stake out a battleground in the legal system. Planned or not, due to its direct involvement with dying persons, it soon found itself entangled in the Washington State court system. Filing a lawsuit, *Compassion in Dying v. the State of Washington* (Ninth Circuit Court, 79f. 3d 790 [1996]), Compassion attempted to invalidate Washington's law criminalizing assisted suicide. The HS filed an amicus brief in support of Compassion's suit and also gave financial help. The HS went so far as to loan the group its mailing list to solicit monetary aid nationwide, although it was the HS's understanding that the mailing list would be used only one time. Compassion continued to utilize the mailing list, creating some hard feelings between the two groups. The decision to retain and use the mailing list apparently was predominantly the brainstorm of Ralph Mero, Compassion's founder and executive director. Mero, a strong, charismatic, and somewhat driven leader, spearheaded the push to bring Compassion's lawsuit to the forefront, believing that this was a way to enact legal change while foregoing the trauma of stalled state bills and failed referendums. Mero's priorities strained relationships somewhat with the parent HS organization. However, with the lawsuit going forward, many in the Right to Die movement saw Compassion as moving to the forefront of the movement (the basis for this suit is discussed below).

Compassion's suit meandered slowly through the legal system, ultimately achieving the glory of being one of two lawsuits to be heard before the U.S. Supreme Court on this topic. The Supreme Court did not support Compassion's case; however, this decision did not dishearten the membership. In an April 1997 interview, a few weeks before the suit was presented to the Supreme Court, John Lee, public relations director for Compassion, was feeling victorious while facing an almost certain loss. He commented:

We don't really expect our case to win. We don't expect Tim Quill's case to win either. However, what we know we have done is extend the dialogue. The medical community has taken a bashing for not really attending to the needs of the dying, and now they are sitting up and paying attention. Sure, we hope one day to get the law changed, but until that happens, we feel we are doing what we should be doing just by focusing attention on the rights of the dying. We feel we have played a very instrumental role in that. Look at what we have done. It was us, Compassion, a small state organization that made its way to the United States Supreme Court. You don't do much better than that. It wasn't Hemlock or any other group who made it to the Supreme Court. While at the court it is true that Tim Quill's case got most of the publicity, but we were right in there with them. We made it there, too, and we got a lot of publicity as our suit hit the Ninth Circuit Court. (Lee 1997)

Compassion in Dying underwent leadership change in 1997. Mero, for personal reasons, relocated to a state in New England. Reluctant to give up the organization that he founded at such a crucial point in its evolution, he attempted to convince the board of directors that the organization should move with him. That suggestion was soundly rejected.

The current director of Compassion is Barbara Coombs Lee. Coombs Lee is multitalented and broadly educated, a nurse as well as an attorney. She was also the chief petitioner and primary spokesperson for Oregon's Death with Dignity Act, Measure 16 (Compassion in Dying 1997). According to Coombs Lee, the group remains energized and motivated, and the Mero departure has apparently not created any loss of momentum.

In 1997 John Lee pointed out possible new directions for the group: "The board of Compassion has already voted to attempt to go national. As you know, we are a Washington-based organization, but there isn't anywhere else for us to go but up. We have what it takes to really move forward the right to die agenda—look at what we have already done" (Lee 1997). When asked by the interviewer how they planned to set up a framework for a national organization, Lee quite freely spoke of the possibility of usurping the already-formed federated chapters of HS:

Compassion came out of Hemlock. Most of us still have joint memberships in Hemlock. But let's face it. What has Hemlock done recently? Of course they have supported us in our struggle, and we really appreciate it, but nothing has been happening with Hemlock for a while now. I think the Hemlock chapters might be well open for a new, more dynamic direction. For example, is your local chapter really satisfied with Hemlock National anymore? What if I were to come down and talk to it, isn't it possible that they might be willing to switch over to us? We are really on the move and Hemlock isn't. (Lee 1997)

Lee's professed strategy is particularly interesting, as the HS chapter in Arkansas held several discussions regarding the possibility of disaffiliating with HS and joining Compassion. Although a decision to do so was not made, this development at least suggests the feasibility of Compassion's political strategy.

On September 16, 1997, the Hemlock Society of Northern California—at one time the largest Hemlock chapter in the United States—voted to disband. In a news release, Dina Smith, treasurer of the group, cited a lack of active supporters, shortage of funds, and more important, a sense that "we are not doing anything worthwhile" (ERGO 1997c). Derek Humphry suggested in the same news release that perhaps the active supporters of right to die organizations are switching over to groups that are involved either in political law reform or direct counseling of the dying. He noted, "Hemlock has done a good job in the field of education, but today seems obsolescent to them; the goal-posts have moved" (ERGO 1997c). Although Humphry's analysis was immediately disputed on the Internet right-to-die listserv by Faye Girsh, the current executive director of the HS, her argument was not entirely persuasive to some (Girsh 1997b).

In a recent special edition of its newsletter, Compassion announced its plans for becoming a national-level organization. A new executive director for the state of Washington was announced, and Barbara Coombs Lee was introduced as the new director for the national Compassion in Dying. According to the newsletter, Compassion in Dying Federation of America will provide leadership in education and advocacy and offer patient consultation through its local affiliated organizations (Compassion in Dying 1997). Along with these startling announcements came the revelation of a newly formed affiliated group, Compassion in Dying of Northern California. Had the Northern California HS chapter jumped ship in order to be picked up by Compassion? Although persons involved in both groups denied this, the coincidence was rather striking.

Following this news, the Arkansas HS chapter received a phone call from a larger HS chapter in another state, inquiring whether the local chapter, like several others, was considering switching over to Compassion. At the October 1997 meeting of the Arkansas chapter, several persons were empowered by the board of directors to seek more information regarding forming an affiliate with Compassion. Thus, while Compassion's immediate future is uncertain, it is apparent that this organization has every intention of being the front-runner in the Right to Die movement.

On April 29 1998, the Hemlock Society of Oregon, whose members helped launch PAS, quietly voted to dissolve their chapter membership. The chapter, founded by Derek Humphry in 1987, formed the base for Oregon Right to Die in 1993. Elven Sinnard, who officially dissolved the organization, commented that it was not an easy decision to make but pointed out that Compassion in Dying, Oregon Right to Die, and the Death with Dignity Legal Defense Center and Education Center operate in Oregon also. "It's just a lot of duplication" (Hofsess 1998m). Humphry announced that he may try to revive Oregon's HS chapter. Although he broke with the national HS leadership over a difference of opinion about the group's direction, he remained a member. Overall national membership of the HS has declined in recent years to 25,000—half of what it was in its heyday in the early 1990s (Hofsess 1998m).

Appealing to Higher Courts

During the summer of 1997, the right of terminally ill patients to die by PAS was given two major court tests. Heard before the U.S. Supreme Court, both failed to find support within that judicial body. However, the failure was not complete.

The two-pronged courtroom assault was led by Compassion, which notes that its strategy was "to bring action in two different federal appeals jurisdictions (Washington and New York), with the expectation that one case would be reviewed by the U.S. Supreme Court" (Mero 1996). To their surprise, the Supreme Court agreed to hear both cases. Compassion's mission with these legal suits was to establish a constitutionally protected right for medical assistance in dying, just as the case of *Roe v. Wade* established a right for medical assistance with abortion (Mero 1996, 1).

Compassion in Dying's Washington State's Litigation: The First Prong

Litigation in Washington was initiated to challenge a state law entitled "promoting a suicide attempt." This law allows for the prosecution of any person who helps a terminally ill patient hasten his or her own death. Compassion in Dying claimed that such a law was unconstitutional under the Liberty and Equal Protection Clauses of the 14th Amendment. Plaintiffs cited previous decisions of the U.S. Supreme

Court that found, for example, "It is a premise of the Constitution that there is a realm of personal liberty which the government may not enter" (Mero 1996, 2; *Planned Parenthood v. Casey* [505 U.S. 833]).

Using the case *Cruzan v. Director, Missouri Dept. of Health* (497 U.S. 261), in which the Supreme Court recognized that competent persons have the constitutional right to direct the removal of life-sustaining medical treatment and thus hasten death, Compassion in Dying argued that this opportunity is denied terminally ill individuals whose life is not being maintained by artificial life support (U.S. Legal Documents 1997b). These individuals, in effect, constitute a class that is being denied equal protection under the law.

On May 3, 1994, Federal District Court Judge Barbara Rothstein declared the Washington State law unconstitutional, supporting Compassion in Dying's position. Judge Rothstein found that "[f]rom a constitutional perspective, the court does not believe that a distinction can be drawn between refusing life-sustaining medical treatment and physician assisted suicide by an uncoerced, mentally competent, terminally ill adult" (quoted in Mero 1996, 2).

Washington State appealed the decision, but Washington's law was ultimately overturned by the U.S. Ninth Circuit Court of Appeals on March 9, 1996. This court's finding also applied to similar laws in the states of Alaska, Oregon, Montana, Idaho, California, Nevada, Arizona, and Hawaii. The majority decision written by Judge Stephen Rienhardt focused on the "liberty interest" inherent in the 14th Amendment:

A competent terminally ill adult, having lived nearly the full measure of his life, has a strong liberty interest in choosing a dignified and humane death rather than being reduced at the end of his existence to a childlike state of helplessness, diapered, sedated, incontinent. How a person dies not only determines the nature of the final period of his existence, but, in many cases, the enduring memories held by those who love him. Those who believe strongly that death must come without physician assistance are free to follow that creed, be they doctors or patients. They are not free, however, to force their views, their religious convictions or their philosophies on all the other members of a democratic society, and compel those whose values differ with theirs to die painful, protracted, and agonizing deaths. (U.S. Legal Documents 1997b; Compassion in Dying 1996)

The Washington State attorney general petitioned for a review of the case by the U.S. Supreme Court.

Litigation Arising in New York: The Second Prong

Meanwhile, on July 29, 1994, the case of *Quill et al. v. Vacco* was filed in the U.S. District Court for the Southern District of New York by three physicians and three terminally ill patients (Second Circuit Court, 95-1858). One of the plaintiffs, Dr. Timothy Quill, had published an article in the *New England Journal of Medicine* on March 7, 1991, in which he described prescribing barbiturates for a dying cancer patient who later ended her life. The Quill case was designed to test the constitutionality of the New York statute on assisted suicide, which is basically a twin to that of the state of Washington. Compassion in Dying was not a plaintiff, but it did sponsor and financially support the litigation.

The constitutionality of the New York assisted-suicide law was upheld in the Southern District Court of New York. The plaintiffs appealed to the U.S. Court of Appeals, and on September 1, 1995, arguments were heard in the Quill case by three judges of the Second Circuit Court of Appeals. All three ruled that the New York laws on assisted suicide violated the Equal Protection clause because "they are not rationally related to any legitimate state interest." Their decision asked:

But what interest can the state possibly have in requiring prolongation of a life that is all but ended? Surely, the state's interest lessens as the potential for life diminishes. And what business is it of the state to require the continuation of agony when the result is imminent and inevitable? What concern prompts the state to interfere with a mentally competent patient's right to define his own concept of existence, of meaning, of the universe, and of the mystery of human life, when the patient seeks to have drugs prescribed to end life during the final stages of a terminal illness? The greatly reduced interest of the state in preserving life compels the answer to these questions: None (Compassion in Dying 1996, 2; U.S. Legal Documents 1997a).

The New York attorney general appealed to the U.S. Supreme Court.

The AMA responded to the flurry of activity supporting PAS. Thomas Reardon, M.D., chair of the AMA Task Force on Quality Care at the End of Life, noted on April 12, 1996, in response to the New York decision by the Second Court of Appeals: "Physicians are healers. When it is clear that healing is no longer an option, the physician is faced with the often difficult challenge of helping patients and their families face death. Nonetheless, the inability of physicians to prevent death does not imply that they are free to help cause death" (Reardon 1996). In response to the Ninth Circuit Court of Appeals decision, he stated: "Physicians do have an obligation to relieve pain and suffering through appropriate palliative care—even if it may hasten the patient's death. However, this must not be in any way confused with assisted suicide, where the sole intent is to cause death. Asking a physician to assist in suicide transforms the instruments of medicine into tools of death" (Reardon 1996).

The Supreme Court: Denying a Constitutional Right to Die

The U.S. Supreme Court agreed to hear the appealed cases from Washington State and New York State and subsequently rejected both arguments in 1997. According to Faye Girsh, executive director of the HS, these decisions were not surprising for a Court decidedly opposed to finding new constitutional rights; the nine justices were unanimous in agreeing that the 14th Amendment did not protect the rights of the terminally ill to hasten death. But the concurring opinions and even the footnotes showed strong ambivalence (Girsh 1997a, 1). Girsh further notes that, although many now think PAS is unconstitutional and therefore can never be codified in the judicial system, that assumption is wrong. In essence, "such laws are now, as it has been, in the hands of the states" (Girsh 1997a, 1).

The implications of the Supreme Court ruling are varied. As it currently stands, states can pass laws banning the practice or permitting physician aid in dying. The Court is still apparently open to looking at other cases with a different emphasis. It additionally encouraged the debate to continue. Despite the Supreme Court decision against PAS for the terminally ill, apparently a majority of adults still believe the law should let doctors aid dying patients who want to end their lives. Harris Poll results published in *USA Today* on September 24, 1997, revealed that 68 percent of those polled believe the law should allow physicians the right to help terminally ill patients die, while 27 percent oppose it (Hofsess 1997a).

Oregon's Death with Dignity Act, Measure 16

In 1994 the state of Oregon, by public referendum, passed Measure 16 by 51 percent to 49 percent, the first PAS legislation that legally allowed physician aid in dying (for the full text of Measure 16, and for a comparison between Measure 16 and model legislation supported by the HS, see appendix 2). This was a stunning victory and in some ways unexpected. Two previous state initiatives in Washington and California had both failed by narrow margins. Here was the first actual victory in the legislative challenge for physician aid in dying.

There was another first in the passage of this proposal also. During the hotly contested debates on the measure prior to turning it over to the voters, the Oregon Medical Association, despite certain pressure from the AMA to publicly oppose Measure 16, voted to remain neutral on the bill. State medical associations in other states previously had come out in opposition to any physician aid–in–dying proposals.

However, passage of the bill did not open the door for physician aid in dying. The bill was immediately challenged in court. On November 23, 1994, an injunction was filed by opponents to PAS in the U.S. District Court stating the law violated the Equal Protection Clause and the Due Process clause of the U.S. Constitution, the Americans with Disabilities Act, and the Religious Freedom Restoration Act. A restraining order was placed to prevent anyone from using the law. After wending its way through the judicial process for three years, Measure 16, Oregon's Death with Dignity Act, finally emerged clear of legal prohibitions. However, its legality did not stand long.

During the three years that Measure 16 was battling legal injunctions, the Oregon legislature, perhaps frightened by the passage of Measure 16, usurped the referendum process by sending the bill back to the voters in November 1997. Thus, while physician aid in dying was legal in the state of Oregon for several weeks—from its emergence from the judicial jungle through the days just prior to the November balloting—according to the guidelines enacted by the 1994 vote, there was not enough time for anyone to use the law before it was due to be voted on again.

Voters were now asked to vote on Measure 51, a bill to repeal Measure 16. Old cast members in this drama had switched sides also. This time the Oregon Medical Association came out in support of rejecting the Death with Dignity Act. However, the governor of Oregon, John Kitzhaber, an M.D., who originally opposed the bill in 1994, now was rejecting the measure to repeal. His perspective was that the voters of Oregon had already made their wishes known when they voted on the bill the first time. He directed his anger at the state legislature, declaring, "They [the legislature] didn't have the courage to repeal the measure. They didn't have the will to make it work, so they just sent it back to the voters" (ERGO 1997h).

For some, the issue began to extend beyond simply the right to die and took on new meaning in terms of the right of the state legislature to ask voters to revote on a bill they had passed once before. A poll released by the *Oregonian* (ERGO 1997e) indicated that 6 out of 10 Oregonians supported the state's assisted-suicide law and did not want to see it repealed. In addition, the same poll indicated that most of those polled felt the law should never have been referred back to the voters.

In opposition to the Oregon Medical Association, a group calling themselves Oregon Physicians for Death with Dignity surfaced. Holding a press conference in the state capital, their message was clearly in support of not repealing the law: "If we repeal measure 16, we take away the tool that has lead to heightened interest in care for the dying. It was not until Oregonians passed this law that we saw the rapid advance in care for the dying we have witnessed in the past three years. It would be a huge mistake to repeal a law that has done so much good without ever having been implemented" (ERGO 1997e).

The major difference between prior proposals and this bill is that the latter focuses purely on prescription. Measure 16 does not allow for a physician to administer a lethal injection. After following all the safeguards written into the bill, a physician may then write a prescription for an oral dose of medication that the patient must self-administer. Although this bill is a compromise when compared to proposals attempted in other states, that is, those that contain a "direct lethal injection by a physician" clause, the opponents to this piece of legislation seized on the oral medication as an example of a "fatal flaw" in the law. They presented the prescribing bill as one whose effectiveness is questionable and that may leave patients still alive, but in worse shape after a suicide attempt. "Fatally flawed" or not, the voters of Oregon reaffirmed their support in physician-assisted suicide by rejecting the repeal of Measure 16 by a 60 percent to 40 percent vote in November 1997 (ERGO 1997g).

The Legacy of Oregon and Measure 16: Comfort Care

Change has come about as a result of Measure 16. According to Dr. Susan Tolle, director of the Center for Ethics in Health Care at the Oregon Health Science University, "[T]he prospect of helping patients kill themselves has forced Oregon's doctors to face up to their failure to provide adequate pain control for the terminally ill" (Shapiro 1997, 63). In support of Dr. Tolle's statements, an article in the *Los Angeles Times* reported that Oregon now leads the nation in the medical use of morphine (Monmaney 1997). According to federal drug data, wholesale, per-capita distribution of the painkilling drug morphine was more than 50 percent higher in the state of Oregon than the U.S. average in the first six months of 1996 (Monmaney 1997). The article goes on to say that Oregon's increasing use of morphine, which is typically given to patients with otherwise untreatable pain, is consistent with its leading role in end-of-life issues. In 1994, when Oregon voters narrowly approved Measure 16, the PAS act, it ranked 11th in morphine distribution. Oregon has increased its medical use of morphine by 70 percent (Hofsess 1998c). Researchers believe that this indicates a sensitization on the part of Oregon physicians to give gravely ill patients comfort care.

Thus, even without the November 1997 right to die victory, the Oregon battle has altered the face of pain care for terminally ill patients. Iowa and California are among the states that have already drafted bills concerning pain management for consideration in their next legislative session, and Florida is discussing one. Others will follow. These laws would make it easier for doctors to prescribe potentially addictive opiates like morphine for their terminally ill patients without facing professional censure. As one journalist noted: "Pain bills are expected to gain popularity. Any politician who can find a compromise between taking a patient's life and easing a patient's pain will make points. The assisted suicide movement has put this debate in the legislature's face and they are feeling pressured to look at it. If they can craft something that improves care for dying people, it will mean something to their constituents and be a winner for them" (Lade 1997).

An example of this is a bill filed in Arizona to strengthen patient-doctor relationships and give patients greater control of end-of-life decisions. This bill, entitled Medical Treatment Options for Terminal Illness, has the full support of the HS. The Arizona measure is the nation's first to cover such a wide range of patient options including curative treatment, hospice care, refusal of medical treatment, do-not-resuscitate instructions, and the removal of life support. The bill also requires doctors to discuss all treatment alternatives with terminally ill patients and requires health care personnel to honor advance directives (HS 1997b). Hearings for this bill were set for mid-January 1998.

Some physicians seem to be heeding the lessons from Measure 16. The AMA, at its 1998 annual conference, announced a new initiative designed to educate physicians in essential clinical end-of-life care skills (Gerhard 1998a). The Education for Physicians on End-of-Life Care Project (EPEC) is a two-year program aimed at helping physicians, who are too often inadequately prepared to care for dying patients.

Although the debate over PAS has driven improvements in care for the dying, Dr. Tolle issued a warning. She noted that state policy makers must make sure that all Oregonians can afford high-level end-of-life care. Without it, she postulates the option of PAS remains essentially a coercive choice for persons without insurance coverage for hospital or comfort measures (Hofsess 1998c).

Advocates on both sides of the assisted-suicide issue observe that it is no surprise that Oregon, with its rich history of social concerns, became the first state in the nation to legalize euthanasia. More than two decades ago, Oregon became the first state to adopt a recycling law that required a refundable deposit on bottles and cans. It is also the only state that requires its entire Pacific coastline to be open to the public.

This has led to some interesting "framing" issues. Dr. Andrew Glass, a member of Oregon's Health Services Commission, notes that "Oregon is a bunch of mavericks who enjoy raising these issues. There's a strong libertarian undercurrent in the state" (Ornstein 1998). Opponents of assisted suicide, such as Dr. Gregory Hamilton, argue, in contrast to Dr. Glass, that Oregon residents may have "a greater moral deficit than the other states." Opponents of assisted suicide point out that recent studies have shown that Oregon has one of the lowest church-going populations and one of the highest divorce rates in the nation (Ornstein 1998). Thus, Oregon is painted as a state of liberal, freedom seekers or as a population of possible moral degenerates, not unlike the different lenses applied to assisted suicide. The populace of Oregon becomes the devil or the liberating angel of assisted death, depending on one's perspective.

Whatever the position one assumes with regard to PAS, and however one characterizes the population of the state of Oregon, it would be difficult to deny that Oregon now practices very good end-of-life care. Its sensitization to the problems associated with terminal care has produced more humane treatment for the dying. The Robert Wood Johnson Foundation announced a major award to Oregon Health Sciences University to study how to break down barriers to good care for dying patients. As noted at the time of the award announcement, "Oregon is providing the road map for a lot of other states in how they can improve care for patients who have life-limiting illness" (Hoover 1998d).

Learning to Live with Measure 16

With voter-decreed reaffirmation of PAS, health care workers in Oregon are now scrambling to provide guidance and support. The day after the reaffirmation of PAS in Oregon brought a stunned realization to many—PAS was a fact, no longer a political or philosophical battle to be fought: "And the recognition dawning for many in health care: . . . It's a different world today, November 5, 1997" (Hogan 1997). As James Kronenberg, spokesperson for the Oregon Medical Association, notes, "For everybody—doctors, this organization—this is all new ground. Legal assisted suicide has never been done before. It's kind of a scary time" (Hogan 1997). No one was really prepared. Assisted suicide turned from theory to detail. Everyone had questions.

On November 11, 1997, the Oregon Medical Association started offering doctors a "Compliance Checklist" outlining their rights and responsibilities under the new law. Physicians for Compassionate Care, which opposes assisted suicide, sent a letter to its 1,000 Oregon members giving them recommendations on how to refuse to participate in the state's Death with Dignity Act (Hogan 1997). In April 1998, Oregon's Task Force to Improve the Care of Terminally Ill Oregonians, after meeting in secrecy for months, finally issued a 91-page *Guidebook on Assisted Suicide.* The new guidebook, which can be purchased from the Center for Ethics in Health Care at the Oregon Health Sciences University, contains helpful hints for those using physician aid in dying. For example, it notes that some proponents of assisted suicide suggest giving patients a test dose of medication before the suicide to assess their tolerance for the medication. Other tips include mixing the drugs with pureed fruit to disguise the bitter taste of the drugs (Stolberg 1998; Hofsess 1998b).

Pharmacists were upset with the new law. The Oregon Pharmacy Board, in an emergency session on November 6, 1997, voted to require physicians to spell out on prescriptions that medication is for assisted suicide so that pharmacists can choose whether to participate (O'Neill 1997a). Physicians want only the name of the drug and the dosage on the label of the drug and believe that labeling the prescription as a drug for suicide would violate patient confidentiality and could lead to family shame or trauma, especially in small towns.

After an initially strong reaction to PAS, pharmacists, six months after passage of the law, seem to be doing better than other health providers in learning to deal with PAS. Unlike the AMA, which emphatically continues to oppose PAS, the American Pharmaceutical Association (APA) passed a resolution recognizing the rights of dying patients to receive medication from their physician and pharmacist under state laws such as the Oregon Death with Dignity law. The AMA, on the other hand, stoutly maintains that PAS is fundamentally inconsistent with the physician's role. By contrast, the APA with its resolution recognizes the right of pharmacists who oppose assisted suicide to refuse to fill lethal prescriptions. They also recognize the rights of patients to have such prescriptions filled by pharmacists willing to do so. According to an editorial published in Oregon's *Register-Guard* editorial page, "That's more sensible than the AMA's moralistic opposition" (ERGO 1998e). The editorial goes on to suggest that all related national health groups should take their cues from the APA rather than the AMA on this issue and recognize their members' right to make their own decisions about handling requests for suicide assistance under Oregon's law (ERGO 1998d, 1998e).

Oregon nurses also are seeking guidance. Many terminally ill people may be too sick to take their own lethal dose of medicine and may be dependent on a nurse's help. By helping a patient mix and swallow a lethal dose of medicine, would they become a violator of the law? Nurses in Oregon have requested an opinion from the state attorney general to guide them as they grapple with their role in assisted suicide (Egan 1998).

A major furor was created in March 1998 by the decision to make suicide part of the list of medical procedures available to residents insured under the state's Medicaid program. Federal money, by law, cannot be used in assisted suicide. Critics argue that the state is subsidizing suicide whereas supporters contend it is only a logical extension of state-financed "comfort care" at the end of life. State Senator Ken Baker, a Republican who is the assistant majority leader, announced that the state legislature may attempt to remove assisted suicide from the list of things covered by the state medical plan (Egan 1998).

Finally, no one is sure what to call this type of death. State medical authorities recommend that doctors put the cause of death as "drug overdose, self-administered, legally prescribed" together with the underlying disease (ERGO 1998c). But no uniform language exists as of yet, and the doorway to linguistically framing the act is wide open (Egan 1998). Members of the task force writing Oregon's *Guidebook on Assisted Suicide* noted that each word in their publication was carefully chosen, most notably the phrase "physician-assisted suicide." The term is not used in the Oregon Death with Dignity Act (Measure 16). Proponents of the law apparently prefer the word "hastened death," whereas opponents wish it to be called "euthanasia." The task force settled on "physician-assisted suicide" because the phrase is commonly accepted in the literature and because it correctly implies participation by both patient and physician" (Stolberg 1998; Egan 1998: Rooney and Blake 1998).

Controversy also exists regarding how much tracking of information should be done by Oregon's Health Division. Some believe that Oregon, as the first state to legalize assisted suicide, should be leading research into how well, or poorly, the law works. Opponents of assisted suicide argue that the Oregon Health Division's plans to collect records on such suicide do not go far enough to gather valuable information that could help people decide whether to take deadly medication. But supporters and the Health Division officials contend that it is not the job of the state to do research into the effectiveness of the suicide law (O'Neill and Hoover 1998).

As it presently stands, if the law is strictly followed, PAS deaths will not be investigated by the medical examiner. And although the medical examiner's office is charged with investigating all unexplained or accidental deaths, including homicide and suicide, legally, the law views the use of a lethal prescription as hastening an already-imminent death and this distinguishes it from suicide (O'Neill and Hoover 1998).

Despite earlier protests concerning the role of the Health Division in collecting PAS information, on June 18, 1998, Oregon health officials announced they will be surveying doctors who help terminally ill people die under the state's landmark assisted-suicide law. A 53-question, voluntary interview covers a range of issues, from why the patient asked for the lethal medication to how many doctors the patient consulted before finding one who would help (Hofsess 1998l). Once enough interviews have been completed to protect the identity of the patients, the Health Division will release a report on the results.

Thus, Oregon health care providers struggle to make sense of the new law within the confines of their health practices. Oregon continues to seek information regarding PAS. In early April 1998, the Task Force on the Care of Terminally Ill Oregonians, the group that published the *Guidebook on Assisted Suicide,* completed a visit to the Netherlands. Their goal was to study ways to improve the state's PAS through better monitoring of deaths and a shared understanding of the Dutch experience with euthanasia (Gianelli 1998). Although it has been difficult for Oregon to struggle with the actual enactment of PAS, perhaps other states will profit in the future from the lessons Oregon is learning (Hoover and O'Keefe 1997b).

Opponents to PAS Continue the Battle

Despite having survived several court challenges and a reconfirmation vote by the population of Oregon, opposition to the newly enacted state law from a federal adversary surprised many scarcely a week after the November 1997 elections. The Drug Enforcement Agency (DEA), with strong encouragement from Senator Orrin Hatch, Republican from Utah, threatened to prosecute any doctor who prescribes drugs to end a life. Although states license physicians, doctors must be registered by the DEA to prescribe controlled substances such as those that would be used under Oregon's new law. Federal law gave U.S. Attorney General Janet Reno the power to revoke a doctor's registration for prescribing controlled substances for anything other than a "legitimate medical" purpose (Suo and Hoover 1997). The DEA appealed to Reno for the power to go forward with their plans (Sarasohn 1997).

However, an internal-review team from the U.S. Department of Justice concluded that the federal law does not prohibit doctors from carrying out Oregon's assisted-suicide law. Barbara Coombs Lee, co-author of the assisted-suicide law and head of Compassion in Dying, concurred with the internal review by the Justice Department. According to Coombs Lee, "It's not the DEA's business to steamroll . . . the people of Oregon and replace the voter's judgement with their own" (Barnett, Hogan, and Green 1998; Hofsess 1998j).

Within a few days of the April 1998 announcement by Oregon that two residents had taken advantage of the act and died as a result of a lethal prescription, with an acknowledgment that ten more had applied for PAS, turmoil erupted. Fifty-three members of Congress, including House Speaker Newt Gingrich, wrote Attorney General Reno to urge that Oregon doctors who assist in their patient's suicide face possible revocation of their license to prescribe drugs (Hogan and Barnett

1998). One hundred and thirty-eight members of Congress urged Reno to overrule the legal judgments of her own staff and "to turn loose the pit bulls of the DEA" on Oregon's physicians who utilize PAS (Enzi 1998).

The Clinton administration had repeatedly voiced opposition to PAS prior to the November vote but has not yet issued any statements regarding the new law. Dr. Thomas Reardon, president of the AMA, announced that he supported a DEA move to pull drug-prescribing privileges for doctors taking part in an assisted suicide, while Oregon Medical Association spokesperson James Kronenberg stated that his group would protect a doctor's legal right to participate in the PAS (Hoover and O'Neill 1998). Accusations of state's rights versus federal law were being bandied about while Reno's ruling was awaited.

On June 6, 1998, Reno announced her conclusion that federal law does not prohibit PAS (Sniffen 1998). She noted that Oregon's assisted-suicide law does not pose a threat to the civil rights of terminally ill patients who want to end their lives (ERGO 1998g). This prompted House Judiciary Chairman Henry J. Hyde, Republican from Illinois, and Assistant Senate Majority Leader Don Nickles, Republican from Oklahoma, to file a bill in Congress to change the Controlled Substances Act to ban the use of medications to assist in suicide or euthanasia (Hughes 1998). This bill, called the Lethal Drug Abuse Prevention Act of 1998, is designed to prohibit the dispensing or distribution of a controlled substance for the purpose of causing, or assisting in causing, the suicide, euthanasia, or mercy killing of any individual (*Congressional Record* 1998; ERGO 1998c). Representative Peter DeFazio, Democrat from Oregon, has said that he has been trying to educate colleagues on PAS. He charged that Republican authors of the new bill are inconsistent in promoting states rights while simultaneously trying to overturn two of Oregon referendums that allow assisted suicide (Hughes 1998).

On July 2, 1998, both Compassion in Dying and the AMA stood side by side officially in opposition to the Hyde bill. They found themselves in the unusual position of being allies. However, both organizations had much to lose with a successful passage of the bill. The AMA feared the bill would have a chilling effect on physicians who prescribe painkilling medication for dying patients. The AMA had just begun a new educational program to teach physicians better end-of-life care and was concerned that physicians would grow fearful of prescribing sufficient amounts of medication to provide comfort care if the bill is enacted. Barbara Coombs Lee saw the bill as a mechanism to subvert the will of the Oregon people. "My take is that it's a pretty audacious attempt by Congress to substitute their own moral judgment for that of Oregonians. It's an attempt to usurp a state's power and replace the local regulatory mechanism through the Board of Medical Examiners and other state authorities with federal power" (O'Neill 1998).

And so the battle continues. Like abortion, even after successful supportive legislation, PAS still faces opponents.

Hemlock and Compassion in Dying Support Oregon

Right to die organizations have joined in the fracas in Oregon as well. Compassion in Dying announced in January 1998 that it plans to move its headquarters to Oregon to help manage requests to use Oregon's PAS law. As Coombs Lee noted in a press release, "Now that there is an area where that is reality (assisted suicide), it would seem irresponsible to not bring our knowledge and experience there" (ERGO 1998a; Hoover 1998a). Although opponents of Compassion argue that the organization will promote assisted suicide in Oregon, Coombs Lee contends that the state needs responsible stewards of the law.

Not to be outdone, Faye Girsh, executive director of the HS, announced it will start a support group for loved ones of terminally ill patients who took their own lives. Nationally, the HS is stepping up efforts to legalize assisted suicide in other states. Girsh asked reporters at a news briefing, "Do we want more Oregons or more Kevorkians?" In the meantime, in states where Compassion is active, local HS chapters will refer members to the former organization. If Compassion is not available, HS will offer members a program to support terminally ill people who decide to hasten their own deaths (Hoover 1998b, 1998c).

Hemlock after Humphry

While much of the Right to Die movement's attention during the past several years had been drawn to the legislative roles of the Supreme Court decisions and Oregon's new PAS law the past several years, the HS struggled to find equilibrium after the retirement of Derek Humphry, its founder. After less than two full years at the helm of the HS, John Pridonoff, who was hired as executive director to replace Humphry, left the organization. During his tenure, Pridonoff, although not receiving the national exposure of Humphry, helped focus the organization's attention on forging alliances with other groups outside the Right to Die movement. For example, he set the stage for opening up at least some dialogue between the hospice movement and HS. His agenda focused on the similarities between the two groups, pointing out that both groups work for the betterment of the rights of the dying and differ only on the actual end of life. Hospice believes in palliative care, supporting the patient who has no hope of cure, but does not encourage the patient to take his or her own life (Hoover and O'Keefe 1997a). Pridonoff claimed the only degree of separation between the two groups is that some patients might opt for self-deliverance after using hospice care up to the point of death.

The hospice movement, for the most part, has chosen to remain distant from HS. Obviously, affiliation with the philosophy of HS might cost them clientele. Patients who are afraid of euthanasists might be fearful of using hospice services if a close association between the two was known. And although the official stance of the hospice movement remains rejection of the Hemlock message, some hospice workers have privately indicated support. The exception to this official distancing from euthanasia has been hospices in Oregon. Due to the legacy of Oregon's PAS, all of Oregon's 57 hospices now accept patients who say they intend to end their lives with drugs prescribed by their doctors under the new law (Claiborne 1998).

The failure of the hospice movement and HS to form a public organizational alliance should not be seen as a failure on Pridonoff's part to meet self-proclaimed goals. He was responsible for opening up previously closed channels of communications. For example, encouraged by his leadership, the Arkansas HS chapter successfully began some discussions with a local hospice group, sending guest speakers to each other's meetings. On a more national level, in 1997 the Boulder Hospice in Colorado publicly proclaimed neutrality in the right to die agenda, stating that such a decision should be given to the patient (ERGO 1997b).

In 1997 an HS chapter and an organization supporting the hospice concept joined forces in a limited way in Florida, asking state officials to give doctors more latitude in managing the pain of terminally ill patients. The director of Florida's Commission on Aging with Dignity and the Hemlock Society of Florida plan to stand together and ask for laws to allow doctors to treat pain aggressively. Although the Commission on Aging with Dignity is actively and publicly opposed to assisted suicide, leaders of that group and the HS note that both organizations have much in common—that is, to help people who are suffering and to have better pain management policies (Peterson 1997). Perhaps Pridonoff's legacy will yet be realized.

The HS Search for a New Home and a New Leader

With Pridonoff's departure, the HS was left in a somewhat troubled state. Although Pridonoff did not have the national recognition of Humphry, he did travel exhaustively on behalf of the HS and engaged in numerous speaking engagements, keeping the name of the HS somewhat visible. After his departure, the HS board was torn regarding what type of new executive director should be hired. Some thought that a highly visible spokesperson would be best, to keep the organization's name in the public eye. Others felt that the HS was successful enough to allow focus on good organizational skills in order to improve the management of the organization. An advertisement for a new executive director was placed, but it became a half-hearted effort, as the HS was running headfirst into some major organizational problems of its own. A former board member, Helen Voorhis, was named acting executive director.

The difficulties HS encountered were the result of a hasty and perhaps not-well-thought-out decision on the part of the board to move the national headquarters to Denver, Colorado, in 1995. It had long been felt that the national headquarters should be relocated given that the current location of Eugene, Oregon, was so closely affiliated with Derek Humphry. Humphry continued to have informal relationships with many of the staff members that he himself had hired and nurtured during his tenure as executive director. Some board members thought it would be difficult to switch old loyalties of the staff from Humphry to another new executive director. Pridonoff apparently ran into a little of this trouble immediately after assuming his leadership role, but that seemed to smooth itself out over time.

The location change from Oregon to Denver, voted on by the board of directors in October 1995, was not the result of any coherent search initiative. In fact, apparently no research was conducted at all. Denver, with an active local chapter and a chapter leader who was willing to oversee the move, became the headquarters as a matter of convenience. A few board members who opposed the move as a rash decision were easily outvoted. To make matters worse, it was planned that a representative from the board, Wiley Morris, would fly to Eugene to discuss the board's decision with the headquarters staff, attempting to solicit as many of the seasoned workers as possible to relocate with the headquarters. Unfortunately for the board, the news of the relocation plan moved faster than the board member assigned to announce the decision. Within hours after the decision had been made, the press had knowledge of the move, and it was Derek Humphry, in Oregon, informing the staff of the upcoming upheaval. Although no longer executive director of the HS, he still resided in Oregon and had no apparent desire to see the national headquarters leave his close proximity. The board's decision to relocate without any consultation with the staff angered many staff members, who felt their dedication and devotion had been discounted.

Within a few days, Humphry sent a letter to chapter leaders asking them to question the board's decision to relocate to Denver. Most chapter leaders were unsure what to make of this letter, and they had no real information regarding the hasty decision by the board. Although his letter generated some questions, Humphry was unable to provoke a groundswell of opposition to the relocation plan among the chapter leaders.

The relocation to Denver was in many ways a shambles. No seasoned staff agreed to relocate. New staff members had to be hired, and as could be expected, there was some early staff turnover and continuity of management was lost. The national HS was still reeling from the problems created by the departure from Oregon when Faye Girsh was named as the new executive director. A hard worker and devoted HS advocate, Girsh came to the position from a background of HS chapter leadership. Although apparently the hands-on general manager type of director some members of the board wished for, she does not have the public visibility or presence of Humphry or Pridonoff. In short, although competent in many ways, she is not a high-profile director.

Thus, the relocation to Denver proved costly to HS in several ways. While HS was engrossed in the move, the social movement landscape began to shift dramatically. The rising visibility of Compassion in Dying and its Supreme Court connection, Oregon's passed state referendum and subsequent court injunction, Australia's Northwest Territories Act (see chapter 7), and the continuing very public behavior of Dr. Kevorkian brought these other players in the movement to the forefront of public attention. Little was heard from the HS at this time, which was struggling to rebuild its organizational framework. Ironically, many of these other players owed much to the HS, particularly in terms of financial resources. In effect, the HS became the sleeping giant of the movement, with the other players pushing to take the lead.

Some local chapters became impatient with the HS. Responding to the precipitous move to Denver and the dazzling rise of other right to die organizations, the Arkansas chapter became disgruntled with the national HS. At several Arkansas chapter board meetings attended by one of the authors, members questioned the inertia of the organization. As one member put it, "I don't feel like they are doing anything. You never hear about Hemlock anymore. What are those guys doing up there?"

Discouraged by a lack of visibility and a clear-cut agenda on the part of the national HS, the Arkansas chapter Board of Directors in April 1997 decided to stop meeting for a period of six months. The purpose of this "sabbatical" was to wait and see what happened with the Supreme Court decisions. The group met again briefly in October 1997. Still discouraged by their perception of the HS's lack of strong leadership in the Right to Die movement but encouraged by the movement's recent political momentum, the chapter discussed the possibility of affiliating with Compassion in Dying. Others suggested simply shutting down the chapter. Finally, on June 5, 1998, a notice of chapter dissolution was sent out to all members. Jim Lilly, president of the Arkansas chapter, wrote the following:

The board's decision to do so was based on several factors. A primary consideration was that the right-to-die movement has changed greatly since the chapter was formed at the beginning of the decade. Consider:

- Derek Humphry's *Final Exit* became a best-seller, and the Worldwide debate over the right-to-die *issue exploded.*
- Dr. Jack Kevorkian has kept the media focused on the issue by helping more than 100 people to end their lives. During this time, no jury has convicted him, even though he has been taken to trial four times.
- Laws allowing physician aid in dying were passed both in the Northern Territories in Australia and in the State of Oregon. . . .
- Numerous radio and television programs—along with many books and videotapes—have kept the issue before the public. The Arkansas Chapter was formed in large part to educate the public on the issue. Thanks in part to the developments listed above, public awareness in Arkansas and in the rest of the country has increased greatly. The next step in the movement is

to change laws, and that really calls for another type of organization, a political action group. (Lilly 1998)

There are no plans to form such a group by the former members of the Arkansas chapter of the HS. Any affiliation with Compassion in Dying was left to the individual choice of each former member. And so the HS lost yet another chapter.

It remains clear that the Right to Die movement is fluid and that a realignment continues to take place among its organizations. Although it is true that various organizations rise and fall—some lose members and others gain members—it is equally clear that the movement appears to be gaining strength. More people than only right to die organization members are concerned with the movement. This movement has implications for entire societies, not just for the handful of people who advocate for PAS. This is even more evident when one examines societal and global dimensions of the movement, as we will see in chapter 7.

Chapter 7

The Right to Die at Home and Abroad: Friends and Enemies

The Right to Die movement involves many more people than just members of SMOs. Decisions on living or dying are played out among the general population on a daily basis. From New York City to the Sonoran Desert, human lives are touched by this issue. It may be the neighbor next door who is terminally ill or a brother who is facing cancer or perhaps even the teenaged babysitter who had an auto accident that left her dependent on life support. These brushes with death that are part of the human experience touch all of us in some way. No one can ever completely escape.

However, until actually faced with quality-of-life or assisted-suicide choices, many people do not investigate the issues proactively. Most would rather wait and hope that the angels of death pass them by one more time. Or they listen with distracted attention to others who talk on the subject. And often, those who are talking are unsure of their stance. However, there are certain groups of people other than SMO members who have a vested interest in the subject of PAS. These particular groups may offer differing, conflicting stands on PAS or turn a deaf ear to it altogether.

Doctors and the Right to Die

As writer Craig Havighurst points out, "Despite their intimate involvement in the time, place, and manner of millions of American deaths each year, health care providers have remained in the background of the debate over the so-called right to die" (1996, 27). To a large extent, physicians represented by the AMA have simply turned away from the issue and refused as a group to confront it, while joining in as one voice to condemn Dr. Jack Kevorkian (Johnson 1995). However critical of Kevorkian, physicians themselves have not escaped condemnation.

A study published in the *Journal of the American Medical Association* documents the poor communication between physicians and their terminally ill patients. This study also suggests that physicians have an inability to confront the issues of the terminally ill. As admitted by the authors of the study, "The care of seriously ill or dying persons is not attractive" (Council on Scientific Affairs 1996). A June 1998 study revealed that daily pain is prevalent among nursing-home residents with cancer and is often untreated, particularly among older and minority patients (Bernabei et al. 1998).

In response to these types of studies, the AMA established a Task Force on Quality Care at the End of Life and found that, in the current system of care, many dying persons suffer needlessly. The 1990 Patient Self-Determination Act, requiring hospitals to offer patients the opportunity to sign an advance directive, in a strong sense encourages patients to take control of their own future despite physician lack of interest. However, another study noted that, despite the 1991 federal law requiring health care institutions to respect patients' wishes on terminal medical care, everyday care is falling short of the law's intent. According to Knox (1998b), health care providers and institutions often do not initiate discussions about patients' preferences, and should a patient be transferred from one facility to another, a record of their wishes frequently does not follow them.

The Massachusetts Health Decision, a nonprofit group concerned with the ethics of medical care, noted that the effort to honor patients' wishes is failing on multiple fronts. Among 190 hospitals, nursing homes, home health agencies, hospice organizations and medical staff leaders responding to the survey, only one-third reported having trained their staffs on advance directives, as the law requires. Additionally, three-quarters of the health care institutions had done no community education on advance directives, another federal requirement, and 42 percent said they had no committee, task force, or designated group to implement the requirements of the federal law. The reason most doctors cite for not raising the issue with patients is that it would "just worry the patient, or the patient is too young and healthy, or too old and sick to discuss it"(Knox 1998b). One problem may be that physicians have not addressed the issue of advanced directives themselves. A survey at one Massachusetts hospital found that fewer than one in five doctors have designated a proxy decision maker for themselves (Knox 1998b).

Not all physicians refuse to deal with matters of impending death. A raising of consciousness among those physicians who work most closely with the dying does seem to have occurred. A 1998 groundbreaking study indicates that, despite the AMA's objections and despite the lack of compliance with the federal Patient Self-Determination Law, a small but significant number of physicians are going along with patients' requests to hasten death with pills or injections (Meier et al. 1998). A national poll, answered by 1,900 physicians in 10 specialties, most involved with dying patients, found that one American doctor in 30 has complied with a patient's request for enough medication to commit suicide. One physician in the anonymous survey indicated that he had done this 25 times. When asked what they would do if there were no laws against assisted suicide or euthanasia, 36 percent said they would prescribe medication for that purpose, and one-quarter said they would give a lethal injection under some circumstances. About one doctor in five reported receiving one or more requests to assist in suicide or administer a life-ending injection under some circumstances.

The authors of this study do not agree on its meaning. Dr. Diane Meier reports that the results provide no basis for liberalizing laws against PAS: "If it is only a rare event, which our study shows, I don't think it makes sense to legalize a practice which carries significant risks to the most vulnerable members of our society, those who are sick and dying" (Knox 1998a). Her coauthor, Dr. Timothy Quill, disagrees: "I think we need to worry about whether that's the only reason they are not assisting patients. Are they turning their backs on their patients now because of legal constraints, because the legally safest thing to do is walk away?" (Knox 1998a).

A recent study reported in the *Archives of Internal Medicine Abstracts* noted that most general internists, especially minority physicians, are personally reluctant to participate in PAS (Sulmasy et al. 1998). Another study conducted in mid-1997, before Oregon's PAS law took effect, indicated that many U.S. neurologists would participate in voluntary active euthanasia if legal constraints were lifted (Fink 1998). In fact, if it were legally allowed, 43 percent of neurologists said they would prescribe a lethal dose of medication for terminally ill patients and half of respondents in the survey indicated their support for PAS. However, the professional organization that represents neurologists, the American Academy of Neurology, has a strongly worded policy opposing PAS.

Neurologists often have patients who are terminally ill from diseases that are quite horrible. These physicians, in dealing with such terminally ill patients, have an overall stronger support for PAS than other doctors, perhaps due to more frequent contact with terribly ill patients. It is worth restating that the reality of their acceptance of PAS differs from the policy advocated by their professional organization and the AMA. Perhaps time spent "in the trenches" spotlights a reality physicians in administrative positions do not see.

The June 1998 AMA meeting in Chicago brought news. It was announced that the Education for Physicians on End-of-Life Care Project (EPEC) intends to start a training program for physicians. New AMA president Dr. Reardon stated: "For decades the medical profession has focused on the growth of medical technology as a means of preserving and extending life. Through the EPEC Project, the AMA is committed to equipping the physicians of tomorrow with the knowledge and skills necessary to ensure that dying patients are comfortable and that their remaining life has value and dignity" (American Medical Association 1998). The educational materials in this new program will address such issues as treating the common symptoms of dying patients, making decisions about life-sustaining treatments, delivering bad news, approaching futility situations, and handling requests for PAS, among other topics. A study published in the *Journal of the American Medical Association* notes the critical need for such training for physicians. This study revealed that between 25 and 40 percent of elderly cancer patients experienced daily pain and 25 percent of these receive no pain medication (Bernabei et al. 1998). Dr. Cleeland of M. D. Anderson Cancer Center explains that "clinical training in pain management, other than for pain specialists, is almost non-existent" ("Science News Update" 1998). Perhaps physicians in the United States are finally paying attention and responding to the critical needs of dying patients. Or perhaps they are merely fearful of the might of the Right to Die movement and see end-of-life education as a mechanism for staving off further invasion of PAS in other states.

Not Dead Yet

While proponents of physician aid in dying closely follow the legal trail of right to die legislation with bated breath and a hope for passage in other states, another small, new group of antieuthanasists hopes for the opposite outcome. Not Dead Yet is a recently formed disability civil rights group that has, in its brief life, been extremely vocal in opposing PAS. From public protests to actually executing a sneak attack on the Right to Die Web sites with announcements of their message, Not Dead Yet claims to be a group of disability activists who are opposed to the legalization of assisted suicide. Denying a partnership with the Christian conservative political movement, their message is as follows:

Promoters of assisted suicide and other related agendas have been successful in presenting the issue as an argument between the religiously based "right to life" movement and advocates of "choice." There is a third voice in this debate, an opposition based in a civil rights perspective. In growing numbers, members of the disability community are alarmed by the stereotypes and discrimination widespread in the medical community and reflected in the language and stories used to promote the legalization of the right, putting it bluntly, to be killed. (Not Dead Yet 1997)

Not Dead Yet is afraid. Members believe that disabled people and sick people deserve to have their health care needs met, including pain management and in-home support services that are often denied. Diane Coleman, a national organizer of the group, notes that "the failings of our health care system are not a justification for killing. This right to die epidemic is based on society's extreme prejudice against people with disabilities—a prejudice that most of the experts won't even acknowledge, much less try to overcome" (Not Dead Yet 1997).

Not Dead Yet made national news not only for its takeover of the right-to-die listserv but also for demonstrations outside the home of Dr. Jack Kevorkian. Although it may be tempting to dismiss this group's arguments as paranoid, it is difficult not to be moved by the parade of individuals with disabilities publicly affirming their human rights.

The Arkansas chapter of the HS, seeking to create a dialogue, invited the local Not Dead Yet group to an HS meeting as guest speakers. The visitors were vocal about their fears of being "put down" because of their disabilities should physician-assisted euthanasia become a legal right. The HS members, although accustomed to guest speakers representing opposing viewpoints, were also accustomed to debate carried out in an orderly and somewhat intellectual manner. The debate grew heated, and eloquent arguments were made on both sides. In the end, little was accomplished, as both sides "agreed to disagree" on the Right to Die movement. The HS chapter appeared genuinely concerned that Not Dead Yet would see them as potential executioners of the disabled, and Not Dead Yet was angry that the HS chapter refused to see the discriminatory possibilities. Not Dead Yet members left the meeting still firm in their resolution to protect the civil rights of the disabled, while HS members continued to affirm that they work on behalf of the civil rights of everyone.

In January 1998, Not Dead Yet assumed a more activist stance. Ten opponents, including Diane Coleman, were charged with trespassing and disruption after taking over the headquarters of the HS in Colorado. About 25 protestors entered the offices and handcuffed themselves to desks and each other, chanting protests against assisted suicide and the HS. The police were called, and the protesters were transported to a community for the disabled in Denver (Young 1998). The image of disabled people in wheelchairs being hauled away from the HS headquarters by police injects a discordant note into the compassionate image the HS wishes to present to the public.

Derek Humphry also had an encounter with Not Dead Yet. Asked to speak at a meeting of the National Council on Disability, Humphry and Diane Coleman engaged in a rather passionate discussion with a somewhat better outcome than that experienced by the Arkansas HS chapter. Coleman argued that her peers were facing a serious issue of discrimination based on health status. Humphry, in response, stressed that neither in spirit nor in law was it now or ever the intention of the Right to Die movement to eliminate disabled persons, poor persons, the aged, or minorities. The National Council on Disability agreed to set up an oversight committee to watch over the interests of disabled persons. As Humphry stated, "Any reasonable complaint made to the right to die movement will be listened to" (Humphry 1997).

PAS and the American Bar Association

Although attorneys might be expected to provide guidance in putting together legislation for good right to die laws, the American Bar Association (ABA) has refused to take a position on legalizing doctor assisted suicide (HS 1997a). In 1997 delegates to the ABA approved a resolution stating that assisted suicide should be left to be resolved by the state legislatures and their electorates. This statement led Faye Girsh, executive director of the HS, to scold the association for ignoring an important legal and social topic that the majority of Americans want to see resolved. She pointed out that the ABA has supported abortion rights and has called for a moratorium on capital punishment in the past and chided attorneys for ducking such a sensitive issue now (HS 1997a).

Attorneys are apparently divided over their role in the debate. David McIntosh of the Beverly Hills (California) Bar Association believes that attorneys need to provide guidance and leadership on the issue, while Washington, D.C., lawyer John Pickering has argued that a proposal from the ABA would rightly be regarded as the ABA model act for PAS (HS 1997a). While debates may occur within the group, the ABA officially remains silent on the subject.

The Maverick and the Martyr

Dr. Jack Kevorkian is seen in many lights as hero or renegade depending on one's perspective. For some, he is the devil incarnate, a murderer of loathsome reputation, and a man of no conscience. There are tales of him whisking people who are not truly terminally ill off into the night to kill them, although always at the behest of the victim. Others herald him as a savior of the suffering, a martyr who is willing to risk his own freedom and reputation for a cause he believes in and is compelled to act upon. Many right to die SMOs condemn him because he is a lone actor, refusing to cooperate in strategy planning or attempts to pass legislation. He has been called "a rogue doctor who should be thrown in jail" by an executive director of Compassion in Dying (Hill 1997). His own peers, physicians, deplore his actions. The AMA has formally condemned his actions and refers to him as "an instrument of death" (Johnson 1995). "For many, mention the term assisted suicide, and what comes to mind? For most people, it's the image of 'Dr. Death,' the passionate but decidedly eccentric ex-pathologist from West Bloomfield, who dabbles in weird painting, talks about 'harvesting' organs from the soon-to-die and makes frequent house calls to area motels" (Bray 1998).

Of course, Kevorkian is also credited with raising the public consciousness with regard to those who need aid in dying. For many Americans, he *is* the Right to Die movement. They may not have even heard of the HS or Compassion. When the Supreme Court ruled that

Americans did not have a constitutional right to die, much of the general population was not aware that the Court was considering such a right. But all have heard of Dr. Kevorkian, and all feel strongly about him, one way or the other.

In one of his more recent releases, one that calls up a ghoulish image of Dr. Frankenstein, Kevorkian announced his decision to start harvesting the organs of individuals he assists to die (Pardo 1997; Murphy 1997). His first effort at organ harvesting met with complete rejection. In June 1998, Kevorkian offered to the medical community at large the kidneys from an individual whose death he attended. There were no takers, but the offer and the act created angry protests (Shepardson 1998). As noted by several well-known transplantation surgeons, Kevorkian's techniques of harvesting do not meet any of the legal or ethical standards of transplantation. State Senator William Van Regenmorter, who chairs the Senate Judiciary Committee and sponsored a bill to make assisted suicide a crime, reacted with dismay to the news: "It's grotesque and outrageous" (Shepardson 1998). Kevorkian, on the other hand, chided doctors for not using the kidneys to save lives. He emphasized that, had he been allowed to harvest the organs in a hospital, six other patients could have benefited (Murphy 1998). In a real sense, Kevorkian is responsible for the study in contrasts found in assisted-suicide issues in Oregon and Michigan. As assisted suicide moves to the forefront of a national debate, these states have assumed radically different positions. Oregon voters have twice affirmed the right of the terminally ill to receive physician aid in dying, while Michigan adopted a law that outlaws such activity on September 1, 1998.

At the same time, Michigan also is contending with an SMO that wants to get PAS accepted into law. Merian's Friends, a right to die organization, although encouraged by polls indicating support for the law, faced difficulties before obtaining the signatures necessary for placing their PAS advocacy bill on the November 1998 ballot in Michigan. On paper, Merian's Friends constructed the same pragmatic approach to assisted suicide that worked in Oregon, with all of the regulatory guidelines borrowed from Oregon's Measure 16 (Hofsess 1998h). However, it is hard for this Michigan group to distance itself from Kevorkian's "have-gas-will-travel" approach to assisted suicide, and even more difficult to separate itself from the image of Dr. Death in the public eye (Bray 1998; Singer and Davis 1998). A May 1998 *Detroit News* poll of likely voters showed that 44 percent favored a November 3 ballot proposal to legalize PAS, while nearly 33 percent opposed it (Cain and Hornbeck 1998). Kevorkian's dramatic action of harvesting organs may have contributed to the defeat on the ballot proposal in November. Interestingly, Kevorkian himself opposed the measure, claiming it was too restrictive ("Kevorkian" 1998). The measure was defeated by approximately 70 percent to 30 percent.

Thus, the image of Dr. Kevorkian has been used as a weapon by both proponents and opponents of PAS. One side claims that, if PAS is not legalized, many more "Dr. Deaths" will spring up everywhere. The opponents use Kevorkian to strike fear into the hearts of people afraid that legally vesting in assisted suicide will also unleash many "Kevorkians."

In early 1998, Kevorkian and his new colleague, Dr. Georges Reding, issued a manifesto, which essentially dared the Michigan legislature to bring them to trial and convict them, vowing to engage in a starvation "fast until death" should that occur. In the manifesto, Kevorkian and Reding pledge: "We shall not submit to that tyranny. Our conviction and death will help future, more enlightened societies gauge the darkness of our plutocratic and theocratic age" (Hofsess 1998a).

Apparently, others are not willing to submit to what they consider tyranny on the part of Kevorkian. On April 9 1998, he delivered a woman's body to a suburban Detroit hospital. The hospital refused to accept delivery of the body, and the body ultimately found its way into the county medical examiner's office. Kevorkian and Reding had dropped off another body the previous month at the same hospital, and the hospital has apparently decided it will not accept deliveries from Kevorkian (Hofsess 1998d).

Kevorkian made headlines again in November 1998 after *60 Minutes* aired portions of a videotape in which he directly injected a fatal dose of potassium chloride into Thomas Youk, a terminally ill man suffering from Lou Gehrig's disease. Claiming that it was his first act of euthanasia, Kevorkian admitted he wanted prosecutors to charge him: "They must charge me. Because if they do not that means they don't think it was a crime" ("Kevorkian" 1998). Kevorkian was arraigned on charges of first-degree murder, criminal assistance to a suicide, and delivery of a controlled substance. Finally, in March of 1999, Kevorkian was found guilty of 2nd-degree murder for his actions involving the death of the man videotaped for *60 Minutes*.

As it presently stands, Kevorkian acknowledges assisting in more than 100 suicides since 1990 and shows no inclination to stop the quantity of his work. Whether one praises him or abhors him, Kevorkian has extended the frontier of the Right to Die movement.

The Right to Die Movement around the World

The Right to Die social movement is not a uniquely American phenomenon. There are worldwide interest in and activism for euthanasia in unexpected parts of the world. For example, Colombia recently became the latest country to legalize voluntary euthanasia and the only one where the legislation seems to be standing (ERGO 1997g). Colombia's Constitutional Court, in June 1997, reaffirmed its May 1997 ruling that allowed euthanasia for terminally ill patients who request it. Although Colombia's congress still has the power to regulate the law, it cannot object to it. Presently, Columbia's congress is working on the guidelines and mechanisms for controlling euthanasia.

Many countries besides the United States are in various stages of consideration of PAS, most with the help of their own right to die organizations and most as members of the World Federation of Right to Die Societies. As we discussed in chapter 2, this organization was founded in 1980 to promote international understanding in dying, with presently 35 different organizations representing almost as many nations. The president of the World Federation of Right to Die Societies, Dr. Aycke O. A. Smook of the Netherlands, in his opening address at the 11th biennial conference, noted the growing worldwide debate on the right to die:

Since our last meetings, nearly two years ago at Bath, England, our movement has come a long way. The Oregon initiative, the Northern Territories act permitting euthanasia, the American court decisions and the acquittals, Kevorkian in his Michigan trials, the recognition of living wills in Geneva and elsewhere, the acquittals of doctors in Japan and Israel—all demonstrate that the world is coming to understand that terminal patients have rights—human rights—to make their own decisions about this most personal right: to decide what they will about their own lives. Their own bodies. (Smook 1998).

There is indeed worldwide activism on behalf of the right to die. Recent attempts in several countries, including Australia, Canada, Great Britain, Holland, and Switzerland, to pass legislative euthanasia law are discussed below.

Australia   In Australia, the Northern Territory Rights of the Terminally Ill Act of 1995, was passed by the territory's Legislative Assembly and enabled a terminally ill patient to request a doctor to administer a lethal drug or provide for self-administration. Under the new law, which went into effect on July 1, 1996, a patient was required to obtain the signatures of two doctors, one a specialist in the patient's illness, who must confirm the diagnosis and prognosis, and the second a psychiatrist, who must state the patient is not suffering a treatable clinical depression.

Doctors were initially reluctant to use the new law because of action taken in the Supreme Court of the Northern Territory by opponents to appeal it. The court heard the appeal in July and supported the law. However, it was negated when the Australian Senate passed the Euthanasia Laws Act on March 23, 1997, which outlawed active euthanasia. The apparent legally usable period of the Northern Territory Rights of the Terminally Ill Act was from July 1, 1996, to March 24, 1997. During that period of time, four people used the law (ERGO 1998b).

The Euthanasia Laws Act of 1997, passed by the Australian Commonwealth Government, infuriated the people of the Northern Territory, who felt they should have the right to make decisions for themselves without fear of federal control. Although the right to die legislation has been thrown out, giving the movement a major setback, life was breathed into a movement designed to seek full statehood for the very angry population of this territory. Unfortunately, the small population of the Northern Territory does easily not lend itself to full statehood.

Australian right to die supporters have not given up. A recent report from the South Australian Voluntary Euthanasia Society (SAVES) indicates that the attorney-general of Australia was aware that the Commonwealth's antieuthanasia act could have an impact on passive-euthanasia legislation, although that was not the intention of those who drafted the act (SAVES 1997). The drafters simply did not want active euthanasia but still supported passive euthanasia. Apparently, a new development is that the attorney-general has instructed the director of public prosecution (DPP) not to prosecute those doctors who practice passive voluntary euthanasia (including those assisting with pain relief even though it may hasten death). According to SAVES, "[I]t is theoretically possible for the Legislative Assembly to have the Attorney-General direct the DPP not to prosecute medical personnel who assist patients with active voluntary euthanasia. This would produce a similar situation to that in the Netherlands, where voluntary euthanasia is illegal, but prosecution does not occur so long as guidelines are followed" (Robinson and Robinson 1998). Although not the ideal situation, it may be the best option available at the present time. Of course, the stumbling block is that a Legislative Assembly vote supportive of voluntary euthanasia would be needed, and that is not likely to occur.

Although the government of Australia may not be willing to support the right of a terminally ill patient to choose the timing of his or her own death, Australian health care providers appear more open to the idea than their counterparts in the United States. One poll indicated that 80 percent of New South Wales nurses support voluntary euthanasia and 22 percent would be prepared to give the lethal injection if it were legalized (Jopson 1998). Seven out of 10 nurses support PAS in which a doctor prepares a lethal dosage and the patient self-administers it.

On May 5, 1998, the Voluntary Euthanasia Research Foundation announced its establishment. Its purpose is to make available up-to-date information on developments in technology and methods for those seeking voluntary euthanasia (Nitschke 1998). Its formation was seen as a response to numerous inquiries regarding euthanasia after the Northern Territory Rights of the Terminally Ill Act was overturned.

In neighboring Tasmania, the Tasmanian Community Development Committee has recommended against the introduction of PAS. The committee suggested instead that more money be spent on palliative care and on publicizing the present laws that enable the ill to refuse treatment (Hofsess 1998i).

Canada According to the *Southam Newspaper,* half of Canada's doctors believe they should have a moral and legal right to help terminally ill patients take their own lives, yet only 20 percent of physicians who responded to a University of Calgary survey said they would actually practice euthanasia or help patients commit suicide if it were legal to do so. This survey, the first of its kind in Canada, queried 3,500 doctors on their views of active euthanasia and PAS (Cunningham 1997a).

Gallup polls report that three-quarters of Canadians believe that doctors should be allowed to end the life of a patient whose life is immediately threatened by a disease that causes the patient to experience great suffering. This statistic has apparently remained quite stable over the past seven years. Canadians are less likely to support a PAS if the patient is suffering from a disease that is not immediately life threatening—the rate of support drops to 57 percent.

In a new development, the Right to Die Society of Canada changed its name and operating procedures (see Hofsess 1997b). Now called the Right to Die Network of Canada, the group has established a toll-free telephone listing and is focusing on the growth and development of local chapters and support groups. It has also moved its head-quarters to Ottawa in order to work more closely with the legislative system in Canada. This SMO appears to be positioning itself for greater political involvement in right to die legislation.

Great Britain   In September 1998, liberal democrats in England backed a full inquiry into the legalization of voluntary euthanasia. The British Medical Association condemned such an inquiry. However, England's physicians appear more likely than American physicians to address the hard decisions of practicing medicine. For example, guidelines issued in 1997 may bring Great Britain closer to euthanasia.

The Senate of Surgery of Great Britain and Ireland says that if a brain-damaged patient will live a "demonstrably awful life," then the surgeon has the moral right not to prevent death. The Senate also pointed out that, although euthanasia is still illegal in Britain, it is necessary for surgeons to respect the "living wills" of patients (ERGO 1997i).

However, on May 7, 1998, concern that Britain could follow Holland along the road to widespread use of euthanasia was voiced in the House of Lords by one of Britain's leading surgeons. Lord McColl announced that there was evidence from the Netherlands to show that "the current practice of euthanasia is out of control" (P. Johnston 1998). This statement may have been stimulated by an expressed concern by church leaders in Great Britain that plans to make living wills legally enforceable marked a further step toward the acceptance of voluntary euthanasia. Lord Irvine, the Lord Chancellor, while considering whether to introduce laws to give statutory force to living wills, was also quoted as saying, "The government's opposition to euthanasia is settled, well-known and unqualified" (P. Johnston 1998).

And so the debate continues in Great Britain. While on one hand appearing to be willing to face up to some very tough decisions, as in the care of brain-dead patients, physicians in England continue to fear legalizing euthanasia.

Holland   Much has been written about euthanasia in the Nether-lands. Various studies have been usurped by both opponents and supporters of euthanasia to support widely divergent positions (Hendin, Rutenfrans, and Zylica 1997; van der Maas, van der Wal, and Haverkate 1996; Benrubi 1992). At times it is difficult to get a clear picture of euthanasia in Holland. It is the only country (until Colombia's new law is controlled by congress) in the world, outside the state of Oregon, where euthanasia is openly practiced. Although it is not allowed by statute, euthanasia is not prosecuted under certain guidelines, as follows: the patient must make a voluntary request, the wish for death is durable over time, the patient is in unacceptable suffering, and the physician must consult a colleague who agrees with the proposed course of action. If these guidelines are followed, then a prosecutor typically declines to prosecute a physician. Rather than a legal enactment of euthanasia by law, each singular act of euthanasia in the Netherlands is examined on a case-by-case basis.

Many American proponents of euthanasia turn to Holland as a shining example of a country in which euthanasia is working well; however, it cannot be an exact comparison. Holland's system of health care is different than that in the United States in some fundamental ways. In Holland, palliative care is quite advanced, while in the United States, physicians are just beginning to grapple with it as a result of the push by the Right to Die movement. Also, Holland has a high standard of medical care, with the majority (over 95 percent) of its population covered by private medical insurance, guaranteeing a large basic foundation of health care, including long-term care. Managed care such as that which many Americans are currently experiencing does not produce a strong trusting relationship between patient and physician, unlike that which is found among the Dutch physician and client. This trust relationship stems back to the Nazi occupation of Holland, when Dutch doctors went to concentration camps rather than divulge the names of their patients. The U.S. physician's trust relationship with patients in an impersonal managed-care health system cannot be compared (ERGO 1997a). Also, too many Americans lack any health insurance of any kind, thus leaving them open to improvised and anonymous medical care.

The situation in the Netherlands with regard to euthanasia is not just a tacit acceptance of a well-engrained governmental policy. In fact, controversial proposals to legalize euthanasia and endorse two decades of tacit medical practice have electrified an otherwise-staid Dutch election campaign (Hofsess 1998e, 1998f). Right to Die campaigners believe existing rules offer doctors insufficient legal protection, while an opposing political party stands as antieuthanasia and antiabortion. An antieuthanasia party leader is quoted as saying, "Thirty-two years of (the opposing political party) has yielded three rights: the right to kill others, . . . the right to kill yourself, . . . and the right to shop on Sundays" (Hofsess 1998f). Euthanasia is becoming a hot topic once more in Holland.

Switzerland   On April 7, 1998, Dr. Meinrad Schaer, president of EXIT (The Society for Human Dying), representing 65,000 members, reported on the current euthanasia situation in Switzerland: "While the USA struggles with controversy regarding the legality of assisted suicide, the Swiss legal system has condoned the practice for sixty years. In contrast to practices in Holland, Australia and the various U.S. proposals where assisted suicide is limited to physician-assisted suicide, Swiss law permits and EXIT practices aid to the dying by lay people" (1998). Although Swiss law permits physicians and nonmedical persons to assist suicides, the Swiss Academy of Medical Sciences, like many medical organizations, opposes doctors helping patients die. Despite this opposition from the medical academy, about 300 doctors are members of EXIT. Swiss laws stipulate that persons who assist a suicide must do so for humane reasons with no chance of personal gain.

In Switzerland, a competent, terminally ill person over the age of 18 may apply to EXIT for euthanasia. An EXIT physician then makes the decision; if there is doubt, the patient is interviewed by a team consisting of a lawyer, a psychiatrist, and another physician. A member of the EXIT team and a witness stay with the patient, and relaxants, followed by barbiturates, are administered. No collaborator of EXIT has ever been made to appear before the court. About 100 to 120 patients are helped in this manner each year (Kerckhoff 1997).

News Briefs from around the World   In 1996 the Beijing Social Investigations Institute interviewed 3,105 people between the ages of 20 and 45 in Shanghai, Wuhan, and Beijing and found that 78 percent believe that doctors should be allowed to help people die if they want to. Suicide is not considered a sin according to traditional Chinese or Taoist beliefs, but many Chinese, particularly those living in rural areas, believe that helping a person to die is taboo. Several Chinese legislators have suggested revising laws to allow terminally ill patients the right to die.

From New Zealand, a news release stated that approximately 75 percent of the population in New Zealand is in favor of appropriate changes in the law to support the right of terminally ill people to seek assisted suicide ("News from around" 1996).

Japan has begun to look more intently at terminal care among its population. The Health and Welfare Ministry released a survey on June 3, 1998, that questioned physicians regarding their views toward life-sustaining medical treatment for terminally ill patients (Hofsess 1998g). The survey noted that 90 percent of the respondents reported doubts about terminal care, with almost 80 percent feeling negative toward giving life-sustaining care for terminal patients. A small number of these physicians (0.7 percent) reported approval for euthanasia. The Health and Welfare Ministry noted that "concern over dignified death is growing worldwide and there is significant opinion among Japanese doctors that patients should be allowed to die peacefully, instead of being kept alive on respirators or other machines" (Hofsess 1998g). Although this issue has become more important in Japan as the society grays, this survey of doctors' views was the first of its kind.

Finally, in Tel Aviv District Court, on June 20, 1998, Israel's Health Minister Yehoshua Matza ordered officials to ask the state attorney's office to appeal a ruling allowing euthanasia. Euthanasia is forbidden by law in Israel but it is clearly a topic of growing concern in that country (Siegel 1998).

The Right-to-Die Internet

News from around the world travels quickly, almost simultaneously, due to the use of the Internet. The Right to Die movement has embraced the technology of computers and worldwide linkages because of its astounding ability to unite people. Derek Humphry founded ERGO in 1993 and by 1994 developed an electronic news service listserv on right to die issues. He has more than 600 subscribers to his news service (ERGO 1997a). Along with Canadian John Hofsess, Humphry cofounded DEATHNET in 1993 (DEATHNET 1993). Both ERGO and DEATHNET offer to the Internet reader a wealth of archived material dealing with right to die issues and concerns. These two Web sites are important sources of information on death issues.

Hofsess also has an electronic news listserv. With ERGO focusing intently on U.S right to die issues and Hofsess's listserv having an international scope, subscribers to these two listservs can be updated on a daily basis. Quite literally, interested readers can be informed on breaking stories as they occur anywhere in the world. Many of these reports would not necessarily appear in local news outlets. For those interested in keeping up to date on right to die concerns, a daily reading of these listservs becomes a necessity. Both Compassion and the HS have used these listservs to make announcements and issue public statements. Right to Die organizations have recognized the importance of instantaneous communication with followers.

The Right to Die social movement is growing in its sophisticated usage of the Internet. An example of this occurred in May 1998: Scottish Association for Voluntary Euthanasia executive secretary, Chris Docker, announced via e-mail to the right-to-die listserv that the SAVE Web site began using a translation engine called Globalink Power Translator in order to make information available to those for whom English is not a first language (Docker 1998).

It is no wonder that the Right to Die movement has gained computer competency very quickly. As written in a 1996 issue of the *World Right to Die Newsletter,* "The right to die is part of one of the basic components of human freedom: the right of Self-determination. Another basic right is freedom of speech, the right to communicate and receive information. The world wide computer network called the Internet has given this freedom a new and wider meaning. We can use it as a tool in order to conquer other rights, and in particular this last right, the right to decide our destiny at the end of our lives" ("News from around" 1996).

A Continuing Discussion

The Right to Die movement is dynamic and diverse, with many ebbs and flows. One organization may rise to power while another slowly loses strength and appeal. State-level SMOs are formed as national-level organizations compete for membership and resources. The strength of a social movement may be calculated roughly by the intensity of its opponents. Delegates to the National Right to Life Conference in Florida during June 1998 found that the hot topic of the day was not abortion, which has been the center of attention ever since the passage of *Roe v. Wade.* Rather, euthanasia and cloning were the most frequent topics. Right to Life officials say they have not changed their goal, and they contend that the group still has a single focus: life (Decker 1998). In addition, in late June 1998, the Catholic Church came out in strong opposition to euthanasia, with Pope John Paul II issuing a stern reminder that carrying out abortions, sterlization, or euthanasia is a "grievous sin." Dissenters from this "definitive truth" of the Catholic Church will be declared "no longer in full communion with the Church" (Wakin 1998). Thus, opponents of PAS can be seen as gathering their forces.

The right to die without pain and with human dignity is a goal that transcends national boundaries. People everywhere are examining the dying process of loved ones, and many are unhappy with their discoveries. The euthanasia laws in various countries are being tested while in the United States the first PAS law is enacted, but not without controversy. Clearly, this is a movement to be reckoned with as it sets off global debates about the nature of life and death and appropriate social intervention. A sociological perspective that systematically examines the movement from multiple angles can make an important contribution. This is the focus of our next chapter.

Chapter Eight

Studying the Right to Die Movement Sociologically: Some Conclusions

We began our book with Ellen's story. Although her story has unique personal elements, its plot is shaped by the cultural beliefs and practices of a particular society. This makes Ellen representative of a large category of people who are negotiating issues surrounding active euthanasia. The sociological side of the story has been the subject of our book, the first systematic study of the Right to Die movement and of the HS's role in the movement.

Our project has been to explore the key features of the Right to Die movement using the combined insights of resource mobilization, framing, and new social movements theories. Our goal has not been to construct new theoretical models or concepts but rather to provide a useful sociological study that blends qualitative and quantitative approaches, involves a three-way collaboration between scholars, inspires future research, and uses triangulation to reveal insights that would not otherwise be evident.

Because social movements do not simply "happen," we asked—and answered—questions such as these: What are the social and cultural circumstances—including existing medical practices—that produce situations such as Ellen's? How are personal and collective identities related to right to die issues? How did a Right to Die movement emerge, and who are the key players? What makes the HS, for a long time on the cutting edge of the movement, different from other right to die SMOs? How is its role changing? Where does the Right to Die movement appear to be going? In our concluding chapter, we return to these questions, reflecting on what we have learned about the movement.

1) How are situations such as Ellen's socioculturally produced? In chapter 3, we discussed the appropriation of technology and control by the U.S. medical establishment, reflected in the dominant medical model and the public health model. We also noted the demographic and epidemiological transitions that led to an aging population with increased longevity and hence a greater likelihood of facing quality-of-life/death issues. The Right to Die movement has challenged existing medical orthodoxy and religious and cultural norms by reclaiming the space in which people die, upholding their right to choose the time and quality of their death. This "heretical model," which redefines the patient as "employer" and the doctor as "consultant," and which emphasizes self-determination, personal dignity, and autonomy, has become an important mobilizing symbol for the Right to Die movement. Its claims have pushed both the government (through such avenues as political referendums and the court system) and the medical profession to redefine their positions. Not surprisingly, it is steadfastly opposed by a countermovement with a strong religious base and cultural norms that criminalize active euthanasia.

2) How are personal and collective identities related to right to die issues? Our book began by revealing—through Ellen's story—the transformative moment that brings people into the Right to Die movement. Aggregate statistics do not reveal this moment, nor do they reveal its importance to the movement. For example, Gallup polls have revealed growing support for euthanasia among younger age cohorts, but little or no change *within* cohorts. With this information, one could assume that the change is merely due to attrition of older populations. It is true that younger people are increasingly exposed to a visible Right to Die movement and the resources (including electronic ones) that it creates, thus making right to die themes more culturally available. However, we know from our own ethnographic observations that making agonizing decisions about the death experiences of loved ones is often deeply transformative. Change takes place not only between but *within* age cohorts. Encounters with human suffering rather than abstractly held principles put the "soul" into the Right to Die movement.

As NSM theory points out, such moments bring individuals face to face with the task of identity negotiation in a society that is often hostile to their efforts. Frequently, the result is family secrets and dissension, forcing people into uncomfortable conspiracies of silence. Although not all individuals will commit an act of active euthanasia, many discover a previously unknown capacity to do so in extreme circumstances (which, we argue in chapters 2 and 3, are increasingly likely).

The power of a movement to provide some form of community to such people should not be underestimated. Although the language of "rights" is frequently focused on the individual, we can safely say that, without an energized collectivity, such rights are rarely created and even more rarely sustained. Community is, in fact, essential to the understanding of the new collective identity that SMOs such as the HS and, more recently, Compassion, have helped to forge.

Because acting alone in a hostile environment to pursue active euthanasia carries a high emotional and social price, the HS played a crucial role in the emergence of the Right to Die movement. It was the first SMO in the United States to provide a national network and resource community for those who believed in active euthanasia as an avenue to death with dignity. Its local-chapter structure (including the Arkansas HS chapter that we studied) permitted like-minded individuals to meet, reduce their feelings of isolation, build solidarity in the face of religious and cultural opposition, and renegotiate their identities as they faced difficult dilemmas in their private and professional lives. Just as important, the HS facilitated the systematic collection of information and its dissemination through books, newsletters, and local chapter meetings. This process continues today in the form of "electronic communities" on the Internet. Individuals faced with decisions concerning active euthanasia now have many more resources than were available to Ellen in her situation.

3) How did a Right to Die movement emerge in the United States? Who are the key players in the movement? In chapter 2, we documented how a social movement field of SMOs began to emerge in the 1960s. Through our chronology of focal events, such as the development of the living will concept, the Karen Quinlan case, and breakthroughs in life-saving medical technology, we witnessed growing activity around the right to die, particularly when combined with an aging population facing quality-of-life issues. We saw how the HS emerged as a leader in the movement, developing cooperative and competitive relationships with other SMOs.

In chapter 4 and subsequent chapters, we examined the emergence of new SMOs such as Compassion in Dying, whose role in the movement is growing. On the countermovement side, the key players have been the Catholic Church, the AMA, federal and state governments (in particular, the courts), and "prolife" SMOs. A relatively new but active player on the countermovement side is the disability rights group Not Dead Yet. Isolated activists such as Dr. Jack Kevorkian have galvanized the movement and played a major role in focusing public attention on the right to die issue. All of these individuals and groups can be defined as key players, and, as shown in chapters 6 and 7, the alignments within and between these groups are changing.

4) How is the HS different from other right to die SMOs? How is its role evolving? We know that the HS was different from other groups due to its early advocacy of active euthanasia. However, other characteristics also make this SMO distinctive. In our study of the HS, we have drawn on several approaches to answer this question—a triangulated theoretical investigation, ethnographic observation, and a national survey of HS membership.

First, using the RM lens, we noted how the HS emerged as a leader in the movement, uniquely offering advocacy for active euthanasia, strengthened by the charismatic leadership of Derek Humphry, organized into a federated chapter structure at the state level, and mobilizing a membership with the crucial resources of time and money (an observation confirmed by our empirical study of HS membership). Our ethnographic observation, interviews, and documents revealed internal organizational struggles as leadership changed and future directions were debated. We saw the HS undergoing goal reorientation as its more activist offshoot, Compassion in Dying, joined the social movement field.

In chapter 6, we saw Compassion emerge nationally as a potential competitor to the HS, displaying energetic leadership and gaining public visibility while the mother organization appeared to stagnate. We also observed that both the HS and Compassion have been affected by a shifting political opportunity structure, and likewise, both have pushed the federal and state governments and the medical profession into a new stance on the right to die; illustrations include the 1997 Oregon political battle that reaffirmed support for PAS and the Supreme Court's consideration of right to die cases.

A framing lens drew our attention to the way in which both individuals (for themselves) and organizations (for themselves and for the public) construct their identities and issues in a way that resonates with actual experience and gains public support. The HS built its organizational identity around a frame of rationality, professionalism, and compassion, distancing itself from more radical activists such as Dr. Kevorkian and constructing a movement community for individuals such as Ellen who were thrown into identity-challenging situations. Our survey data revealed that a large number of respondents framed active euthanasia in human rights/civil rights terms. Elsewhere, the frame was subject to negotiation, as internal debates in the HS revealed tension over how political the organization should be and what kind of connection should be made with the issue of AIDS, hospice, or disability rights groups. Perhaps because compassion has been one of the key elements of the HS frame, Compassion's attempt to lay a more valid claim to this element has seriously challenged the legitimacy of the HS agenda.

NSM theory, in turn, helps explain why there was a pool of people available to connect with the HS agenda in the first place. Grappling with difficult issues arising out of standard medical and technological practices in the United States, individuals were forced to carve out meaningful spaces wherein they could make decisions about death without being subordinated to a doctor-controlled technology that valued longevity over quality of life (and death). Many who were caught in this situation desperately sought resources for "self-deliverance" even as outside authorities tried to prevent their actions. Professionals (particularly those in medical and social-work fields) found themselves caught in new dilemmas.

Connecting these individual problems with structural changes characteristic of information-based advanced capitalist societies, NSM theory provides a general rationale for the rise of the Right to Die movement, and a more specific one for HS active euthanasia advocates who resisted the colonization of their final moments of life. Because of its well-organized structure and early support for active euthanasia, the HS made it possible for a collective identity and a movement community to emerge out of scattered individual battles.

Given the pioneering role of the HS in the Right to Die movement, it is important to know exactly who the participants in the HS are and whether they exhibit significant differences from the general population. In chapter 5, we presented a social profile of HS members based on our survey. It revealed not only social and cultural characteristics of that population but also information about framing and identity. We found that the majority of HS members were White, female, and over 65. They had considerably higher incomes, much higher levels of educational attainment, and fewer children than would be expected in the general population. They reported lower religious affiliations with mainstream churches. They were geographically concentrated in New England, the Pacific, and the Mountain states (with the exception of Utah). When we examined the trends, however, we found increasing similarity to the general population; for example, demographically, male membership has been growing and age has been dropping over time.

Regarding issue framing, we found strong support for the organization's goals to educate the public and advocate for the right to die. The most prominent reasons for joining the HS were (1) the belief that the government does not have the right to legislate certain personal choices and (2) support of right to die legislation. There was strong support for the right to die as an undeniable human right, a matter of personal choice, and a question of civil rights. The strong support for Dr. Kevorkian uncovered in our survey is consistent with these framings of the right to die. Interestingly, about 75 percent of HS members supported Kevorkian, with 65 percent doing so "wholeheartedly."

Regarding organizational participation, although they express strong support for the HS, a majority of members do not feel compelled to participate directly. Most members were not active in their local chapters, with a trend away from direct grassroots involvement over time (as pointed out, early joiners were more likely to participate in the organization and held stronger beliefs than later joiners).

What does all of this mean? Our membership profile outlined in chapter 5 led us to argue that HS members were societal elites and culturally different from the general population. For example, in the general population, men and younger people are more likely to support active euthanasia. Does this mean that the Right to Die movement is supported only by a small, elite subset of the population? There is much evidence to the contrary. It does mean, however, that the HS organization itself, using the avenues through which it channels resources, is likely to attract a higher-income, White, and highly educated subgroup.

This subgroup behaves, especially as time goes by, in a way consistent with NSM theory. "Submerged networks," instead of traditional political and formal organizational involvement, seem to characterize participation (with the exception of some activists, such as Humphry, who espouse political action). Again resonating with NSM theory, HS members very strongly disagree with the "colonization" of the death experience, defining their personal autonomy as a human and/or civil right. New social movements, it has been argued, are energized by resistance to such colonization of everyday life by the administrative, economic, political, and technological organization of complex modern societies. Making the case that the decision-making process should be displaced away from the medical professional and toward the patient, the HS—and even more so, Compassion—affirm an individual's right to shape his or her own identity, even in the death experience. At the same time, the critique rarely incorporates corporatized medicine; indeed, as societal and economic elites, one would not expect HS members to engage in a class-based critique of the medical system.

What about the issue of community as sustained by organizational participation? We have been making the case throughout our book that the HS provided an important face-to-face community for proponents of active euthanasia, particularly in the earlier phases of the movement. Clearly, timing and the life cycle of the movement are important to consider here. Early joiners, who had fewer social resources available and who provided the founding energy for the movement, participated actively in HS chapters and benefited from this kind of community. As time has gone on, and as the movement has made its impact, some of the initial fervor appears to have subsided or been displaced. For example, a subset of HS members has put its energy into building Compassion in Dying; in this new organization with a more radical agenda, face-to-face community appears to be thriving. At the same time, even our demographic data show HS membership characteristics moving closer to the societal norm, making a case for a slow mainstreaming of the organization.

Finally, it is relevant that more societal resources are available in general, thanks to the Right to Die movement. For example, comfort care, a relatively recent concept in health care for dying patients, has been institutionalized in many hospital settings. Such developments alter the environment for later joiners of the movement. This leads us into our last question.

5) Where is the Right to Die movement heading? What kinds of resources is it creating locally and globally? There are many people such as Ellen living in the United States, but due to the influence of the Right to Die movement, their stories are changing. Although active euthanasia and PAS continue to be controversial topics, there is no doubt that the movement itself is reshaping the dialogue between doctor and patient and is sensitizing medical practitioners to death-with-dignity issues as never before.

This shift is reflected in hospital regulations, legal documents, medical journals, internal debates in professional associations, voter referendums, Internet resources, and in changing medical technology itself. Medical practitioners, as well as the general public, are engaged in an active debate over patient autonomy and the right to choose not to suffer. Although Dr. Kevorkian's solution is still seen by many as extreme, the rise of SMOs such as the HS and Compassion reveals public support for a heretical model that puts the patient and his or her loved ones at the heart of the decision-making process. This grassroots movement, in which the HS has played an essential role, appears to be part of a larger late-twentieth-century movement challenging scientific expertise that has become detached from the bodies and the communities of actual, living people. For example, in the grassroots environmental movement, "popular" or "lay" epidemiology has begun to transform the orthodox medical model by incorporating citizens' knowledge alongside that of the experts (P. Brown 1992). In the case of the Right to Die movement, a revisioning of the doctor-patient relationship has originated among patients and their families who felt that the medical system was failing them. In both of these movements, there is resistance to a top-down scientific model that appears to ignore the lived experience of ordinary citizens, hence undermining their autonomy and dignity.

Chapters 6 and 7 elaborated on the diversity and dynamism presently found in the Right to Die movement. Although particular SMOs move in and out of the social movement landscape, evidence clearly shows that the movement is growing and is reaching a worldwide audience. The electronic media make this possible, as do the growing number of SMOs that address right to die issues. In the United States, the unprecedented (and twice-voted-on) approval for PAS in Oregon sends a strong message to the public about support for active euthanasia as a route to death with dignity. A patient's freedom of choice can only be meaningful if he or she has access to information needed to make a good decision. The HS made it a goal to provide this information when no other group would do so. Although the HS may be losing its position on the cutting edge of the movement, its contributions to the struggle for death with dignity have been crucial.

As we look toward the future, framing battles continue to be visible in the broader landscape of the movement. In the 1997 Oregon referendum, opponents of right to die legislation called it "fatally flawed," while Oregon's governor framed the right to die as a states' rights issue. The Catholic Church, opposed to active euthanasia, criticized euthanasists for "playing God," while supporters of euthanasia characterized doctors and the Catholic Church in this way. The AMA has publicized a frame that attempts to demonstrate sensitivity to right to die issues while opposing active euthanasia. As suggested in chapter 6, many of the recent court battles, including the Supreme Court cases, reveal frame ambiguity. Is the right to die a "liberty" issue? Is it a civil rights issue? Is it a states' rights issue? The Supreme Court, for example, has said it would hear another right to die case if it were to be based on a different framework than those already heard. Such a moment can provide a favorable opportunity for a well-organized SMO with a viable frame.

What is certain is that the voter approval of Measure 16 in Oregon now opens up a series of practical questions that no other state has faced. The Supreme Court decision in effect invites other statewide initiatives, and the degree of contested terrain in future elections is likely to be high, drawing on the entire array of RM and framing tactics of a variety of SMOs. Even if the movement is not successful in passing any more PAS legislation, it has created an unprecedented awareness among the public and among physicians of the special needs of the dying patient. That dialogue is only beginning. The new global electronic community connects previously isolated groups and provides models of successes and failures that are shared throughout the Right to Die movement.

The movement thus finds itself in a highly creative moment. Commenting on the 1997 U.S. Supreme Court decision, Chief Justice Rehnquist summed up this moment: "Throughout the Nation, Americans are engaged in an earnest and profound debate about the morality, legality and practicality of physician assisted suicide. Our holding permits this debate to continue, as it should in a democratic society" (Compassion in Dying 1997).

This book has only begun to tell the story of the Right to Die movement, mapping out its landscape and engaging in systematic inquiry without, we hope, dehumanizing our subjects, the brave human beings who stand against the tide and seek to alleviate human suffering. It is our hope that our work will be a contribution to the scholarly and the movement communities, both of whom are engaged in the search for a better society.

Appendix 1

Selected World Right to Die Organizations

Source: http://www.FinalExit.org/world.fed.html

AUSTRALIA
South Australia Voluntary Euthanasia Society
http://www.on.net/clients/saves/
Voluntary Euthanasia Society of New South Wales, Inc.
Voluntary Euthanasia Society of Queensland
Voluntary Euthanasia Society of Victoria, Inc.
http://www.vicnet.net.au/~vse/v1.htm
Voluntary Euthanasia Society of West Australia
Northern Territory Voluntary Euthanasia Society

BELGIUM
Recht op Waardig Sterven (Flemish-speaking; known as RWS)
Association pour le Droit de Mourir dans la Dignité

BRITAIN
Voluntary Euthanasia Society of England and Wales (EXIT)
http://www.ves.org.uk

CANADA
Dying with Dignity
http://www.web.apc.org/dwd
Goodbye, A Choice-in-Dying Society
Surrey/White Rock Choice in Dying Society

COLOMBIA
   Fundacion Pro Derecho a Morir Dignamente
      http://www.laplazamall.com/dmd/

FINLAND
   Exitus Ry
   Pro Gratia of Helsinki

FRANCE
   Association pour le Droit de Mourir dans la Dignité

GERMANY
   Deutsche Gesellschaft Für Humanes Sterben e.V (DGHS)

INDIA
   Society for the Right to Die with Dignity

JAPAN
   Japan Society for Dying with Dignity

LUXEMBOURG
   Association pour le Droit de Mourir dans la Dignité

NETHERLANDS
   Nederlandse Vereniging voor Vrijwillige Euthanasie

NEW ZEALAND
   Voluntary Euthanasia Society
   Voluntary Euthanasia Society (Auckland), Inc.

NORWAY
   Landsforeningen Mitt Livestement

SOUTH AFRICA
   SAVES—The Living Will Society

SPAIN
   Derecho a Morir Dignamente
      http://www.ma.utexas.edu/~mlerma/dmd

SWEDEN
Rätten Til Var Död

SWITZERLAND
Exit/ADMD (Suisse Romande)
EXIT/Vereinigung für Humanes Sterben (German-speaking)
www.exit.ch

UNITED STATES
Compassion in Dying
http://www.CompassionInDying.org
Death with Dignity Education Center
Euthanasia Research and Guidance Organization (ERGO)
http://www.FinalExit.org
Hemlock Society, USA
http://www.hemlock.org/hemlock/

ZIMBABWE
Final Exit—Zimbabwe

Right to Die Organizations in the United States

Americans for Death with Dignity
President: John Brooke
1783 Terrace Dr., Belmont, CA 94002
Telephone: 415-593-2863
E-mail: JohnBrooke@aol.com
Choice in Dying
Executive Director: Karen O. Kaplan
200 Varick Street, New York, NY 10014-4810
Telephone: 212-366-5540, 800-989-9455
FAX: 212-366-5337
Web site: http://www.choices.org
E-mail: cid@choices.org (general inquiries)
pr@choices.org (media inquiries)
services@choices.org (membership and publications)
Compassion in Dying
President: Susan J. Dunshee
Vice-President: John Lee
Acting Executive Director: Barbara Coombs Lee

410 E. Denny Way, Suite 111, Seattle, WA 98122
Telephone: 206-624-2775
FAX: 206-624-2673
Web site: http://www.CompassionInDying.org
E-mail: cid@CompassionInDying.org
Death with Dignity Education Center
  President: [none listed]
  Vice-President: Fred S. Marcus, M.D.
  Executive Director: Charlotte P. Ross
  520 South El Camino Real, Suite 710, San Mateo, CA 94402
  Telephone: 415-344-6489
  FAX: 415-344-8100
  E-mail: ddec@aol.com
Dying Well Network
  President: Rob Neils, Ph.D.
  Vice-President: Jay Toews, Ed.D.
  P.O. Box 880, Spokane, WA 99210-0880
  Telephone: 509-926-2457
  FAX: 509-927-8819
  Web site: http://www.ior.com/~jeffw/homepage.htm
  E-mail: Rob.Neils@ior.com
Euthanasia Research and Guidance Organization (ERGO)
  President: Derek Humphry
  Directors: Faye J. Girsh, Luis A. Gallop, Stephen M. Jamison
  Legal Analyst: Mary C. Clement, J.D.
  24829 Norris Lane, Junction City, OR 97448-9559
  Telephone/FAX: 541-998-1873
  Web site: http://www.FinalExit.org
  E-mail: Ergo@efn.org
Hemlock Society USA
  President: John Westover
  Vice-President: Ilene Kaplan
  Executive Director: Faye J. Girsh, Ed.D.
  Medical Director: Richard MacDonald, M.D.
  Associate Executive Director: Helen Voorhis
  P.O. Box 101810, Denver, CO 80250
  Telephone: 303-639-1202, 800-247-7421
  FAX: 303-639-1224
  Web site: http://www.hemlock.org/hemlock/
  E-mail: hemlock@privatei.com

Merian's Friends
   Chairman: Edward C. Pierce, MD
   Telephone: 313-761-1066 (chairman)
   P.O. Box 272, Northville, MI 48167-0272
   E-mail: merians@aol.com
Oregon Death with Dignity Legal Defense and Education Center
   Contact Person: John Duncan
   625 SW 10th Ave., Suite 284c, Portland, OR 97205
   Telephone: 503-228-6079
   FAX: 503-228-7454
   E-mail: JDuncan49@aol.com
Oregon Right to Die
   Contact Person: Loretta Johnston
   P.O. Box 19328, Portland, OR 97280
   Telephone: 503-297-6388
   FAX: 503-228-7454

Appendix 2

The Oregon Death with Dignity Act
Oregon Right to Die press release, December 14, 1993.

Section 1
General Provisions

1.01 Definitions
The following words and phrases, whenever used in this Act, shall have the following meanings:

(1) "Adult" means an individual who is 18 years of age or older.
(2) "Attending physician" means the physician who has primary responsibility for the care of the patient and treatment of the patient's disease.
(3) "Consulting physician" means the physician who is qualified by specialty or experience to make a professional diagnosis and prognosis regarding the patient's disease.
(4) "Counseling" means a consultation between a state licensed psychiatrist or psychologist and a patient for the purpose of determining whether the patient is suffering from a psychiatric or psychological disorder, or depression causing impaired judgment.
(5) "Health care provider" means a person licensed, certified, or otherwise authorized or permitted by the law of this State to administer health care in the ordinary course of business or practice of a profession, and includes a health care facility.

(6) "Incapable" means that in the opinion of a court or in the opinion of the patient's attending physician or consulting physician, a patient lacks the ability to make and communicate health care decisions to health care providers, including communication through persons familiar with the patient's manner of communicating if those persons are available. Capable means not incapable.

(7) "Informed decision" means a decision by a qualified patient to request and obtain a prescription to end his or her life in a humane and dignified manner, that is based on an appreciation of the relevant facts and after being fully informed by the attending physician of:
(a) his or her medical diagnosis;
(b) his or her prognosis:
(c) the potential risks associated with taking the medication to be prescribed;
(d) the probable result of taking the medication to be prescribed;
(e) the feasible alternatives, including, but not limited to, comfort care, hospice care, and pain control.

(8) "Medically confirmed" means the medical opinion of the attending physician has been confirmed by a consulting physician who has examined the patient and the patient's relevant medical records.

(9) "Patient" means a person who is under the care of a physician.

(10) "Physician" means a doctor of medicine or osteopathy licensed to practice medicine by the Board of Medical Examiners for the State of Oregon.

(11) "Qualified patient" means a capable adult who is a resident of Oregon and has satisfied the requirements of this Act in order to obtain a prescription for medication to end his or her life in a humane and dignified manner.

(12) "Terminal disease" means an incurable and irreversible disease that has been medically confirmed and will, within reasonable medical judgment, produce death within six (6) months.

Section 2
Written Request for Medication to End One's Life in a Humane and Dignified Manner

2.01 Who may initiate a written request for medication
An adult who is capable, is a resident of Oregon, and has been determined by the attending physician and consulting physician to be suffering from a terminal disease, and who has voluntarily expressed his or
her wish to die, may make a written request for medication for the purpose of ending his or her life in a humane and dignified manner in
accordance with this Act.

2.02 Form of the written request
    (1)   A valid request for medication under this Act shall be in sub-
stantially the form described in Section 6 of this Act, signed
and dated by the patient and witnessed by at least two individuals who, in the presence of the patient, attest that to the
best of their knowledge and belief the patient is capable, acting voluntarily, and is not being coerced to sign the request.
    (2)   One of the witnesses shall be a person who is not:
        (a) A relative of the patient by blood, marriage, or adoption;
        (b) A person who at the time the request is signed would be
entitled to any portion of the estate of the qualified patient
upon death under any will or by operation of law; or
        (c) An owner, operator or employee of a health care facility
where the qualified patient is receiving medical treatment or is a resident.
    (3)   The patient's attending physician at the time the request is
signed shall not be a witness.
    (4)   If the patient is a patient in a long-term care facility at the
time the written request is made, one of the witnesses shall
be an individual designated by the facility and having the
qualifications specified by the Department of Human
Resources by rule.

Section 3
Safeguards

3.01 Attending physician responsibilities
The attending physician shall:

    (1)   Make the initial determination of whether a patient has a ter-
minal disease, is capable, and has made the request voluntarily;

(2) Inform the patient of:
 (a) his or her medical diagnosis;
 (b) his or her prognosis;
 (c) the potential risks associated with taking the medication to be prescribed;
 (d) the probable result of taking the medication to be prescribed;
 (e) the feasible alternatives, including, but not limited to, comfort care, hospice care, and pain control.

(3) Refer the patient to a consulting physician for medical confirmation of the diagnosis, and for determination that the patient is capable and acting voluntarily;

(4) Refer the patient for counseling if appropriate pursuant to Section 3.03;

(5) Request that the patient notify next of kin;

(6) Inform the patient that he or she has an opportunity to rescind the request at any time and in any manner, and offer the patient an opportunity to rescind at the end of the 15-day waiting period pursuant to Section 3.06;

(7) Verify, immediately prior to writing the prescription for medication under this Act, that the patient is making an informed decision;

(8) Fulfill the medical record documentation requirements of Section 3.09;

(9) Ensure that all appropriate steps are carried out in accordance with this Act prior to writing a prescription for medication to enable a qualified patient to end his or her life in a humane and dignified manner.

3.02 Consulting physician confirmation

Before a patient is qualified under this Act, a consulting physician shall examine the patient and his or her relevant medical records and confirm, in writing, the attending physician's diagnosis that the patient is suffering from a terminal disease, and verify that the patient is capable, is acting voluntarily, and has made an informed decision.

3.03 Counseling referral

If in the opinion of the attending physician or the consulting physician a patient may be suffering from a psychiatric or psychological disorder, or depression causing impaired judgment, either physician shall refer the patient for counseling. No medication to end a patient's life in a humane and dignified manner shall be prescribed until the person performing the counseling determines that the person is not suffering from a psychiatric or psychological disorder, or depression causing impaired judgment.

3.04 Informed decision
No person shall receive a prescription for medication to end his or her life in a humane and dignified manner unless he or she has made an informed decision as defined in Section 1.01(7). Immediately prior to writing a prescription for medication under this Act, the attending physician shall verify that the patient is making an informed decision.

3.05 Family notification
The attending physician shall ask the patient to notify next of kin of his or her request for medication pursuant to this Act. A patient who declines or is unable to notify next of kin shall not have his or her request denied for that reason.

3.06 Written and oral requests
In order to receive a prescription for medication to end his or her life in a humane and dignified manner, a qualified patient shall have made an oral request and a written request, and reiterate the oral request to his or her attending physician no less than fifteen (15) days after making the initial oral request. At the time the qualified patient makes his or her second oral request, the attending physician shall offer the patient an opportunity to rescind the request.

3.07 Right to rescind request
A patient may rescind his or her request at any time and in any manner without regard to his or her mental state. No prescription for medication under this Act may be written without the attending physician offering the qualified patient an opportunity to rescind the request.

3.08 Waiting periods
No less than fifteen (15) days shall elapse between the patient's initial and oral request and the writing of a prescription under this Act. No less than 48 hours shall elapse between the patient's written request and the writing of a prescription under this Act.

3.09 Medical record documentation requirements

The following shall be documented or filed in the patient's medical record:

(1) All oral requests by a patient for medication to end his or her life in a humane and dignified manner;

(2) All written requests by a patient for medication to end his or her life in a humane and dignified manner;

(3) The attending physician's diagnosis and prognosis, and determination that the patient is capable, acting voluntarily, and has made an informed decision.

(4) The consulting physician's diagnosis and prognosis, and verification that the patient is capable, acting voluntarily, and has made an informed decision;

(5) A report of the outcome and determinations made during counseling, if performed;

(6) The attending physician's offer to the patient to rescind his or her request at the time of the patient's second oral request pursuant to Section 3.06; and

(7) A note by the attending physician indicating that all requirements under this Act have been met and indicating the steps taken to carry out the request, including a notation of the medication prescribed.

3.10 Residency requirements

Only requests made by Oregon residents, under this Act, shall be granted.

3.11 Reporting requirements

(1) The Health Division shall annually review a sample of records maintained pursuant to this Act.

(2) The Health Division shall make rules to facilitate the collection of information regarding compliance with this Act. The information collected shall not be a public record and may not be made available for inspection by the public.

(3) The Health Division shall generate and make available to the public an annual statistical report of information collected under Section 3.11(2) of this Act.

3.12 Effect on construction of wills, contracts, and statutes

(1)   No provision in a contract, will, or other agreement, whether
      written or oral, to the extent the provision would affect
      whether a person may make or rescind a request for medica-
      tion to end his or her life in a humane and dignified manner,
      shall be valid.

(2)   No obligation owing under any currently existing contract
      shall be conditioned or affected by the making or rescinding
      of a request, by a person, for medication to end his or her
      life in a humane and dignified manner.

3.13 Insurance or annuity policies

The sale, procurement, or issuance of any life, health, or accident
insurance or annuity policy or the rate charged for any policy shall not
be conditioned upon or affected by the making or rescinding of a
request, by a person, for medication to end his or her life in a humane
and dignified manner. Neither shall a qualified patient's act of ingest-
ing medication to end his or her life in a humane and dignified manner
have an effect upon a life, health, or accident insurance or annuity
policy.

3.14 Construction of act

Nothing in this Act shall be construed to authorize a physician or any
other person to end a patient's life by lethal injection, mercy killing, or
active euthanasia. Actions taken in accordance with this Act shall not,
for any purpose, constitute suicide, assisted suicide, mercy killing or
homicide, under the law.

Section 4
Immunities and Liabilities

4.01 Immunities

Except as provided in Section 4.02:

(1)   No person shall be subject to civil or criminal liability or pro-
      fessional disciplinary action for participating in good faith
      compliance with this Act. This includes being present when
      a qualified patient takes the prescribed medication to end
      his or her life in a humane and dignified manner.

(2) No professional organization or association, or health care provider, may subject a person to censure, discipline, suspension, loss of license, loss of privileges, loss of membership, or other penalty for participating or refusing to participate in good faith compliance with this Act.

(3) No request by a patient for or provision by an attending physician of medication in good faith compliance with the provisions of this Act shall constitute neglect for any purpose of law or provide the sole basis for the appointment of a guardian or conservator.

(4) No health care provider shall be under any duty, whether by contract, by statute, or by any other legal requirement to participate in the provision to a qualified patient of medication to end his or her life in a humane and dignified manner. If a health care provider is unable or unwilling to carry out a patient's request under this Act, and the patient transfers his or her care to a new health care provider, the prior health care provider shall transfer, upon request, a copy of the patient's relevant medical records to the new health care provider.

4.02 Liabilities

(1) A person who without authorization of the patient willfully alters or forges a request for medication or conceals or destroys a rescission of that request with the intent or effect of causing the patient's death shall be guilty of a Class A felony.

(2) A person who coerces or exerts undue influence on a patient to request medication for the purpose of ending the patient's life, or to destroy a rescission of such a request, shall be guilty of a Class A felony.

(3) Nothing in this Act limits further liability for civil damages resulting from other negligent conduct or intentional misconduct by any persons.

(4) The penalties in this Act do not preclude criminal penalties applicable under other law for conduct which is inconsistent with the provisions of this Act.

Section 5
Severability

5.01 Severability

Any section of this Act being held invalid as to any person or circumstance shall not affect the application of any other section of this Act which can be given full effect without the invalid section or application.

Section 6
Form of the Request

6.01 Form of the request

A request for a medication as authorized by this Act shall be in substantially the following form:

REQUEST FOR MEDICATION TO END MY LIFE IN A HUMANE AND DIGNIFIED MANNER

I, _____, am an adult of sound mind.

I am suffering from _____, which my attending physician has determined is a terminal disease and which has been medically confirmed by a consulting physician.

I have been fully informed of my diagnosis, prognosis, the nature of medication to be prescribed and potential associated risks, the expected result, and the feasible alternatives, including comfort care, hospice care, and pain control.

I request that my attending physician prescribe medication that will end my life in a humane and dignified manner.

INITIAL ONE

____ I have informed my family of my decision and taken their opinions into consideration.

____ I have decided not to inform my family of my decision.

____ I have no family to inform of my decision.

I understand that I have the right to rescind this request at any time.

I understand the full import of this request and I expect to die when I take the medication to be prescribed.

I make this request voluntarily and without reservation, and I accept full moral responsibility for my actions.

Signed: _____

Dated: _____

DECLARATION OF WITNESSES
We declare that the person signing this request:

    (a) Is personally known to us or has provided proof of identity;
    (b) Signed this request in our presence;
    (c) Appears to be of sound mind and not under duress, fraud, or undue influence;
    (d) Is not a patient for whom either of us is attending physician.

_____Witness 1
Date

_____ Witness 2
Date

Note: One witness shall not be a relative (by blood, marriage, or adoption) of the person signing this request, shall not be entitled to any portion of the person's estate upon death and shall not own, operate, or be employed at a health care facility where the person is a patient or resident. If the patient is an inpatient at a health care facility, one of the witnesses shall be an individual designated by the facility.

A Model State Act to Authorize and Regulate Physician-Assisted Suicide

Source: http://www.FinalExit.org/mdlact.shtml

Section 1. Statement of Purpose
The principal purpose of this Act is to enable an individual who requests it to receive assistance from a physician in obtaining the medical means for that individual to end his or her life when he or she suffers from a terminal illness and is otherwise qualified under the terms

of the Act. Its further purposes are (a) to ensure that the request for such assistance is complied with only when it is fully informed, reasoned, free of undue influence from any person, and not the result of a distortion of judgment due to clinical depression or any other mental illness, and (b) to establish mechanisms for continuing oversight and regulation of the process for providing such assistance. The provisions of this Act should be liberally construed to further these purposes.

Section 2. Definitions
As used in this Act,

(a) "Commissioner" means the Commissioner of the Department.

(b) "Department" means the Department of Public Health [or similar state agency].

(c) "Health care facility" means a hospital, hospice, nursing home, long-term residential care facility, or other institution providing medical services and licensed or operated in accordance with the law of this state or the United States.

(d) "Medical means of suicide" means medical substances or devices that the responsible physician prescribes for or supplies to a patient for the purpose of enabling the patient to end his or her own life. "Providing medical means of suicide" includes providing a prescription therefor.

(e) "Patient's medical record" means (1) in the case of a patient who is in a health care facility, the record of the patient's medical care that such facility is required by law or professional standards to compile and maintain, and (2) in the case of a patient who is not in such a facility, the record of the patient's medical care that the responsible physician is required by law or professional standards to compile and maintain.

(f) "Person" includes any individual, corporation, professional corporation, partnership, unincorporated association, government, government agency, or any other legal or commercial entity.

(g) "Responsible physician" means the physician, licensed to practice medicine in this state, who (1) has full or partial responsibility for treatment of a patient who is terminally ill, and (2) takes responsibility for providing medical means of suicide to the patient.

(h) "Terminal illness" means a bodily disorder that is likely to cause a patient's death within six months.

Section 3. Authorization to Provide Assistance

(a) It is lawful for a responsible physician who complies in all material respects with Sections 4, 5, and 6 of this Act to provide a patient with medical means of suicide, provided that the responsible physician acts on the basis of an honest belief that

1. the patient is eighteen years of age or older;
2. the patient has a terminal illness; and
3. the patient has made a request of the responsible physician to provide medical means of suicide, which request
   (a) is not the result of a distortion of the patient's judgment due to clinical depression or any other mental illness;
   (b) represents the patient's reasoned choice based on an understanding of the information that the responsible physician has provided to the patient pursuant to Section 4(d) of this Act concerning the patient's medical condition and medical options;
   (c) has been made free of undue influence by any person; and
   (d) has been repeated without self-contradiction by the patient on two separate occasions at least fourteen days apart, the last of which is no more than seventy-two hours before the responsible physician provides the patient with the medical means of suicide.

(b) A responsible physician who has provided a patient with medical means of suicide in accordance with the provisions of this Act may, if the patient so requests, be present and assist the patient at the time that the patient makes use of such means, provided that the actual use of such means is the knowing, intentional, and voluntary physical act of the patient.

Section 4. Discussion with Patient and Documentation

Before providing medical means of suicide to a patient pursuant to Section 3 of this Act, the responsible physician shall

(a) offer to the patient all medical care, including hospice care if available, that is consistent with accepted clinical practice and that can practicably be made available to the patient for the purpose of curing or palliating the patient's illness or alleviating symptoms, including pain and other discomfort;

(b) offer the patient the opportunity to consult with a social worker or other individual trained and experienced in providing social services to determine whether services are available to the patient that could improve the patient's circumstances sufficiently to cause the patient to reconsider his or her request for medical means of suicide;

(c) counsel the patient to inform the patient's family of the request if the patient has not already done so and the responsible physician believes that doing so would be in the patient's interest; and

(d) supply to and discuss with the patient all available medical information that is necessary to provide the basis for a reasoned decision concerning a request for medical means of suicide, including all such information regarding the patient's diagnosis and prognosis, the medical treatment options, and the medical means of suicide that can be made available to the patient, and their benefits and burdens, all in accordance with the following procedures:

1. at least two adult individuals must witness the discussion required by this paragraph (d), at least one of whom (a) is not affiliated with any person that is involved in the care of the patient, and (b) does not stand to benefit personally in any way from the patient's death;
2. the responsible physician shall inform each witness that he or she may question the responsible physician and the patient to ascertain that the patient has, in fact, heard and understood all of the material information discussed pursuant to this paragraph (d); and
3. the responsible physician shall document the discussion with the patient held pursuant to this paragraph (d), using one of the following methods:
   (a) an audiotape or a videotape of the discussion, during which the witnesses acknowledge their presence; or
   (b) a written summary of the discussion which the patient reads and signs and which the witnesses attest in writing to be accurate.

The documentation required by this subparagraph (3) must be included and retained with the patient's medical record, and access to and disclosure of such records and copies of them are governed by the provisions of Section 10 of this Act.

Section 5. Professional Consultation and Documentation

Before providing medical means of suicide to a patient pursuant to Section 3 of this Act, the responsible physician shall

(a) secure a written opinion from a consulting physician who has examined the patient and is qualified to make such an assessment that the patient is suffering from a terminal illness;

(b) secure a written opinion from a licensed psychiatrist, clinical psychologist, or psychiatric social worker who has examined the patient and is qualified to make such an assessment that the patient has requested medical means of suicide and that the patient's request meets the criteria set forth in Sections 3(a)(3)(A), 3(a)(3)(B), and 3(a)(3)(C) of this Act to the effect that the request is not the result of a distortion of the patient's judgment due to clinical depression or any other mental illness, is reasoned, is fully informed, and is free of undue influence by any person; and

(c) place the written opinions described in paragraphs (a) and (b) of this section in the patient's medical record.

Section 6. Recording and Reporting
by the Responsible Physician

Promptly after providing medical means of suicide to a patient, the responsible physician shall (a) record the provision of such means in the patient's medical record, (b) submit a report to the Commissioner on such form as the Commissioner may require pursuant to Section 8(a) of this Act, and (c) place a copy of such report in the patient's medical record.

Section 7. Actions by Persons
Other Than the Responsible Physician

(a) An individual who acts on the basis of an honest belief that the requirements of this Act have been or are being met may, if the patient so requests, be present and assist at the time that the patient makes use of medical means of suicide, provided that the actual use of such means is the knowing, intentional, and voluntary physical act of the patient.

(b) A licensed pharmacist, acting in accordance with the laws and regulations of this state and the United States that govern the dispensing of prescription drugs and devices and controlled substances, may dispense medical means of suicide to a person who the pharmacist reasonably believes presents a valid prescription for such means.

(c) An individual who acts on the basis of an honest belief that the requirements of this Act have been or are being met may counsel or assist the responsible physician in providing medical means of suicide to a patient.

Section 8. Record Keeping by the Department

(a) The Commissioner shall by regulation specify a form of report to be submitted by physicians pursuant to Section 6(b) of this Act in order to provide the Department with such data regarding the provision of medical means of suicide as the Commissioner determines to be necessary or appropriate to enable effective oversight and regulation of the operation of this Act. Such report shall include, at a minimum, the following information:

1. the patient's diagnosis, prognosis, and the alternative medical treatments, consistent with accepted clinical practice, that the responsible physician advised the patient were practicably available;
2. the date on which and the name of the health care facility or other place where the responsible physician complied with the patient's request for medical means of suicide, the medical means of suicide that were prescribed or otherwise provided, and the method of recording the discussion required by Section 4(d) of this Act;
3. the patient's vital statistics, including county of residence, age, sex, race, and marital status;
4. the type of medical insurance and name of insurer of the patient, if any;
5. the names of the responsible physician, the medical and mental health consultants who delivered opinions pursuant to Section 5 of this Act, and the witnesses required by Section 4(d) of this Act; and
6. the location of the patient's medical record.

(b) The Commissioner shall require that the report described in paragraph (a) of this section not include the name of the patient but shall provide by regulation for an anonymous coding or reference system that enables the Commissioner or the responsible physician to associate such report with the patient's medical record.

Section 9. Enforcement and Reporting by the Department

(a) The Commissioner shall enforce the provisions of this Act and shall report to the Attorney General and the appropriate board of registration [or similar state agency] any violation of its provisions.

(b) The Commissioner shall promulgate such rules and regulations as the Commissioner determines to be necessary or appropriate to implement and achieve the purposes of this Act and shall, at least ninety days prior to adopting any rule or regulation affecting the conduct of a physician acting under the provisions of this Act, submit such proposed rule or regulation to the Board of Registration in Medicine [or similar state agency] for such Board's review and advice.

(c) The Board of Registration in Medicine [or similar state agency] may promulgate no rule or regulation inconsistent with the provisions of this Act or with the rules and regulations of the Department promulgated under it and shall, at least ninety days prior to adopting any rule or regulation affecting the conduct of a physician acting under the provisions of this Act, submit such proposed rule or regulation to the Commissioner for the Commissioner's review and advice.

(d) The Commissioner shall report to the Legislature annually concerning the operation of this Act and the achievement of its stated purposes. The report of the Commissioner shall be made available to the public upon its submission to the Legislature. In order to facilitate such annual reporting, the Commissioner may collect and review such information as the Commissioner determines to be helpful to the Department, the Board of Registration in Medicine [or similar state agency], or the Legislature and may by regulation require the submission of such information to the Department.

Section 10. Confidentiality of Records and Reports

(a) The information that a person acting under this Act obtains from or about a patient is confidential and may not be disclosed to any other person without the patient's consent or the consent of a person with lawful authority to act on the patient's behalf, except as this Act or any other provision of law may otherwise require.

(b) The report that a responsible physician files with the Department pursuant to Section 6(b) of this Act is confidential, is not a public record, and is not subject to the provisions of [the state public records statute or freedom of information act].

Section 11. Provider's Freedom of Conscience

(a) No individual who is conscientiously opposed to providing a patient with medical means of suicide may be required to do so or to assist a responsible physician in doing so.

(b) A health care facility that has adopted a policy opposed to providing patients with medical means of suicide and has given reasonable notice of such policy to its staff members may prohibit such staff members from providing such means to a patient who is within its facilities or under its care.

Section 12. Patient's Freedom from Discrimination

(a) No physician, health care facility, health care service plan, provider of health or disability insurance, self-insured employee health care benefit plan, or hospital service plan may require any individual to request medical means of suicide as a condition of eligibility for service, benefits, or insurance. No such physician or entity may refuse to provide medical services or medical benefits to an individual because such individual has requested medical means of suicide, except as Section 11 of this Act permits.

(b) A patient's use of medical means of suicide to end such patient's life in compliance with the applicable provisions of this Act shall not be considered suicide for the purpose of voiding a policy of insurance on the life of such patient.

Section 13. Liability

(a) No person who has acted in compliance with the applicable provisions of this Act in providing medical means of suicide to an individual shall be subject to civil or criminal liability therefor.

(b) No individual who has acted in compliance with the applicable provisions of this Act in providing medical means of suicide to a patient shall be subject therefor to professional sanction, loss of employment, or loss of privileges, provided that such action does not violate a policy of a health care facility which complies with Section 11(b) of this Act.

(c) Except as provided in paragraphs (a) and (b) of this section, this Act does not limit the civil, criminal, or disciplinary liability of any person for intentional or negligent misconduct.

Section 14. Criminal Penalties

In addition to any other civil, criminal, or disciplinary liability which he or she may otherwise incur thereby, an individual who willfully violates Section 3, 4, 5, 6, or 7 of this Act is guilty of a [specify grade of offense].

Appendix 3

The Hemlock Society USA Survey

This is a survey of the membership of The Hemlock Society USA. The following questionnaire is divided into four parts: (1) Demographic Information; (2) The Hemlock Society; (3) Right-to-Die Issues; and (4) Miscellaneous Questions. The survey is entirely voluntary and confidential. Circle only one response for each item unless otherwise specified. Thank You.

DEMOGRAPHIC INFORMATION

1. **Sex:**   a. Male   b. Female
2. **Ethnicity:**
   a. African-American
   b. Asian
   c. Caucasian
   d. Hispanic
   e. Native American
   f. Other_____
3. **Current age:**
   a. 85 years or more
   b. 75–84 years
   c. 65–74 years
   d. 55–64 years
   e. 45–54 years

    f. 35–44 years

    g. 25–34 years

    h. Less than 25 years

4. Marital status:

    a. Widowed and remarried

    b. Divorced and remarried

    c. Widow/Widower

    d. Divorced

    e. Legally separated

    f. Married

    g. Cohabitating

    h. Never married

5. Current age of spouse or significant other:

    a. No significant other

    b. 85 years or more

    c. 75–84 years

    d. 65–74 years

    e. 55–64 years

    f. 45–54 years

    g. 35–44 years

    h. 25–34 years

    i. Less than 25 years

6. Number of children:

    a. None

    b. One

    c. Two

    d. Three

    e. Four

    f. Five or more

7. Number of children over 21 years of age:

    a. None

    b. One

    c. Two

    d. Three

    e. Four

    f. Five or more

8. Number of grandchildren:

    a. None

    b. One

    c. Two

    d. Three

    e. Four

    f. Five or more

9. Religious affiliation:

    a. Jewish

    b. Protestant

    c. Roman Catholic

    d. None

    e. Other_____

10. Registered voter:

    a. Yes

    b. No

11. Formal education:

    a. Doctorate

    b. Master's

    c. Post Baccalaureate

    d. Bachelor's

    e. Associate

    f. High School Diploma or equivalent

    g. Other_____

12. Present employment status (Circle all that apply):

    a. Self-employed

    b. Employed full time

    c. Employed part time

    d. Laid-off/Disabled

    e. Semi-retired

    f. Retired

    g. Never employed

13. Major occupational field:

    a. Health

    b. Business/Commerce

    c. Government

    d. Social Service

    e. Education

    f. Legal

    g. The Arts

    h. Other_____

14. Yearly household income:

    a. $160,000 or more

    b. $140,000–$159,999

    c. $120,000–$139,999

    d. $100,000–$119,999

    e. $ 80,000–$ 99,999

    f. $ 60,000–$ 79,999

    g. $ 40,000–$ 59,999

    h. $ 20,000–$ 39,999

    i. Less than $20,000

15. How would you rate your present standard of living:

    a. Very comfortable

    b. Good

    c. Adequate

    d. Poor

    e. Unacceptable

16. Total net worth of your present estate:

    a. $ 1 million or more

    b. $ 500,001 to $ 1 million

    c. $ 100,000 to $ 500,000

    d. $ 50,000 to $ 99,999

    e. Less than $ 50,000

17. Living circumstances:

  a. Renting an apartment

  b. Renting a house

  c. Own a condominium

  d. Own a house

  e. Live in a retirement community

18. Living situation:

  a. Alone

  b. With spouse only

  c. With spouse and family

  d. With family only

  e. With non-family relations

19. Do you have a second residence?

  a. Yes

  b. No

20. Political party affiliation:

  a. Democrat

  b. Independent

  c. Libertarian

  d. Republican

  e. Other_____

21. How would you describe your general political views:

  a. Very conservative

  b. Conservative

  c. Middle-of-the-road

  d. Liberal

  e. Very liberal

22. Did you vote in your last state election:

  a. Yes

  b. No

23. State of residence:

  _____

THE HEMLOCK SOCIETY

24. How long have you been a member of the Hemlock Society?

    a. Less than one year

    b. 1 to 5 years

    c. 6 to 10 years

    d. 11 years or more

25. With whom are you comfortable in discussing your membership in the Hemlock Society? (Indicate all that apply).

    a. Immediate family members

    b. Extended family

    c. Close friends

    d. Casual acquaintances

    e. Co-workers

    f. Family physician

    g. Family attorney

    h. Anyone who will listen

26. How did you first find out about the Hemlock Society?

    a. Television

    b. Radio

    c. Newspapers

    d. Direct mail

    e. Magazines

    f. Friends

    g. Other_____

27. Are you aware that the Hemlock Society has local chapters?

    a. Yes, I am involved with it.

    b. Yes, but I'm not involved with it.

    c. No

28. How often do you attend chapter meetings?

    a. Always

    b. Often

    c. Occasionally

    d. Never

29. What would be your primary reason for not attending a chapter meeting?

    a. Not interested in attending the meetings

    b. Transportation difficulties

    c. Health condition

    d. Inconvenient meeting times or locations

    e. Lack of information about meeting times or locations

    f. Other_____

For the items 30 through 33, use the following rating scale:

    SD = Strongly Disagree   A = Agree

    D = Disagree   SA = Strongly Agree

                N = Neutral

30. To what extent were the following the reasons for your joining the Hemlock Society?

    a. You had a personal experience with the terminal condition of a loved one.

        SD   D   N   A   SA

    b. You were diagnosed as having a terminal condition.

        SD   D   N   A   SA

    c. You have professional experience as a care-giver for terminal patients.

        SD   D   N   A   SA

    d. You wanted to investigate potential options should you develop a terminal condition in the future.

        SD   D   N   A   SA

    e. Your decision to support right-to-die legislation.

        SD   D   N   A   SA

    f. You believe that the government does not have the right to legislate certain personal choices.

        SD   D   N   A   SA

31. **Please indicate to what extent the following list of goals are essential to your conception of the Hemlock Society's mission:**

    a. To educate the public about physician assisted suicide.

    SD   D   N   A   SA

    b. To advocate for legislation on physician assisted suicide.

    SD   D   N   A   SA

    c. To provide direct information about different euthanasia techniques to people.

    SD   D   N   A   SA

    d. To empower patients regarding options for the terminally ill.

    SD   D   N   A   SA

    e. To disseminate information to the medical community about aid in dying.

    SD   D   N   A   SA

32. **Are the following reasons essential to your actual or future attendance at chapter meetings?**

    a. Obtaining new information on the political status of the right-to-die movement.

    SD   D   N   A   SA

    b. To be educated about the right-to-die movement by programs and outside speakers.

    SD   D   N   A   SA

    c. As a social support group of people who feel as I do about individual rights.

    SD   D   N   A   SA

    d. As a social support group of people who feel as I do about social justice issues in general.

    SD   D   N   A   SA

    e. As a social support group of people who have had similar experiences with the terminal condition of a loved one.

    SD   D   N   A   SA

    f. As a social support group of people who can help you if you are terminally ill.

    SD   D   N   A   SA

33. **Have you ever contacted your local or the national Hemlock Society for help with any end of life decisions?**

    a. Both

    b. The national office only

    c. The local chapter only

    d. Neither

34. **Would you be more or less likely to support the Hemlock Society if it had a different name?**

    a. More likely to support

    b. Would make no difference

    c. Less likely to support

RIGHT-TO-DIE ISSUE QUESTIONS

35. **Of the following, pick the one that best describes your views toward Dr. Jack Kevorkian.**

    a. You whole-heartedly support his actions and believe he is helping the right-to-die movement.

    b. You agree with his assisting of suicides, but have some reservations regarding the people he has assisted.

    c. You support his actions, but believe he may be hurting the right-to-die movement.

    d. You strongly condemn his actions and believe that he hurts the right-to-die movement.

    e. Other_____

36. **Of the following, pick the one that you think is the best option for national right-to-die legislation.**

    a. Lethal injection by a physician

    b. Lethal pharmaceutical prescription written by a physician for a medication overdose

    c. Law providing for both options

    d. Other_____

37. **Right-to-Die legislation should be written to include the hopelessly ill in addition to the terminally ill.**

    a. You are not aware of the distinction between the terms hopelessly and terminally ill.

  b. Strongly agree

  c. Agree

  d. Neutral

  e. Disagree

  f. Strongly disagree

38. Do you believe that physician aid-in-dying will be legalized during your lifetime?

  a. Yes, definitely

  b. Yes, probably

  c. Doubtful

  d. No, impossible

For the items 39 through 42, use the following rating scale:

SD = Strongly Disagree	A = Agree
D = Disagree	SA = Strongly Agree

N = Neutral

39. You view the movement for the legislation of voluntary physician aid-in-dying:

  a. As a matter of personal insurance for your own future.

   SD   D   N   A   SA

  b. As a question of civil rights.

   SD   D   N   A   SA

  c. As a philosophical and religious battle with forces that want to dictate to others.

   SD   D   N   A   SA

  d. As a humane measure that should have been available to someone you have cared about.

   SD   D   N   A   SA

  e. As a human right that is undeniable but has nonetheless been denied by society.

   SD   D   N   A   SA

40. If physician aid-in-dying becomes available, it will be because of:

  a. Court action

   SD   D   N   A   SA

b. Legislative action.

SD   D   N   A   SA

c. Voters passing an initiative.

SD   D   N   A   SA

41. You would move to another state if physician aid-in-dying were legally available there.

SD   D   N   A   SA

MISCELLANEOUS QUESTIONS

42. Which of the following would most likely serve as your primary caregiver in cast of terminal illness?

a. Children

b. Nursing home

c. Hospice

d. Hospital

e. Spouse

f. Friends

g. Other relatives

h. Other_____

43. Have you made out a will?

a. Yes

b. No

44. Have you made out a living will?

a. Yes

b. No

45. Have you made out a durable power of attorney for health care decisions?

a. Yes

b. No

46. With which of the following national organizations are you a member? (Circle all that apply.)

a. ACLU

b. Sierra Club

   c. NOW

   d. Amnesty International

   e. Greenpeace

   f. AARP

   g. League of Women Voters

   h. Common Cause

   i. NRA

   j. ACT-UP

   k. NARAL

   l. OWL

   m. Others_____

   n. None

47. Which of the following publications do you read? (Circle all that apply and specify where appropriate.)

   a. The National Review

   b. Humanist Magazine

   c. The Nation

   d. New Republic

   e. Harper's

   f. Advocate

   g. Mother Jones

   h. The New Yorker

   i. The Progressive

   j. Rolling Stone

   k. Atlantic Monthly

   l. Spin

   m. National newspapers

   _____

   n. State newspapers

   _____

   o. Local newspapers

   _____

p. Women's magazines

_____

q. Men's magazines

_____

r. News magazines

_____

s. Professional journals

_____

t. Others _____

48. How would you rate your present physical health?

a. Excellent

b. Above average

c. Good

d. Below average

e. Poor

49. How would you rate your present mental health?

a. Excellent

b. Above average

c. Good

d. Below average

e. Poor

50. Rank the following types of health care systems from '1' (most desirable) to '6' (least desirable):

___a. Strict fee-for-service

___b. Private health insurance

___c. Private health maintenance organizations

___d. Private preferred provider organizations

___e. Publicly funded national health insurance

___f. Government managed socialized medicine

51. Do you believe that there is spiritual afterlife?

a. Yes

b. No

52. **How important an issue is AIDS for the Hemlock Society?**
    a. Very important
    b. Important
    c. Undecided
    d. Not important
    e. Not at all important

53. **Should the Hemlock Society focus more attention on the AIDS issue?**
    a. More attention
    b. About the same attention
    c. Less attention

54. **If you could have a major impact on the debate over legalized physician aid-in-dying, what would you be willing to do to achieve that goal?**

    _____

    _____

    _____

Notes

Preface

1. The Hemlock Society has at times claimed a membership of over 50,000, but their actual current paid-in-full membership as of 1998 is 25,000. The 50,000 figure more accurately reflects the mailing list.

Throughout our book we refer to the Hemlock Society (HS) because that is the organization's original name and the name under which it continues to be known informally. To distinguish the national organization from newly forming local state chapters, the name was changed officially by the board of directors in 1992 to Hemlock Society U.S.A. In 1995, the punctuation was taken out and the name written simply as Hemlock Society USA. During the transitional period, a number of variations were used in newsletters and other documents.

Chapter Two

1. Although each tradition is more complex than can be captured here, we believe that a summary of major tendencies of each perspective is both possible and useful at this stage.

Chapter Four

1. In the Right to Die movement, there is presently some evidence that Choice in Dying is moving toward the more socially interactive and locally based HS model, providing indirect evidence of its grassroots-level success.

2. In an interview with Elaine Fox, a representative of Choice in Dying stated that the organization was focusing on mainstream issues because the HS and Kevorkian were "not mainstream."

3. *Infrastructural conduciveness* is a term that emerged in a conversation with one of our colleagues, Ken Mackintosh.

4. Recent developments in social movement scholarship support this view. Hunt, Benford, and Snow (1994) and Friedman and McAdam (1992) have pointed out that NSM theory has no monopoly on "identity" issues. Certain strands of NSM theory (Melucci 1985) usefully call attention to the ongoing, processual, constructed nature of collective identity, offering an analytical lens quite different from RM theory but having much in common with the framing literature. Hunt, Benford, and Snow (1994, 186) have made the connection explicit by conceptualizing identity in terms of fluid and overlapping "identity fields," which incorporate relationships between protagonists, antagonists, and audiences over time, and which intersect with organizational fields as discussed by RM theorists. This image is consistent with, and useful for, our triangulated viewpoint on the Right to Die movement. Although Choice in Dying has experienced growth in the past decade, it has not been as publicly visible as the HS, probably due not only to an isolated adherent membership but also to its more conservative position of support for passive euthanasia. However, in a recent interview with former executive director of the HS, John Pridonoff, Elaine Fox learned that Choice in Dying and HS representatives met and agreed to share some limited information (Pridonoff 1993a). Choice in Dying was interested in securing literature the HS has developed regarding forming federated chapters.

Chapter Five

1. It should be noted, however, that these were closed-ended items. As a result, respondents could only indicate their level of agreement or disagreement with these items. They were not given the opportunity to write in what they wanted. However, because these were the stated goals of the HS, we felt that the questions were justified.

Selected Bibliography

Abercrombie, Nicholas, Stephen Hill, and Bryan S. Turner, eds. 1988. "Sociology of Medicine." In *The Penguin Dictionary of Sociology,* 238–39. New York: Penguin Books.

American Medical Association. 1998. "The EPEC Project Home Page." <http://www.ama-assn.org/ethic/epec/index.htm> (February 3, 1999).

American Medical News. 1997. "Revoke Oregon's License to Kill." September 15. <http://www.ama-assn.org>(February 3, 1999).

Anderson, Douglas M., ed. 1989. *Dorland's Pocket Medical Dictionary.* Philadelphia, Penn.: W. B. Saunders.

Babbie, Earl. 1994. *The Sociological Spirit.* Belmont, Calif.: Wadsworth.

Barnett, Jim, and Dave Hogan. 1998. "Assisted Suicide Opponents Go on the Attack." *Religious News Service.* June 16. <jh@rights.org> (August 1998).

Barnett, Jim, Dave Hogan, and Ashbel Green. 1998. "DEA Policy on Suicide Law in Doubt." *Oregonian,* January 24. <http://www.oregonian.com> (August 1998).

Baudrillard, Jean. 1988. *Jean Baudrillard: Selected Writings.* Translated by Mark Poster. Stanford, Calif.: Stanford University Press.

Becker, Howard. 1986. *Doing Things Together: Selected Papers.* Evanston, Ill.: Northwestern University Press.

Benford, Robert D. 1993a. "Frame Disputes within the Nuclear Disarmament Movement." *Social Forces* 71:677–701.

———. 1993b. "You Could Be the Hundredth Monkey: Collective Action Frames and Vocabularies of Motive within the Nuclear Disarmament Movement." *Sociological Quarterly* 34(2):196–216.

Benrubi, G. I. 1992. "Euthanasia: The Need for Procedural Safeguards." *New England Journal of Medicine* 326:197–99.

Berger, Peter, and Thomas Luckmann. 1966. *The Social Construction of Reality.* Garden City, N.Y.: Doubleday.

Bernabei, Roberto, with Giovanni Gambassi, Kate Lapane, Francesco Landi, Constantine Gatsonis, Robert Dunlop, Lewis Lipsitz, Knight Steel, and

Vincent Mor. 1998. "Management of Pain in Elderly Patients with Cancer." *Journal of the American Medical Association* 279(23):1877–82.

Bray, Thomas J. 1998. "Problems for Merian's Friends: Kevorkian." *Detroit News.* March 8. <http://www.detnews.com> (August 1998).

Brown, E. Richard. 1979. *Rockefeller Medicine Men.* Berkeley: University of California Press.

Brown, Phil. 1992. "Popular Epidemiology and Toxic Waste Contamination: Lay and Professional Ways of Knowing." *Journal of Health and Social Behavior* 33:267–81.

Buechler, Steven M. 1993. "Beyond Resource Mobilization? Emerging Trends in Social Movement Theory." *Sociological Quarterly* 34(2):217–35.

———. 1995. "New Social Movements Theories." *Sociological Quarterly* 36(3):441–64.

Bushnell, O. A. 1993. *The Gifts of Civilization.* Honolulu: University of Hawaii Press.

Cain, Charlie, and Mark Hornbeck. 1998. "44% Favor Assisted Suicide: Undecided Voters Hold Key to Fate of State Ballot Issue." *Detroit News.* May 31. <http://detnews.com/1998/metro/9805/31/05310060.htm> (February 3, 1999).

Calhoun, Craig. 1993. "New Social Movements of the Early Nineteenth Century." *Social Science History* 17:385–427.

Claiborne, William. 1998. "Oregon Statute Is Blunting Death's Sting." *Washington Post,* April 29, sect. A, p. 1. <right_to_die@efn.org> (August 1998).

Clark, Elizabeth, and Austin Kutscher. 1992. *The Thanatology Movement and the Needs of the Community.* New York: Haworth Press.

Cockerham, William C. 1991. *The Aging Society.* Englewoods Cliffs, N.J.: Prentice-Hall.

———. 1995. *Medical Sociology.* Englewood Cliffs, N.J.: Prentice-Hall.

Cohen, Jean. 1985. "Strategy or Identity: New Theoretical Paradigms and Contemporary Social Movements." *Social Research* 52(4):663–716.

Coleman, Diane. 1997. "Not Dead Yet Web Page." December 8. <http://www.acils.com/notdead> (February 5, 1999).

Compassion in Dying. 1996. *Compassion in Dying Newsletter,* Spring.

———. 1997. "Compassion in Dying Goes National." *Compassion in Dying Newsletter,* special edition.

Congressional Record. 1998. 105th Cong., 1st sess. *Hyde Bill S.2151.* <right_to_die@efn.org> (June 9).

Couch, Carl. 1984. *Constructing Civilizations.* Greenwich, Conn.: Jai Press.

Council on Scientific Affairs. 1996. "Good Care of the Dying Patient." *Journal of the American Medical Association* 275(6):474–78.

Cunningham, Jim. 1997a. "Doctors Not At All Sure They Have Right to Play God." April 10. <http://www.islandnet.com/~deathnet/> (August 1998).

———. 1997b. "Kevorkian File." September 30. <http://www.islandnet.com/~deathnet/> (August 1998).

Curtis, Russell, and Louis Zurcher. 1971. "Social Movements: An Analytical Exploration of Organizational Forms." *Social Problems* 21:356–70.

DEATHNET. 1993. <http://www.rights.org/deathnet/home_frame.html>

Decker, Twila. 1998. "Orlando: Pro-Lifers Gear Up for PAS Fight." *St. Petersburg (Fla.) Times.* June 24. <jh@rights.org> (August 1998).

Denzin, Norman K. 1989. *The Research Act: A Theoretical Introduction to Sociological Methods.* Englewood Cliffs, N.J.: Prentice Hall.

———. 1992. "The Suicide Machine." *Society* 29(5):7–10.

Docker, Chris. 1998. "Help Sought." May 11. <right_to_die@efn.org> (August 1998).

Doyal, Lesley, with Imogen Pennell. 1981. *The Political Economy of Health.* Boston, Mass.: South End Press.

Dumont, Richard, and Dennis Foss. 1972. *The American Way of Death.* Cambridge, Mass.: Schenkman.

Dungan, Tracie. 1992. "Author of *Final Exit* Differs from Kevorkian." *Arkansas Democrat Gazette,* March 25, p. 6b.

Eder, Klaus. 1993. *The New Politics of Class: Social Movements and Cultural Dynamics in Advanced Societies.* London: Sage.

Egan, Timothy. 1998. "No One Rushing in Oregon to Use New Suicide Law." *New York Times.* February 15. <jh@islandnet.com> (August 1998).

Ehrenreich, Barbara, and John Ehrenreich. 1970. *The American Health Empire.* New York: Random House.

Enzi, Michael. 1998. "Senators Write Reno on Suicide Stance." *Federal Document Clearing House, Inc.* January 22. <jh@islandnet.com> (August 1998).

Euthanasia Research and Guidance Organization (ERGO). 1997a. "What Is ERGO?" *Euthanasia Research and Guidance Organization: Right to Die Listserv.* January 1. <http://www.rights.org/~deathnet/what_is_ergo.html> (February 4, 1999).

———. 1997b. Private e-mail communication (regarding hospices), September 11. <ERGO@efn.org>

———. 1997c. "Hemlock Chapter Closes." September 16. <right_to_die@efn.org> (August 1998).

———. 1997d. "World Federation of Right to Die Societies." September 20. <right_to_die@efn.org> (August 1998).

———. 1997e. " Nearly 400 Oregon Physicians Join in Just Six Weeks." October 1. <right_to_die@efn.org> (August 1998).

———. 1997f. "Active Voluntary Euthanasia in Columbia." October 3. <right_to_die@efn.org> (August 1998).

———. 1997g "Campaign to Repeal the Oregon Death with Dignity Act." October 22. <right_to_die@efn.org> (August 1998).

———. 1997h. "Kitzhaber Chides Legislators." October 22.
<right_to_die@efn.org> (August 1998).

———. 1997i. "UK Surgeons Take Step towards Euthanasia." December 19.
<right_to_die@efn.org> (August 1998).

———. 1998a. "Seattle Right to Die Group Plans Move into Oregon." *Associated Press.* January 5. <right_to_die@efn.org> (August 1998).

———. 1998b. "ACT Australia Contribution." February 4.
<right_to_die@efn.org> (August 1998).

———. 1998c. "Fierce Lobbying on Guidebook Terms." *American Medical News.* March 19. <right_to_die@efn.org> (August 1998).

———. 1998d. "Congress, Mind Your Own Business." *Willamette (Oregon) Weekly Newspaper.* April 12. <right_to_die@efn.org> (August 1998).

———. 1998e. "National Pharmacist Association Endorses Right of Dying Patients and Rights to Pharmacist Concerning Life-Ending Medication." (Press release from the Oregon State Pharmacists Association.) April 16. <ERGO@efn.org> (August 1998).

———. 1998f. "Sensible Pharmacists:On Oregon Suicide Law" (editorial). *Register Guard.* April 24. <right_to_die@efn.org> (August 1998).

———. 1998g. "Attorney General Says She Examined Civil Rights Issue." June 6. <right_to_die@efn.org> (August 1998).

Fink, Sheri. 1998. "Half of US Neurologists Support Assisted Suicide for the Terminally Ill." *Oregonian.* April 29). <right_to_die@efn.org> (August 1998).

Foucault, Michel. 1973. The Birth of the Clinic. London: Tavistock.

———. 1980. *Power/Knowledge, Selected Interviews and Other Writings 1972–1977.* Brighton: Harvester Press.

Fox, Elaine. 1993. Letter to Jean Holmes Gillett, Board of Directors, Hemlock Society USA, January 28.

Fox, Elaine, and Stella M. Čapek 1993. "The Hemlock Society in Transition: A Case Study." Paper presented at the Annual Meetings of the American Sociological Association, August 14, Miami Beach, Fla.

Fox, Elaine, and Jeffrey J. Kamakahi. 1995. "The National Hemlock Survey." *TimeLines,* September–October.

Friedman, Debra, and Doug McAdam. 1992. "Collective Identity and Activism: Networks, Choices, and the Life of a Social Movement." In *Frontiers in Social Movement Theory,* ed. Aldon D. Morris and Carol McClurg Mueller, 156–73. New Haven, Conn.: Yale University Press.

Friedson, Eliot. 1970. *Profession of Medicine.* New York: Harper and Row.

Gale, Richard P. 1986. "Social Movements and the State: The Environmental Movement, Countermovement, and Government Agencies." *Sociological Perspectives* 29:202–40.

Gallop, Luis. 1993. Letter to Hemlock Chapter Leaders, January 16.

Gamson, William. 1975. *The Strategy of Social Protest.* Homewood, Ill.: Dorsey Press.

————. 1988. "Political Discourse and Collective Action." *International Social Movements Research* 1:219–44.

Gamson, William, Bruce Fireman, and Steve Rytina. 1982. *Encounters with Unjust Authority.* Homewood, Ill.: Dorsey Press.

Garrett, Laurie. 1994. *The Coming Plague.* New York: Penguin Books.

Gerhard, Sylvia. 1998a. "AMA Annual Meeting: Initiative to Improve Care of Dying." June 15. <http://www.ama-assn.org/meetings/public /annual98/reports/index.htm> (August 1998).

————. 1998b. "Catholics Who Accept Euthanasia Automatically Excommunicated." *UPI Report.* July 3. <Sgerhard@world.std.com> (August 1998).

Gianelli, Diane. 1998 "Praise, Criticism Follow Oregon's First Reported Suicides." *AMA News.* April 13. <jh@rights.org> (August 1998).

Giddens, Anthony. 1981. *A Contemporary Critique of Historical Materialism.* London: Macmillan.

Girsh, Faye. 1997a. Editorial. *TimeLines,* June <jh@islandnet.com> (August 1998).

————. 1997b. "Hemlock Chapter Closes." September 17. <right_to_die@efn.org> (August 1998).

Glaser, Barney, and Anselm Strauss. 1975. *Awareness of Dying.* Chicago: Aldine.

Goffman, Erving. 1974. *Frame Analysis.* Cambridge, Mass.: Harvard University Press.

Gould, Stephen J. 1981. *The Mismeasure of Man.* New York: Norton.

Habermas, Jurgen. 1975. *Legitimation Crisis.* Boston: Beacon Press.

Harrington, Michael. 1968. *Toward a Democratic Left: A Radical Program for a New Majority.* New York: Macmillan.

Havighurst, Craig. 1996. "Hospitals, Doctors, and the Right to Die." *Health Systems Review,* May–June, pp. 27–30.

Hemlock Society USA (HS). 1992. *Hemlock Society Chapter Leaders' Newsletter,* September.

————. 1993. *Hemlock Society Chapter Leaders' Newsletter,* special edition, January 13.

————. 1997a. "American Bar Association Ducks the Issue." October 30. <http://www2.privatei.com/hemlock/press> (August 1998).

————. 1997b. "Arizona Legislature Would Expand End-of-Life Medical Options" (press release) November 17. <jh@islandnet.com> (August 1998).

————. n.d.a. [*Membership Application Form*] (pamphlet).

————. n.d.b. *Q. and A. on the Hemlock Society* (pamphlet).

Hendin, Herbert, Chris Rutenfrans, and Zbigniew Zylica. "Physician Assisted Suicide and Euthanasia in the Netherlands: Lessons from the Dutch." *Journal of the American Medical Association* 277:1720–22.

Herrmann, Robert. 1991. "Participation and Leadership in Consumer Movement Organizations." *Journal of Social Issues* 47:119–33.

Hill, Gail. 1997. "Oregon Could Set Course on Suicide Debate in U.S." *Oregonian,* September 25, sect. A, p. 1. <jh@islandnet.com> (August 1998).

Hofsess, John. 1997a. "USA Today: 68% of Americans Support PAS." *USA Today,* September 24, sect. A, p. 1. <jh@islandnet.com> (August 1998).

———. 1997b. "The Right to Die Network of Canada." December 17. <jh@islandnet.com> (August 1998).

———. 1998a. "Kevorkian and Reding Manifesto." January 4. <jh@islandnet.com> (August 1998).

———. 1998b. "Guide to Assisted Suicide: Oregon Releases Assisted Suicide Book for Doctors." March 5. <jh@islandnet.com> (August 1998).

———. 1998c. "Care for Dying Improves with Debate over Assisted Suicide, Doctors Say." April 1. <jh@islandnet.com> (August 1998).

———. 1998d. "Kevorkian Brings Body to Hospital." April 9. <jh@islandnet.com> (August 1998).

———. 1998e. "Euthanasia Row Looms Large in Dutch Election." *Reuters.* April 11. <jh@rights.org> (August 1998).

———. 1998f. "Netherlands: Pro-Euthanasia Party Suffers Setback." *Agence France-Presse.* May 7. <jh@rights.org> (August 1998).

———. 1998g. "Doctors and Public Differ over Terminal Care." *Japan Economic Newswire.* May 11. <jh@rights.org> (August 1998).

———. 1998h. "Physician Aid in Dying Will Be on Ballot." (Press release from Merian's Friends.) June 6. <jh@islandnet.com> (August 1998).

———. 1998i. "Tasmania: Thumbs Down to Euthanasia Law." *Mercury,* June 5, p. 5. <jh@rights.org> (August 1998).

———. 1998j. "Reno Confirms Non-Interference in Oregon." June 6. <jh@islandnet.com> (August 1998).

———. 1998k. "Hawaii Governor to Put Euthanasia before Legislature." *Congress Daily.* June 15. <jh@rights.org> (August 1998).

———. 1998l. "Questionnaire Compiled for Doctors Who Aid in Deaths." *Associated Press.* June 18. <jh@rights.org> (August 1998).

———. 1998m. "Humphry Tries to Revive Oregon Hemlock Society Chapter." June 22. <jh@rights.org> (August 1998).

Hogan, Dave. 1997. "Doctors Get Advice on Suicide Question." *Oregonian,* November 12. <ERGO@efn.org> (August 1998).

Hogan, Dave, and Jim Barnett. 1998. "Aided Suicide Causes Storm in Congress." *Oregonian.* April 3. <jh@rights.org> (August 1998).

Holden, J. 1993. "Demographics, Attitudes, and Afterlife Beliefs of Right-to-Life and Right-to-Die Organization Members." *Journal of Social Psychology* 133: 521–27.

Hoover, Erin. 1998a. "Right to Die Group Plans Move to Oregon." *Oregonian.* January 5. <jh@islandnet.com> (August 1998).

———. 1998b. "Assisted Suicide Law Redefines Activism." *Oregonian.* March 25. <jh@islandnet.com> (August 1998).

———. 1998c. "Assisted Suicides Cause Reflection." *Oregonian,* March 27. <jh@islandnet.com> (August 1998).

———. 1998d. "OSHU Wins Grant for End-of-Life Care." *Oregonian.* June 16. <ERGO@efn.org> (August 1998).

Hoover, Erin, and Mark O'Keefe. 1997a. "Care Issue Colors Debate on Suicide Law." *Oregonian.* September 30. <jh@islandnet.com> (August 1998).

———. 1997b. "Patients, Doctors Seek Answers." *Oregonian.* November 6. <jh@islandnet.com> (August 1998).

Hoover, Erin, and Patrick O'Neill. 1998. "The AMA Is Wary of Legislation's Effect on Pain Management but Remains Opposed to Assisted Death." *Oregonian.* June 8. <ERGO@efn.org> (August 1998).

Hughes, John. 1998. "Lawmakers Are Getting Ready for a Battle over Assisted Suicide." *Associated Press.* June 20. <jh@rights.org> (August 1998).

Humphry, Derek. 1981. *Let Me Die before I Wake.* Eugene, Ore.:Hemlock Society.

———. 1991. *Final Exit.* New York: Harper and Row.

———. 1992. Interview by Elaine Fox. March.

———. 1993. Information letter sent to all Hemlock Chapter Leaders. January 5.

———. 1997. "Hearing the Anxieties of the Disabled." *TimeLines,* July–September.

Humphry, Derek, and Ann Wickett. 1978. *Jean's Way.* New York: Fontana.

———. 1986. *The Right to Die.* New York: Harper and Row.

Hunt, Scott A., Robert D. Benford, and David A. Snow. 1994. "Identity Fields: Framing Processes and the Social Construction of Movement Identities." In *New Social Movements: From Ideology to Identity,* ed. Enrique Larana, Hank Johnston, and Joseph R. Gusfield, 185–208. Philadelphia, Penn.: Temple University Press.

Illich, Ivan. 1976. *Medical Nemesis.* New York: Pantheon Books.

Inglehart, Ronald. 1977. *The Silent Revolution: Changing Values and Political Styles among Western Publics.* Princeton, N.J.: Princeton University Press.

Johnson, Kirk. 1995. "The AMA's Response to Jack Kevorkian." *Ohio Right to Life.* October 10. <life@infinet.com> (August 1998).

Johnston, Hank, Enrique Larana, and Joseph R. Gusfield. 1994. "Identities, Grievances, and New Social Movements." In *New Social Movements: From Ideology to Identity,* ed. Enrique Larana, Hank Johnston, and Joseph R. Gusfield, 3–35. Philadelphia, Penn.: Temple University Press.

Johnston, Philip. 1998. "Lords Warned over Following Dutch Road to Euthanasia." *Daily (London) Telegraph,* May 7, p. 10. <jh@rights.org> (August 1998).

Jopson, Debra. 1998. "Strong Support for Euthanasia in Nurses' Poll." *Sydney Morning Herald* February 13, p. 5. <jh@rights.org> (August 1998).

Kamakahi, Jeffrey J. 1997. "Longitudinal Analysis of Right to Die Attitudes in Age Cohorts, 1977 to 1989." Unpublished paper.

Kamakahi, Jeffrey J., and Elaine Fox. 1996. "Extra-Organizational Affiliations of Hemlock Society USA Members." Paper presented at the Annual Meetings of the American Sociological Association, August 20, New York.

Kamakahi, Jeffrey J., Elaine Fox, and Stella Čapek. 1997. "The Right to Die Movement: Extrapolating from the National Hemlock USA Membership Survey." Paper presented at the Annual Meetings of the American Sociological Association, August 9, Toronto.

Kerckhoff, Richard. 1997. "Swiss Have Assisted Suicide." *TimeLines,* July–August.

"Kevorkian Faces Murder Charge for Televised Death." 1998. *Arkansas Democrat Gazette,* November 26, p. 4a.

Klandermans, Bert. 1986. "New Social Movements and Resource Mobilization: The European and the American Approach." *Journal of Mass Emergencies and Disasters* 4:13–39.

———. 1992. "The Social Construction of Protest and Multi-Organizational Fields." In *Frontiers in Social Movement Theory.* ed. Aldon D. Morris and Carol McClurg Mueller, 77–103. New Haven, Conn.: Yale University Press.

Klandermans, Bert, and Sidney Tarrow. 1988. "Mobilization into Social Movements: Synthesizing European and American Approaches." *International Social Movements Research* 1:1–38.

Knox, Richard. 1998a. "Doctors Accepting of Euthanasia, Poll Finds Many Would Aid in Suicide Were It Legal." *Boston Globe,* April 23, sect. A, p. 5.

———. 1998b. "Patients' Last Wishes Found Often Overlooked." *Boston Globe,* April 17, sect. A, p. 1.

Kriesi, Hanspeter. 1988. "The Interdependence of Structure and Action: Some Reflections on the State of the Art." *International Social Movements Research* 1:349–68.

Kriesi, Hanspeter, Ruud Koopmans, Jan Willem Duyvendak, and Marco G. Giugni. 1992. "New Social Movements and Political Opportunities in Western Europe." *European Journal of Political Research* 22:219–44.

Kubler-Ross, Elizabeth. 1969. *On Death and Dying.* New York: Macmillian.

———. 1975. *Death: The Final Stage of Growth.* Englewood Cliffs, N.J.: Prentice-Hall.

Kurian, George Thomas, ed. 1994. *Datapedia of the United States 1790–2000.* Series A 29–37. Lanham, Md.: Benham Press.

Kurtz, Richard, and Paul Chalfant. 1984. *The Sociology of Medicine and Illness.* Boston, Mass.: Allyn and Bacon.

Kutner, Louis. 1969. "Due Process of Euthanasia: The Living Will, a Proposal." *Indiana Law Review* 543.

Lade, Diane C. 1997. "Florida: Easing Pain at the End of Life." *(Fort Lauderdale, Fla.) Sun-Sentinel,* October 13, p. 1A. <jh@islandnet.com> (August 1998).

Larana, Enrique, Hank Johnston, and Joseph R. Gusfield, eds. 1994. *New Social Movements: From Ideology to Identity.* Philadelphia, Penn.: Temple University Press.

Larue, Gerald. 1993. Letter to the Hemlock Society—Board of Directors, Hemlock Society Consultants, Chapter Leaders, Derek Humphry, John Pridonoff, and Cheryl Smith, January 21.

Lee, John. 1997. Personal interview by Elaine Fox. April 22.

Lilly, Jim. 1998. "Notice of Chapter Dissolution." Letter to Arkansas Hemlock Board of Directors, June 10.

Lipsky, Michael. 1970. *Protest in City Politics: Rent Strikes, Housing, and the Power of the Poor.* Chicago: Rand McNally.

Luke, Timothy. 1989. "Class Contradictions and Social Cleavages in Informationalizing Post-Industrial Societies: On the Rise of New Social Movements." *New Political Science* 16–17 (Fall–Winter):125–53.

Marker, Rita. 1993. *Deadly Compassion.* New York: William Morrow.

Marwell, Gerald, and Pamela Oliver. 1984. "Collective Action Theory and Social Movements Research." *Research in Social Movements, Conflict and Change* 7:1–27.

McAdam, Doug. 1982. *Political Process and the Development of Black Insurgency, 1930–1970.* Chicago: University of Chicago Press.

———. 1986. "Recruitment to High-Risk Activism: The Case of Freedom Summer." *American Journal of Sociology* 92:64–90.

McAdam, Doug, and David A. Snow. 1997. *Social Movements: Readings on Their Emergence, Mobilization, and Dynamics.* Los Angeles, Calif.: Roxbury.

McCarthy, John D., David Britt, and Mark Wolfson. 1991. "The Institutional Channeling of Social Movements in the United States." *Research in Social Movements, Conflict and Change* 13:45–76.

McCarthy, John D., and Mayer Zald. 1973. *The Trend of Social Movements in America: Professionalization and Resource Mobilization.* Morristown, N.J.: General Learning Press.

———. 1977. "Resource Mobilization and Social Movements: A Partial Theory." *American Journal of Sociology* 82:1212–41.

McKeown, Thomas. 1965. *Medicine in Modern Society.* London: Routledge and Kegan Paul.

———. 1979. *The Role of Medicine.* Oxford: Basil Blackwell.

McKinlay, John B. 1984. *Issues in the Political Economy of Health Care.* London: Tavistock.

Mechanic, David. 1989. *Mental Health and Social Policy.* Englewood Cliffs, N.J.: Prentice Hall.

Meier, Diane, Carol Annemons, Sylvan Wallenstein, Timothy Quill, R. Sean Morrison, and Christine Cassel. 1998. "A National Survey of Physician-Assisted Suicide and Euthanasia in the United States." *New England Journal of Medicine* 338(17):1193–1201.

Melucci, Alberto. 1980. "The New Social Movements: A Theoretical Approach." *Social Science Information* 19:199–226.

———. 1985. "The Symbolic Challenge of Contemporary Movements." *Social Research* 52:789–816.

Mero, Ralph. 1993. Telephone interview with Elaine Fox, April.

———. 1996. "Victory through the Courts!" *Compassion in Dying Newsletter,* Spring, pp. 1–3.

Mills, C. Wright. 1940. "Situated Actions and Vocabularies of Motive." *American Sociological Review* 5:904–14.

———. 1967. *The Sociological Imagination.* London: Oxford University Press.

Monmaney, Terence. 1997. "Oregon's Medical Use of Morphine Leads Nation." *Los Angeles Times,* September 26, sect. A, p. 20. <jh@islandnet.com> (August 1998).

Morris, Desmond. 1996. *The Human Zoo.* New York: Kodansha Press.

Mottl, Tahi. 1980. "The Analysis of Countermovements." *Social Problems* 27:620–35.

Mueller, Carol M. 1994. "Conflict Networks and the Origins of Women's Liberation." In *New Social Movements: From Ideology to Identity,* ed. Enrique Larana, Hank Johnston, and Joseph R. Gusfield, 234–63. Philadelphia, Penn.: Temple University Press.

Murphy, Brian. 1997. "Kevorkian to Harvest Patient's Organs: Donation Second Phase of His Plan." *Detroit Free Press.* October 23. <http://www.freep.com/news/extra2/qkevo23.htm> (February 3, 1999).

———. 1998. "Kevorkian Lashes Out at Officials." *Detroit Free Press.* June 10. <jh@rights.org> (August 1998).

Nash, Bradley, Jr., and Mark Wardell. 1993. "The Control of Sociological Theory: In Praise of the Interregnum." *Sociological Inquiry* 63:276–92.

Navarro, Vicente. 1986. *Crisis, Health, and Medicine.* New York: Tavistock.

"News from around the World." 1996. *World Right to Die Newsletter,.* June. <http://www.efn.org/~ergo/wfn28.html> (August 1998).

Nitschke, Philip. 1998. "Welcome to Deliverance: Site of the VES Research Foundation." May 5. <jh@rights.org> (August 1998).

Not Dead Yet. 1997. Web site. June. <http://www.acils.com/notdeadyet> (February 5, 1999).

Offe, Claus. 1985. "New Social Movements: Challenging the Boundaries of Institutional Politics." *Social Research* 52:817–68.

Omandam, Pat. 1998. "Legalize Euthanasia, Hawaii Panel Reports." *Star-Bulletin.* June 1. <ERGO@efn.org> (August 1998).

O'Neill, Patrick. 1997a. "Pharmacy Board Requires Notification." *Oregonian.* November 7. <ERGO@efn.org> (August 1998).

———. 1997b. "Pharmacy Panel Affirms Suicide Disclosure." November 19. <http://www.oregonian.com/todaysnews/1197/st11193.html> (February 4, 1999).

———. 1998. "The AMA and Compassion in Dying Federation Oppose the Congressional Legislation for Different Reasons." *Oregonian.* July 2. <ERGO@efn.org> (August 1998).

O'Neill, Patrick, and Erin Hoover. 1998. "Testimony Differs on How Much Information the Oregon Health Division Should Collect on Physician-Assisted Suicide and What Then Should Be Done with the Data." *Oregonian,* March 21, sect. D, p. 1. <jh@islandnet.com> (August 1998).

Ornstein, Charles. 1998. "Oregon and Michigan: A Study in Contrasts on Assisted Suicide." *Dallas Morning News,* March 30, p. 1A. <jh@islandnet.com> (August 1998).

Pardo, Steve. 1997. "Marlinga Warns against Organ Harvesting." *Detroit News.* November 26. <http://www.detnews.com/1997/metro/9711/26/11260023.htm> (February 3, 1999).

Parrillo, Vincent. 1997. *Strangers to These Shores.* Fifth Edition. Boston, Mass.: Allyn and Bacon.

Peterson, Lindsay. 1997. "Comfort Care of Dying Patients Sought." *Tampa Tribune,* September 23, p. 1. <jh@islandnet.com> (August 1998).

Pius XII. 1957a. "Religious and Moral Aspects of Pain Prevention in Medical Practice." *Irish Ecclesiastical Record* 88:193–209 (February 24).

———. 1957b. "Allocution on Ordinary and Extraordinary Means." *Acta Apostolicae Sedis* (November 24).

Plotke, David. 1990. "What's So New about New Social Movements?" *Socialist Review* 90:81–102.

Pridonoff, John A. 1993a. Telephone interview by Elaine Fox, February.

———. 1993b. "Friends Form Organizations to Join Right to Die Family." *Hemlock Quarterly* 15:1–2.

Reardon, Thomas. 1996. "AMA on the 2nd U.S. Circuit Court of Appeals Decision on Physician Assisted Suicide." April 2. <http://www.ama-assn.org/ad-com/releases/1996/tr329.htm> (February 2, 1999).

Robinson, Dagmar, and Barrie Robinson. 1998. "Australia Contribution." February 4. <right_to_die@efn.org> (August 1998).

Rooney, Brian, and Asha Blake. 1998. "Oregon Releases Assisted Suicide Books for Doctors." March 4. <jh@rights.org> (August 1998).

Rosen, G. 1983. *The Structure of American Medical Practice 1875–1941.* Philadelphia: University of Pennsylvania Press.

Rosen, Patty. 1993. Letter to Hemlock Chapter Leaders, Board Members, Office Staff and John Pridonoff, January 15.

Sarasohn, David. 1997. "Odd Couple on Oregon." *Oregonian,* November 12, sect. E, p. 10. <jh@islandnet.com> (August 1998).

Sartre, Jean-Paul. 1965. *Essays in Existentialism.* Saracuse, N.J.: Citadel Press.

———. 1976. *Critique of Dialectical Reason,* trans. Alan Sheridan-Smith. Atlantic Highlands, N.J.: Humanities Press.

Schaer, Meinrad. 1998. "How Assisted Suicide Happens in Switzerland." April. <ERGO@efn.org> (August 1998).

Schutz, Alfred. 1962. "On Multiple Realities." In *Collected Papers, Vol. 1,* 207–59. The Hague: Martinus Nijnof.

"Science News Update." 1998. June 17. <http://www.ama-assn.org/sci-pub/sci-news1998/snr0617.htm> (August 1998).

Shapiro, Joseph. 1997. "On Second Thought. . . . Oregon Reconsiders Its Pioneering Assisted-Suicide Law." *U.S. News and World Report,* September 1, pp. 58–63.

Shepardson, David. 1998. "Kevorkian Harvests Kidneys in Assisted Suicide." *Detroit News.* June 8. <http://www.detnews.com> (February 3, 1999).

Siegel, Judy 1998. "Ministry to Appeal Pro-Euthanasia Ruling." *Jerusalem Post,* June 5, p. 5. <jh@rights.org> (August 1998).

Simmons, Roberta G., Susan Kleinmarine, and Richard Simmons. 1977. *Gift of Life: The Social and Psychological Impact of Organ Transplantation.* New York: Wiley.

Singer, Christopher M., and Larry Davis. 1998. "Kevorkian's Effort Hurts Group." *Detroit News.* July 3. <http://www.detnews.com/1998/metro/9807/03/07030019.htm> (February 3, 1999).

Singer, Eleanor, and Phyllis M. Endreny. 1993. *Reporting on Risk.* New York: Sage.

Sivard, Ruth Leger. 1991. *World Military and Social Expenditures 1991.* Washington, D.C.: World Priorities.

Smook, Aycke O. A. 1996 "From the Presidency." *World Federation of Right to Die Societies Newsletter,* no. 8 (June). <http://www.efn.org/!ERGO> (August 1998).

Sniffen, Michael. 1998. "Reno Won't Block Oregon's Assisted-Suicide Law." *Associated Press.* June 5. <jh@rights.org> (August 1998).

Snow, David A., and Robert D. Benford. 1988. "Ideology, Frame Resonance, and Participant Mobilization." *International Social Movement Research* 2:197–217.

———. 1992. "Master Frames and Cycles of Protest." In *Frontiers in Social Movement Theory,* ed. Aldon D. Morris and Carol McClurg Mueller, 133–55. New Haven, Conn.: Yale University Press.

Snow, David, E., Burke Rochford Jr., Steven Worden, and Robert Benford. 1986. "Frame Alignment Process, Micromobilization and Movement Participation." *American Sociological Review* 56:464–81.

South Australian Voluntary Euthanasia Society (SAVES). 1997. "What Next in South Australia?" *SAVES Newsletter, The VE Bulletin* 14:3 <http://www.on.net/clients/saves/blevy.htm> (February 5, 1999).

Spector, Malcolm, and John I. Kitsuse. 1973. "Social Problems: A Re-formulation." *Social Problems* 21:145–59.

Stannard, David E. 1989. *Before the Horror.* Honolulu: Social Science Research Institute, University of Hawaii Press.

Starr, Paul. 1982. *The Social Transformation of American Medicine.* New York: Basic Books.

Stolberg, Sheryl Gay. 1998. "Guide Covers Territory Suicide Law Does Not Explore." *New York Times,* science section. April 21. <jh@islandnet.com> (August 1998).

Suber, Monica, and Virginia Quinn. 1983. "Who Believes in Voluntary Euthanasia?" *Hemlock Quarterly* 12:4–8.

Sudnow, David. 1967. *Passing On: The Social Organization of Dying.* Englewood Cliffs, N.J.: Prentice-Hall.

Sulmasy, Daniel, Benjamin Linas, Karen Gold, and Kevin Schulman. 1998. "Physician Resource Use and Willingness to Participate in Assisted Suicide." *Archives of Internal Medicine Abstracts* 158:974–78.

Suo, Steve, and Erin Hoover. 1997. "Administration Studies Suicide Sanctions." *Oregonian,* November 7, p. 7. <jh@islandnet.com> (August 1998).

Tarrow, Sidney. 1991. "Struggle, Politics and Reform:Collective Action, Social Movements, and Cycles of Protest." Western Societies Occasional Paper No. 21, Center for International Studies. Ithaca, N.Y.: Cornell University Press.

Thomas, Lewis. 1983. *The Youngest Science.* New York: Bantam Books.

Tilly, Charles. 1978. *From Mobilization to Revolution.* Reading, Mass.: Addison-Wesley.

Timms, Dana. 1993. "Humphry Trying to Regain Control of National Hemlock Society." *Oregonian,* January 5, sect. B, p. 8.

Touraine, Alain. 1971. *The Post-Industrial Society.* New York: Random House.

———. 1985. "An Introduction to the Study of Social Movements." *Social Research* 52:749–87.

Turner, Bryan, with Colin Samson. 1995. *Medical Power and Social Knowledge.* Thousand Oaks, Calif.: Sage.

Turner, Jonathan H. 1989. "The Disintegration of American Sociology." *Sociological Perspectives* 32:419–33.

Turner, Ralph. 1969. "The Public Perception of Protest." *American Sociological Review* 34:815–31.

———. 1983."Figure and Ground in the Analysis of Social Movements." *Symbolic Interaction* 6:175–86.

Turner, Ralph, and Lewis Killian. 1972. *Collective Behavior,* 2nd ed. Englewood Cliffs, N.J.: Prentice-Hall.

Turner, Stephen P., and Jonathan H. Turner. 1990. *The Impossible Science: An Institutional Analysis of American Sociology.* Newbury Park, Calif.: Sage.

United Nations Population Fund. 1990. *Global Outlook 2000.* New York: United Nations.

United Nations Population Fund. 1991. *Population and the Environment.* New York: United Nations.

U.S. Bureau of the Census. 1918. *Mortality Statistics 1916.* Washington, D.C.: Government Printing Office.

U.S. Bureau of the Census. 1975. *Historical Statistics of the United States.* Washington, D.C.: Government Printing Office.

U.S. Bureau of the Census. 1994. *Statistical Abstracts of the United States 1994.* Washington, D.C.: Government Printing Office.

U.S. Bureau of the Census. 1997. *Statistical Abstracts of the United States 1997.* Washington, D.C.: Government Printing Office.

U.S. Department of Health and Human Services. 1991. *Vital Statistics of the U.S. 1991.* Washington, D.C.: Government Printing Office.

U.S. Legal Documents. 1997a. "Compassion in Dying: New York State." <http://www.rights.org/deathnet/us2.html> (February 2, 1999).

U.S. Legal Documents. 1997b. "Compassion in Dying: Washington State." <http://www.rights.org(deathnet)/us9.html> (February 2, 1999).

U.S. Legal Documents. 1997c. "Oregon's Death with Dignity Act." <http://www.rights.org/deathnet/ergo_library2.html#law> (February 2, 1999).

van der Maas, P. J., Gal van der Wal, and I. Haverkate. 1996. "Euthanasia, Physician Assisted Suicide and Other Medical Practices Involving the End of Life in the Netherlands, 1990–1995." *New England Journal of Medicine* 335:1609–1705.

Voorhis, Helen, Bob Blizard, Kay Gleichman, Bill Eichelberger, and Don Scheuer. 1993. Letter to Sidney Rosoff, President, Hemlock Society USA, January 19.

Wakin, Daniel. 1998. "Vatican Closes Church Law Loophole on Theological Dissent." *Associated Press.* June 30. <jh@rights.org> (August 1998).

Wallerstein, Immanuel. 1974–1989. *The Modern World System.* 3 vols. New York: Academic Press.

Weber, Max. 1968. *Economy and Society.* New York: Bedminster.

Weeks, John R. 1996. *Population.* New York: Wadsworth.

Westover, John. 1993. Telephone interview by Elaine Fox, February 11.

Whitman, Walt. 1991. "When Lilacs Last in the Dooryard Bloom'd," In *Walt Whitman: Selected Poems,* ed. Stanley Appelbaum. New York: Dover.

Williams, Rory. 1989. "Awareness and Control in Dying: Some Paradoxical Trends in Public Opinion." *Sociology of Health and Illness* 11:201–12.

Wilson, Janet, Elaine Fox, and Jeff Kamakahi. 1998. "Who Is Fighting for the Right to Die? Older Women's Participation in the Hemlock Society." *Health Care of Women International* 19:101–16.

Wood, Floris, ed. 1990. *An American Profile: Opinions and Behavior, 1972–1989.* Detroit, Mich.: Gale Research.

Young, Ricky. 1998. "Ten Euthanasia Foes Charged." *Denver Post Online.* January 24. <http://www.denverpost.com> (August 1998).

Zald, Mayer, and Roberta Ash. 1966. "Social Movement Organizations: Growth, Decay, and Change." *Social Forces* 44:327–42.

Zald, Mayer, and John McCarthy. 1980. "Social Movement Industries: Competition and Cooperation among Movement Organizations." *Research in Social Movements, Conflict and Change* 3:1–20.

Zald, Mayer, and Bert Useem. 1987. "Movement and Countermovement Interactions: Mobilization, Tactics, and State Involvement." In *Social Movements in an Organizational Society,* ed. Mayer Zald and John McCarthy, 247–72. New Brunswick, N.J.: Transaction Books.

Zurcher, Louis, and David A. Snow. 1981. "Collective Behavior: Social Movements." In *Social Psychology: Sociological Perspectives,* ed. Morris Rosenberg and Ralph Turner, 447–82. New York: Basic Books.

Index

The Authors

Stella M. Čapek is associate professor in the Sociology/Anthropology Department at Hendrix College. She received her B.A. in Soviet and East European Studies at Boston University and her M.A. and Ph.D. in Sociology at the University of Texas at Austin, where she first became interested in studying social movements. She has coauthored *Community versus Commodity: Tenants and the American City* with John I. Gilderbloom (SUNY, 1992) and has published articles on environmental justice, tenants' rights, grassroots movements, and community issues. Her present areas of interest include social change and social movements, urban/community studies, medical sociology, and interdisciplinary approaches to environmental studies.

Elaine Fox's interest in quality of life and right to die issues began when she was an army nurse in the 95th Evacuation Hospital in Vietnam in 1969. As medical staff in a terrible war, she knew she was helping to save lives, but due to the severity of many of the head wounds of her patients, she was led to wonder if she was saving people. That compelling question has stayed with her through her professional life. Several years after her military duty, she returned to undergraduate school to earn a degree in Sociology, completing her graduate education at Oklahoma State University in 1982. She is currently professor of Sociology at the University of Central Arkansas, teaching courses in medical sociology and death and dying. Her secondary interests are in anthropology and traditional medical care of indigenous people. Dr. Fox has published in the areas of medical sociology and traditional folk health practices. She is currently on a sabbatical leave to help in the relief effort in post–Hurricane Mitch Honduras, where she also expects to study the effects of societal devastation on a traditional population.

Jeffrey J. Kamakahi was born and raised in Hawaii. He received his B.S. from Willamette University in Oregon, his M.A. from the University of Iowa, and his Ph.D. from the University of Hawaii at Manoa. He is currently an assistant professor of Sociology at the College of Saint Benedict and Saint John's University in Minnesota. His course offerings include ethnicity, statistics, sociological theory, and medical sociology. Much of his research involves the sociological study of Hawaii and Native Hawaiians.

The Editor

Robert D. Benford received his Ph.D. from the University of Texas at Austin in 1987 and is currently associate professor of sociology at the University of Nebraska-Lincoln. His published works include *The Nuclear Cage* (with Lester Kurtz and Jennifer Turpin) and numerous articles and book chapters on social movements, nuclear politics, war and peace museums, environmental controversies, and qualitative research methods. His current research focuses on the linkages between the social construction of movement discourse, collective identity, and collective memory.